OUR Eternal INHERITANCE

A Guide to a Biblically-Integrated Estate Plan

❖ by ❖

Cory Wessman

ISBN 979-8-218-35651-4

PREFACE

Web search the term *biblical estate planning,* and you might encounter a short article written by an estate planning attorney. This attorney references a popular 1960s advertising slogan used by a hair cream company: "A little dab'll do ya." The attorney suggests Christians who are planning their estates should use the Bible like hair cream, or "A little dab'll do ya." The suggestion is that Christians should use the *same* estate planning framework as our secular or non-believing neighbors or friends, but with just a little "dab" of the Bible here or there. He asserts that the estate-planning decisions of Bible-believers is not discernibly different from the framework of our secular friends.

As demonstrated by the fact that this book is in your hands, I could not disagree more with this suggestion. The goal of this book is to demonstrate the transformational implications of a biblical worldview on your personal legal estate-planning decisions. In this book, I provide a summary of your key legal estate-planning decisions and then contrast a secular approach to a biblical approach in making these important decisions. I pray that each of us will use the opportunity occasioned by personal estate-planning decisions to bring glory and honor to the Lord. Our eternal inheritance in Christ should have a transformational impact on our planning decisions.

PERSONAL DEDICATION

My parents and grandparents have left the type of inheritance that benefits multiple generations. The legacy of faith left by my parents and grandparents pointed us to a personal assurance of eternal salvation in Christ and an eternity in Christ with the Lord. I pray that just as my parents and grandparents left our family an inheritance focused on the eternal, that I would likewise leave my three living children a legacy of faith. Owen, Brendan, and Kinsley, I pray that your financial inheritance will be viewed inseparably from a narrative of God's provision for our family, to His glory.

TABLE *of* CONTENTS

Introduction 1

1. Identity 9

2. Trustee 25

3. Story 43

4. Communicate 59

    A. Disclose 61

    B. Plan 78

    C. Blessing 90

5. Fiduciary 103

6. Memorial Stones 119

7. Children 133

    B. Honor 136

    C. Equity 152

    D. Wisdom 168

    E. Limit 182

    F. Trust 195

8. Charity 205

    B. Share: 207

    C. Joy 215

    D. Impact 230

9. End of Life 245

10. Testament 265

Conclusion 281

INTRODUCTION

In the April 24, 1983, volume of the periodical *GRIT,* the following story appeared: *Grandpa Gives Boy Lesson in Immortality.*

One sunny day in Minnesota, grandpa and his five-year-old grandson decided to go fishing using grandpa's boat and motor. On the way to the lake, they drove past the village cemetery.

"Who's buried there?" asked the grandson.

"Several are buried there," answered grandpa. "And do you know what? Your grandpa and grandma are going to be buried there, too."

Noticing the sad look on the grandson's face, Grandpa continued, "We don't want you to be sad, though, because we'll be up in heaven."

"Will you die first, grandpa?" asked the grandson.

"Yes, I suppose I'll die first and then grandma will die, but then we'll be together forever in heaven," Grandpa replied.

Grandpa felt he was really getting through to his grandson, but after a time of silence, the boy piped up, "Can we have your boat when you're gone?"

The grandson in that story, me, eventually entered the practice of law, where I now provide legal advice on the very topics discussed by my grandfather and me. This area of law, generally called "estate planning," addresses the legalities of who gets earthly possessions—

whether my grandfather's boat and motor, the valuable business, grandmother's dinner plate, or the substantial retirement account. Little did I know, as a five-year-old boy conversing with my grandfather about his boat, that this conversation would be the backdrop to the emotional and spiritual questions of inheritance that I have with my clients every day. My five-year-old self was focused on questions of specific earthly items, such as Grandpa's boat and motor, to avoid more significant questions of eternal consequence. My grandfather was attempting, to no apparent immediate benefit, to leverage the conversation about earthly stuff into a conversation yielding spiritual benefits. In my law practice, my clients who are parents and grandparents feel the same weight of significance to their earthly inheritance decisions because most of us wish to leave an inheritance of eternal significance. Whether they recognize it or not, my clients wish for their estate plan to be imbued with such a deep meaning and purpose that it lasts longer than it takes for their family to spend the cash they left behind.

The purpose of this book, therefore, is to encourage those who proclaim Christ as their Lord and Savior to make wise earthly estate-planning decisions with an eternal perspective in view. The Bible provides us with sufficient guidance to truly transform our legal decisions so that our earthly estate plan is not an end in itself, but a means to point others toward an eternal inheritance. It is my hope that this book allows you to apply this biblical wisdom at a practical level to your earthly estate-planning decisions.

The apostle Peter describes the nature of our eternal inheritance as Christians in 1 Peter 1:3–5. There, he writes, "*According to his great mercy, has caused us to be born again to a living hope through the resurrection of Jesus Christ from the dead to an inheritance that is imperishable, undefiled, and unfading, kept in heaven for you, who by God's power are being guarded through faith for a salvation ready to be revealed in the last time.*"

This verse offers four ways in which a biblical estate plan has transformative practical implications on our earthly estate-planning decisions.

1. Our Inheritance Is Unmerited

First, since our eternal inheritance in Christ is unmerited, our earthly inheritances to our children and churches must likewise be unmerited. Peter writes that apart from God's mercy, we have no entitlement to be a member of God's family. Only *according to His great mercy* have we been adopted into God's family. By reason of our own sin, we ought to have no share in any eternal inheritance. Before God adopted us as His daughters and sons, we were on the outside looking in. We were legal debtors to God. But by God's grace manifested in Christ, we no longer stand as debtors but as beneficiaries of God's boundless and matchless estate, enjoying the riches of His glory as vessels of His mercy.

The good news of salvation is not just for us only; Christ is also the sole Hope of an eternal inheritance for our children or grandchildren. It is the redeeming work of Christ in *their* lives that saves our children and grandchildren, not any good works they might accomplish. **Therefore, the single most profound disparity between a biblical estate plan and a secular estate plan is the unmerited and conditional nature of our gifts to our beneficiaries.** By reason of the gift of salvation we have received from our God, we must withhold any sense of moral superiority in allocating a financial inheritance to our family, to our churches, and to our supported ministries.

The principle of an unmerited inheritance implicates important legal estate-planning decisions:

- Our children are the recipients of a financial inheritance from us not because of their success or personal financial needs, but only by reason of their status as a son or daughter.

- Our children and supported churches and charities are not perfect; we can give unconditional gifts even with the knowledge that gifts may not be used to maximal financial effect.

- We ought not leverage our earthly wealth to make gifts conditional or otherwise require family or charities to act in a certain way.

- Our children or other family members are not required to act as our key decision-makers (what we attorneys call "fiduciaries") when we are no longer able to act.

2. Our Inheritance Is Complete

Second, since our eternal inheritance in Christ is already complete, we have the freedom to follow God's leading in our earthly estate-planning decisions. Peter states that God has already accomplished the eternal inheritance plan on our behalf. Peter says that *"he has caused us…to be born again."* Our secular friends and neighbors are generally anxious about the uncertainties in life and whether it will be possible to accomplish their legacy endeavors. Our inheritance, in contrast, has already been set for us "... *not with perishable things such as silver or gold, but with the precious blood of Christ.*" We believe that God sovereignly intervened on our behalf two thousand years ago in the person of Jesus Christ to provide us with an eternal identity. God's completed and ongoing control over the universe extends to our individual lives, such that God will merge our life story into the broader metanarrative of God's redemption of all things. Our eternal identity in Christ has already been set such that no earthly events can change that identity.

The completeness of our identity in Christ transforms our estate-planning decisions in the following ways:

- We should implement an estate plan immediately, not awaiting the completion of a set of life circumstances that we perceive would make us complete.

- We share personal stories of God's work in our lives with family and friends, trusting that God will finish the seemingly "unfinished" elements of our story into His broader metanarrative of redemption.

- We periodically review and update our legal decisions, admitting that past mistakes and/or lack of information require us to change our minds.

- We financially support the favorite ministry endeavors of our friends and family, free from the fear of lack of financial resources.

3. Our Inheritance Is Inexhaustible

Third, since our eternal inheritance in Christ is inexhaustible, our earthly estate-planning decisions can be made with joy and purpose even with the full knowledge that we might exhaust our earthly resources. There is merit in accumulating assets to plan for future personal financial events. However, in most instances, the end result of a client's accumulated assets is simply a larger inheritance to that client's children. The result of a larger financial inheritance is simply a larger boat, a more expensive vacation, or a more expensive college. One study found that the average inheritance is spent in as little as twelve to eighteen months.[1] The law of diminishing returns dictates that we need a greater and greater amount of consumption to enjoy the same items even during our lifetimes. For the same reasons, our children will need a greater amount of financial inheritance after our death to achieve the same level of desired pleasure in their personal living standards. In any secular estate plan, the benefits of a financial inheritance will fade.

In contrast, our eternal adoption provides us with exponentially increasing returns, for our *inheritance will not fade and is stored for us in heaven* to enjoy for all eternity. In heaven, we will revel in God's unique and unparalleled attributes, the ways in which He has befuddled scientists and cynics for thousands of years, worship the power by which He formed the universe, and marvel at how He controls the course of all human events, from humbling Nebuchadnezzar to eat grass like an ox to orchestrating the birth of our Savior in a cattle stall. In heaven, we will tell of the wonders of God's love to us, through good times and bad.

We should use what will burn up—that is, our earthly treasures—to tell the narrative of God's work in our own lives. Using earthly assets, we can point others to the story of God's redeeming work. We can use earthly goods to encourage our children and friends in ministry to follow God in the unique narratives God is telling through their personal stories. Our sentimental household items as well as our valuable stock portfolios should be used to elevate the metanarrative of God's work in our lives. If we can use our perishable goods to tell our story of God's redemption to our family and supported ministries, the inheritance will indeed last into eternity.

This principle of an inexhaustible inheritance should be played out in a Christian's estate plan in the following ways:

- We use sentimental items to share stories of God's provision and redemption in our lives, pointing them to God's sustaining grace.

- We limit the size of a financial inheritance to our children so that they trust in God, not money, as their provider and sustainer.

- We use our broken bodies as vessels to demonstrate to our

---

1 Survey findings from the 2005 Allianz American Legacies Study.

Christian community God's sustaining grace.

4. Our Inheritance Is Unfading

Fourth and finally, since my eternal inheritance in Christ is undiminished by your enjoyment of Christ, we should make earthly estate-planning decisions to encourage a multiplicative mindset among fellow brothers and sisters in Christ. An earthly inheritance is a good example of a "zero-sum" game. With a "zero-sum" game, the only way for one beneficiary to receive more is for the other beneficiaries to receive less. The more dinner guests enjoying my wife's dinner, the less leftovers there are for me later in the week. In contrast to this type of "zero sum" problem with an earthly inheritance, Peter references our inheritance in Christ as one that is *"unfading."* Among other attributes, one's enjoyment of an "unfading inheritance" cannot be reduced by reason of the participation of others. Our heavenly and eternal inheritance will be shared with other believers, yet that enjoyment will not reduce our enjoyment. In Christ, we find a never-ending well of living water that satisfies all who drink of His infinite goodness.

An earthly financial inheritance can be multiplied at our death if we cast a vision for the use of the inherited or gifted financial assets for eternal purposes in the lives of family and ministry partners. If successful, our financial assets will not simply be split at death like my wife's dinner is split among our guests. Rather, our financial inheritance will have a multiplicative effect of increasing, eternally significant joy in the lives of our children and in our supported ministry partners.

A multiplicative approach will impact our estate-planning decisions as follows:

- We strategically transfer assets to our children for the purpose of teaching them the inexhaustible blessings of wisdom.

- We articulate a purpose for lifetime gifting among children based not on strict financial equality, but to achieve eternally and spiritually significant outcomes.

- We make sacrificial charitable gifts to spread a contagious joy in the gospel and in giving in the lives of others.

- We consider how our end-of-life decisions will bless the relationships that our children and our community members have with one another.

Two Books in One

My ambition for this book is to fulfill two goals. First, and less significantly, I hope you might use it as a comprehensive outline of your legal estate-planning decisions. Second, and more significantly, I hope that you use it to consider how to apply a biblical worldview to critical earthly estate-planning decisions. Whether you are already well-acquainted with your own personal estate-planning decisions or are considering these decisions for the first time, I hope that you will use this book as the biblical framework for your personal estate-planning decisions.

In each of the sections, I summarize the decision to be made and apply biblical principles to help guide your decisions. Illustrations taken from my law practice are included, with actual names redacted. I conclude each section with questions or other application materials that provide you the opportunity to personally consider and apply a biblical worldview to your estate plan. I pray your estate-planning decisions reflect a certainty in an eternal inheritance, to the glory of God.

I never received the boat and motor from my late grandfather. But because my grandparents and parents have been purposeful about planning discussions and leveraging those discussions for eternal purposes, these ancestors of mine left an inheritance of eternal inheritance to me and, Lord willing, subsequent generations. I pray that your children, as well as mine, will reap the benefits of the type of inheritance described by King Solomon in Proverbs 13:22, who wrote, *"A good man leaves an inheritance for his children's children."* I pray that you would fully leverage the opportunity presented by an earthly estate plan to have eternal impact on your family and your community.

LESSON ONE
Identity

Our identity in Jesus Christ frees us to make grace-based legal estate-planning decisions.

"There is more than one way to get to heaven, but this is a great way." In 2006, billionaire investor Warren Buffett made this comment as he publicly announced his pledge to make annual gifts of $1.5 billion per year to the Bill and Melinda Gates Foundation.[1] Buffett's charitable commitments are generally viewed in secular circles with awe. In Buffett's mind, he has "earned" heaven many times over by the size of his financial commitments. Many in our culture would agree with Buffett's underlying assumption that, if there is an afterlife, Buffett's charitable gifts are certain to "earn" his salvation. Even among self-described Christians, there seems to be an attempt to use the financial value of an inheritance or good works to justify their righteousness to God, others, and themselves.

The most transformative characteristic of a biblical estate plan is how our identity in Jesus Christ frees us from the constraints of a secular estate plan. Our inheritance in Jesus Christ is an inheritance of eternal significance far superior to the size of Buffett's bequests. By the work of Jesus on our behalf, we now have standing before God to receive His great grace and mercy. Nothing we can accomplish will add to,

---

1 Gates: Buffet Gift may help cure worst diseases. NBC News, June 25, 2006. https://www. nbcnews.com/id/wbna13541144

or subtract from, our eternal inheritance in Christ. *"For by grace you have been saved through faith. And this is not your own doing; it is the gift of God, not a result of works, so that no one may boast."*[2] Our eternal inheritance is secured by Christ's work regardless of the status of any earthly financial inheritance.

In this chapter and throughout the rest of this book, I want to show how our identity in Christ transforms our earthly estate-planning decisions in the following ways:

- *Freedom from Self-Focus.* We are freed from any obligation to make estate-planning decisions to defend ourselves in the eyes of God or others.

- *Extension of God's Grace to Others.* We create a grace-based earthly estate plan as a symbol of the greater grace-based eternal estate plan we received from God.

- *Make an Estate Plan.* We take steps to implement an earthly estate plan.

- *Communicate in Joy.* Freed from the fear of death, we communicate our plan to others.

- *Update Our Estate Plan.* Freed from maintaining a façade of control, we periodically review and update our plan as life unfolds before us.

- *Fidelity to God.* Freed from the need to create a perception of success for ourselves, we demonstrate our fidelity to God and our desire to achieve eternally significant outcomes.

I pray that you would integrate your identity in Jesus Christ in the manner outlined in this book and perhaps other practical ways that demonstrate your status as a beloved child of God.

Freedom from Self-Focused Estate Planning

Our identity in Jesus Christ frees us from the bondage of using our estate plan to defend ourselves before God or others. A secular estate plan is used to point to one's own achievements as assuring one's moral worth before God. The rich young ruler was prompted to come to Jesus in search of this assurance, and he asked, *"Good Teacher, what*

---

2 Ephesians 2:8–9.

good deed must I do to inherit eternal life?" Jesus sent the ruler away disappointed, as Jesus commanded him to relinquish the very personal attribute, his money, which formed his identity. Jesus' response forever forecloses the possibility of self-justification through one's wealth. "If you want to be perfect," Jesus says, "sell all you have, give it away, and follow me."[3] Cut to the heart, the rich young ruler went away sad, knowing that he could not use his assets to make himself appear righteous.

Like the rich young ruler, many of my secular clients suffer from the uncertainty as to whether their lives have been lived with sufficient merit. Even ostensibly successful people like Buffett suffer from the uncertainty of whether they truly have done enough. In the absence of an understanding of God's grace to us, our estate plan will be drawn up in a manner to focus on self, rather than to thank God for His grace toward us. From my professional perspective as a planner, I see too many of my clients create a plan not necessarily to benefit their family or favorite charities, but as a means of justifying their own behavior. To the extent that we make decisions to try to defend ourselves, we miss the point of the gospel, and our decisions will be no different from our secular neighbors.

My secular clients create a benchmark for success that involves the demonstration to others of how they have accumulated more assets or accolades than their neighbor. An estate plan could be structured as a reminder to others of our (past) lifetime successes. Those embarking on such a secular estate plan would have the pleasure now of receiving desired recognition after death. As noted by C.S. Lewis, "Pride gets no pleasure out of having something, only out of having more of it than the next man…It is comparison that makes you proud: the pleasure of being above the rest. Once the element of competition is gone, pride is gone."[4]

The area of the cemetery where my eldest son is buried has the oldest gravestones in the city of Minneapolis. It was the fashion, in the late 19th century, for wealthy Minnesota families to create gargantuan stone obelisks to mark the family's burial plots. Based on the size of these obelisks, there was a race for recognition among these families even based on the size of one's gravestone. Whether the value of our house or car, the size of the stone obelisk, or the financial size of the trust

---

3 Matthew 19:21.
4 C.S. Lewis, *Mere Christianity* (San Francisco, Harper Collins, 2001), 122..

account left behind, a secular approach requires us to outdo everyone else to demonstrate our successes.

My secular clients also have a difficult time with creating and maintaining "finish lines" for professional or financial success. Other than simply having more than one's colleagues or neighbors, these finish lines must be arbitrarily chosen. A secular estate-planning approach might create an efficient transfer of assets, but to no certain eternal outcome. In fact, a secular approach provides no certainty of a solid set of objectives. It is not a matter of whether the ground shifts below our feet, but when that ground shifts and to what degree. A secular mindset requires us to be, in the words of David in Psalm 16, "chasing after other gods." The secular estate plan is never quite complete. The whims of society and family relationships will change with time; hence, any objectives founded on society and family relationships will change. Any sense of completion is only temporary, as we will end up only moving the goal line further down the proverbial football field of life. Since the finish line is uncertain, the next goal, the next achievement, the next level is always on the horizon.

In Psalm 16, King David compares the strivings of those who don't know God with the certainty of God's promises to him. "The sorrows of those who run after another god shall multiply; their drink offerings of blood I will not pour out or take their names on my lips. The Lord is my chosen portion and my cup; you hold my lot."[5] The world's way is to encourage people to "find their own way" and "find their truth" regarding the meaning and significance in life. But this never-ending search for meaning and significance provides no framework for a finish, no certainty that the self-determined purpose of one's life today will be the same self-determined purposes tomorrow, let alone ten years from now.

As for your own legacy, will you be like the world, always striving after the next big thing? Or will you be like Peter, who made his confession, *"Lord, to whom should we go? You have the words of eternal life."*[6] As Christians, our own inheritance in Christ exceeds the value of Warren Buffett's riches. We have the boundless riches of Christ, promised riches beyond our searching out, human measure, or even human understanding.[7] While our earthly circumstances will

5 Psalm 16:4–5.
6 John 6:68.
7 Ephesians 3:8.

change, our eternal inheritance is set. The certainty of this eternal inheritance means, therefore, that we can structure our plan pointing the attention of others to what God has accomplished, not what we did. We structure our plan so that others can have a joy in what God can accomplish in the future, not necessarily pointing others to our good deeds. We are freed from the secular pressures to use worldly wealth to create a legal estate plan to promote or justify ourselves to God and others.

Freedom to Extend God's Grace to Others

Our identity in Christ means we can use our estate-planning decisions to extend grace to family and community. Left to our own devices, we could throw up our hands at the first sign of financial mismanagement by our spouse and children and disinherit them on account of likely mismanagement of funds in the future. But Jesus calls us to implement a grace-based plan toward our spouse, children and charities to an uncomfortable degree. The Parable of the Wicked Servant in Mathew 18 must be in our minds as we consider the conditions on our inheritance toward others. [8] There, a servant had been forgiven a great debt by the king. Fresh off the forgiveness of his own greater debt, this servant then encounters a fellow servant who owed him a far lesser amount than the amount of the debt he had owed to the king. The "wicked" servant's heart was apparently unchanged by the king's great mercy toward him, as he demanded a fellow servant repay him the smaller amount. In a similar manner, Jesus admonishes us to forgive others because Jesus has forgiven us, as debtors to Him, an otherwise insurmountable debt that exists between us.

In a subsequent chapter, we will take time to reflect on how God has blessed us in our own lives despite, or perhaps even using, our own previous mistakes. If we recognize the extent of the costliness of God's grace to us, we will not demand a certain requisite level of behavior from others. Just as we have been forgiven by Jesus "seventy times seven times," Jesus calls us to forgive past mistakes "seventy times seven times." Our estate-planning decisions will therefore be transformed by the grace of God in our lives. If we have worked with our children on their previous mistakes, and they seem to demonstrate a heart to learn from their mistakes, we would give them chance after chance, perhaps 490 chances, to improve financial stewardship skills.

Our identity in Christ means that we do not use the financial

8 Matthew 18:21–23.

mismanagement of our children, our church or supported charities as a means of defending the identity we have with our accumulated wealth. If our identity is wrapped up in the size of our financial gifts to children or grandchildren, we will take steps to make sure that others laud us, even after our death, for our good works in accumulating assets. What would have otherwise been the means to an end—our financial assets assisting others—becomes the end in itself. We take steps to preserve our financial inheritance as a symbol of our own inheritance. But if our identity is in Jesus Christ, we are freed to extend grace to the earthly beneficiaries of our estate, even in spite of the fact that they might make poor decisions.

Freedom to Complete a Plan

Our identity in Christ means that we have the freedom to complete an estate plan now, having no fear that our death will cut short our eternal purposes. Rather than assume on a future known by God but unknown to us, we should plan immediately for the possibility that we will die tomorrow. The rich fool, as described by Jesus in Luke 12, acted as if nothing could harm him. "Eat, drink and be merry" was his approach.[9] He built bigger barns to enjoy those goods through the end of what he believed to be his life expectancy. Jesus' admonition to store our wealth in heaven, not earth, ought to encourage those of us seeking eternal riches to plan as if we will die tomorrow. The certainty that drives our decisions is not that we will live to the end of our life expectancy, but that our eternal inheritance is already secure.

In the absence of our biblical faith, a secular approach fears death. This fear ultimately results in many secular individuals never properly completing their legal plan. Some never engage with estate-planning professionals because they decide to bury their head in the sand, avoiding questions of existential meaning and purpose, never bringing to full fruition planning decisions.[10]

Alternatively, fear of death might result in "paralysis by analysis." The sociologist Earnest Becker used the term *partialization* to refer to our human tendency to avoid existential questions by focusing on smaller, less significant questions that can be controlled. Some clients are overly concerned about the punctuation of their legal documents, even while ignoring the fact that significant legal decisions go unanswered.

9 Luke 12:13–21.
10 This approach is most appropriate under a secular approach. Under an evolutionary worldview, one's perceived affections for one's community are merely the result of evolutionary forces. If this is true, there is no need to bother with estate planning decisions.

It provides our children and family little benefit after our deaths that we had appropriate punctuation in draft documents, but blanks in the legal documents where the beneficiaries need to be listed. Rather than attempt to control all elements of our future existence, we must not be paralyzed by indecision. According to the philosopher Voltaire, "Perfect is the enemy of good." Let us therefore make decisions for the benefit of our families, knowing that our future inheritance is secure.

Freedom to Review and Revise Our Legal Plan

Our identity in Christ frees us to admit past mistakes in our estate plan and to revise our plan as life unfolds before us. As we will describe in this book, most of our legal estate-planning decisions are subject to change. Since we cannot possibly know the future and God's plans for us, we must be ready to accept the fact that we made some wrong predictions about the future and be willing to change course. We know that our eternal inheritance is already certain and known by a loving and good God and be willing to complete an estate plan even with imperfect information.

Our identity in Christ means that our estate plan is eternally complete, even while our earthly estate plans need to be tidied up. I've yet to administer an estate where there was not a stray asset, an unpaid bill (*e.g.,* my legal fees charged after death), or final tax returns filed and paid. No one dies with an empty email inbox. As imperfect creatures in fellowship with a perfect, omnipotent God, we trust that God will reveal more about us and His plans for us in the future. *"I am the Lord almighty,"* God told Abraham, so *"walk before me faithfully."*[11] Our estate-planning decisions need to change because we cannot possibly know the future. As in so many other areas of the Christian life, there is an "already-but-not-yet" dynamic with estate-planning decisions. While our identity in Christ is certain and unchangeable, our earthly estate plan must change with our changing life circumstances. As the sovereign Lord shows us more of His plan, we can change the key estate-planning decisions previously aligned to make them more consistent with our current life situation. The efficiency of your earthly estate plan at your death will depend on how closely aligned your legal plan is with your life situation at the time of your death.

Freedom to Publicly Demonstrate Fidelity to God

Our identity in Christ frees us to use financial assets to boast in Christ by spending or giving away financial assets in ways that our

11 Genesis 17:1.

secular neighbors would be wise to avoid. One attribute of successful secular clients is that they take steps in their planning to be perceived as successful. We use the legal term "advancement" to mean any lifetime gift made to adult children who will receive an even greater amount of assets as an inheritance following the death of her parents. The flashy car or extravagant house becomes a means of showing off the wealth and perceived significance of the family to which they belong. The advancement is a means of allowing the parents to boast in the extent of their wealth to their friends and neighbors. If mom and dad have enough to buy the sixteen-year old son the fancy new car, the neighbors reason, how much more do mom and dad own to back up that spending? The ownership of the asset says to friends and neighbors, "Do you know the wealth of the family to which I belong?"

In Ephesians 1, Paul says that after receiving Christ, we are "sealed with the promised Holy Spirit, who is the guarantee of our inheritance until we acquire possession of it, to the praise of his glory." We are called to "show off" our membership in the family of God by demonstrating the fruits of the Holy Spirit. As members of the richest household in the universe, how much more should we be showcasing the identity of the family to whom we belong? God gives us the fruit of the Spirit as an advancement against our ultimate inheritance in Christ.

If we boast in anything in this world, it is about our worldly weaknesses, not successes, because those weaknesses clearly demonstrate that our identity is in Jesus Christ. We share our personal weakness so that God's power can be displayed in our lives.[12] To the Galatians, Paul writes, *"But far be it from me to boast except in the cross of our Lord Jesus Christ, by which the world has been crucified to me, and I to the world."*[13] In his letter to the Philippian church, the Apostle Paul even suggests that his good works are worse than garbage because those good works might be perceived as the source of his moral authority with God.[14] At every opportunity, we can joyfully exert influence, financially and relationally, to identify ourselves as Christians.

Our earthly estate plan can also be structured to conspicuously demonstrate our identity in Christ as well as the implications this has for our children and our church community. As we will discuss in this

---

12 Paul writes, "If I must boast, I will boast of the things that show my weakness." 2 Corinthians 11:30. See also 1 Corinthians 1:31. "Let him who boasts boast in the Lord."
13 Galatians 6:14.
14 Philippians 3:8.

book, we should make lifetime asset transfers for our children not for the purpose of increasing their living standards or our reputation, but to demonstrate the power of godly wisdom in their lives. Just as God gives us the Holy Spirit to "show off" our identity in Christ, we can use financial assets to attempt to *advance wisdom* to our children. Ultimately, it is our hope that our children receive an advancement of an inheritance that benefits each of them in their personal walk with the Lord. Similarly, we should be careful not to boast in past ministry accomplishments through our estate-planning decisions. Since God has promised to use our past efforts to accomplish His purposes regardless of the health of any particular church or ministry, we are freed from any personal obligation to financially support ministries or churches through our estate plan.

ILLUSTRATIONS FOR APPLICATION

As an estate-planning attorney with eighteen years of private practice experience, I observe first-hand the spiritual dimension of estate-planning decisions. To illustrate the far-reaching implications of a grace-based biblical estate plan, in this chapter and most of the chapters that follow, I share three illustrations. May you implement a biblical estate plan based on your identity in Christ, not your current or future earthly accomplishments.

Already Past the Finish Line

"My current net worth is approximately $10 million," Steve tells me during a telephone call before he hired me. "But I'm not done yet. Once I get to $12 million," Steve reflects, "I will feel like then I will have enough, and then I can start with my retirement and estate planning in earnest. Once I hit $12 million, I will contact you to implement a plan." Eventually, Steve was convinced to hire me even while failing to hit his self-determined identity goal of a $12 million net worth.

Like many other high achievers, Steve's mindset makes it difficult to complete a legal plan. If someone can justify their legacy only upon the completion of their determination of "success," why even bother creating a plan before then? Many of these clients are so self-driven that, even after obtaining the original goal, what had been a 100-yard football field becomes a 150-yard football field. Rather than enjoying the touchdown, the goal posts get moved further down the field. Self-driven and success-oriented individuals are truly "limitless" in their pursuits.

Steve's business efforts are laudable and noteworthy; after all, he genuinely cares for his family and his coworkers. However, the constant striving means that there is little time to reflect on what has been accomplished and how the narrative of his story should impact family, friends and ministries once the Lord calls him home to heaven. Steve had originally set for himself a $12-million finish line before he considered his legacy. But upon arrival at this mark, if Steve compares himself to the colleagues in his industry worth $50 million or even $100 million, then from a secular perspective, Steve will say, "Why bother?

As a child of God, Steve's identity is already secure regardless of whether he meets his $12-million threshold. When Jesus proclaimed, "It is finished" from the cross, He was not merely proclaiming that His sacrificial work was complete, but that our strivings for a sense of proving ourselves was finished. If we are serious about implementing a biblical estate plan based upon our identity in Christ, we ought to avoid "if only" considerations when implementing our plan. Steve's response should be to consider his further strivings in light of the gospel. Through the Great Exchange of our lives for Jesus' life, Steve should stop, consider the narrative of his life, and diligently plan for his family as if he were going to die today, knowing that God's provision for Him, in Christ, is sufficient.

Don't Forget My Success

Bill was a successful banker whom a colleague introduced to me early in my law career. Bill made it clear to me how he and his wife, Sandra, disagreed on everything related to money. Bill believed that Sandra, as well as his two young adult children, overspent and under-saved. Regardless of the validity of Bill's concerns about his family, it was clear that Bill wanted to remind others of the extent of Bill's success. Bill's estate plan was therefore designed to be a perpetual reminder to others of his successes. Bill established trusts for Sandra and his children, but structured the trusts with restrictive provisions so that it was difficult to use the assets for living expenses. I disagreed with Bill and what should be done with regards to his estate plan. Hence, I was not Bill's attorney.

No one doubts that Bill worked hard to accumulate the assets that he eventually left behind. But it was ultimately God who provided Bill with the wealth through his banking businesses. By establishing restrictive trusts for Sandra and his children, Bill's estate plan is like the giant stone obelisks in my son's graveyard, vestiges of human attempts to "one-up" friends and families with conspicuous demonstration of good works. If we believe that our story is part of God's broader story, we can release a sense of entitlement over the assets that we have under our stewardship.

A Darwinian Survival of the Fittest

"I'm not giving my son any more money after I die." Frank expressed exasperation has he explained to me why he decided to disinherit one of his sons. "He has already received a significant gift from me, and he blew it all on bad business decisions." About ten years before our conversation, Frank gifted a restaurant business to one of his sons who, according to Frank, "ran the business into the ground." As a result, Frank was determined to cut out his son from all planning, despite the fact that Frank professed a faith in God. Frank's reticence in considering his son as a possible beneficiary demonstrates a misunderstanding of God's grace towards him. As far as I know, Frank has not been able to bring himself to provide for his son in his estate plan by reason of his son's past mistakes.

Under a secular plan, one might say that some of our children are simply not "cut out" to handle business matters. If we took a Darwinian "survival-of-the-fittest" approach, it would be appropriate to exclude family members after bad decisions. We take steps to reward those who succeed like we think we succeeded (at least in our own minds). Frank admitted making some mistakes in his own business career, which he blamed on market conditions. But in turning a blind eye toward his own past failings, Frank is losing tremendous opportunities for mentorship in wisdom with his son. A biblical approach would require Frank to give his son 490 opportunities (70 times 7). The financial cost of such business losses is well worth the benefit of attempts to instill biblical wisdom in our children.

Living Out Our Eternal Inheritance

Jesus, as the perfect human and Son of God, would have been justified in accumulating the greatest single estate in human history, one that would have made the wealthy Warren Buffett look like a pauper. But rather than leverage his wealth for worldly gain, Jesus made Himself lower than the angels, took the form of a servant, and went to death for us on the cross. He left no assets, no vast estate, not even anything to give at His death in support of His surviving mother. The only assets

He possessed, up to the moments immediately before His death, were the garments taken from Him by the mocking Roman soldiers. ***In legal terms, Jesus died insolvent.***

At the cross of Calvary, Christ took sin on our behalf and exchanged His life for ours. He took the death we deserved and, in exchange, provided us with the eternal inheritance that only He deserved. Our debt was buried with Christ,[15] paid for by that insurmountable and incomparable pain experienced at Calvary. Our inheritance was then solidified as Christ rose from the dead, bringing us with Him into His rightful inheritance. Our earthly estate-planning decisions should therefore be shaped by our eternal inheritance in Christ. If we follow the rest of the world in making estate-planning decisions, our inheritance will never be complete, it being the product of "chasing other gods." We will use the estate planning decision-making process to justify our own behavior. But, in Christ, we know we have already received our perfect inheritance and have no need to convince God, others or ourselves that we deserve an inheritance. Through the gift of grace to us in Christ, we are freed to use financial assets for His purposes.

---

15 In Colossians 3:3, Paul says, "For you died, and your life is hidden with Christ in God."

REFLECTIONS
On Your Identity

In this chapter and those that follow, I include several questions to encourage you to reflect on, and then act on, your personal estate planning. May you prayerfully integrate the identity you have in Christ into your personal estate-planning decisions.

Freedom from Self-Focused Estate Planning

Imagine the moment you die. You are immediately escorted into the grand throne room before God Himself. God asks you, "Why should I let you into heaven?" Would any part of your answer include what you did on earth? Do you, like Warren Buffett, believe that your salvation is based on certain successes, relationships, or achievements?

Even though you have not accomplished all the goals you set for yourself, are you ready to die now? Or do you feel you must achieve certain goals, whether financially, relationally, or professionally, before you feel that your life has been successful? Is there anything in your life, other than Jesus, that you feel like you "must have" and that you cannot die without having?

Have you used your earthly estate-planning decisions to defend past behavior? Are you providing a large inheritance to your children because you regret how you raised them? Are you providing a larger amount to charity to make up perceived past shortcomings?

Freedom to Extend God's Grace to Others

In what ways are you conditioning an inheritance based on the behavior of your children?

Have you stopped sacrificing for your children because of their mistakes? How many chances will you give your children to learn from their mistakes?

Have you ceased giving to a church or charity by reason of financial stewardship decisions? In giving or not giving to a church or ministry, how many financial mistakes is "too many" when it comes to ceasing make further contributions?

Freedom to Complete an Estate Plan

What assumptions are you currently making about your longevity on earth?

Are you putting off your own planning because you have not achieved personal goals?

Is the success of your estate plan conditional upon circumstances outside of your control?

Freedom to Update Your Estate Plan

If you have already created an estate plan, have you reviewed it recently to confirm that all decisions continue to be appropriate?

Do you know of any changes to your existing estate plan you ought to make, but have not yet done so?

Freedom to Demonstrate Fidelity to God

Is it more important to you that your children make good decisions so that you are perceived as being successful, or that they learn financial decisions to gain long-term wisdom?

Have you ever gone out of your way to make sure that others perceive you as successful? Are you enjoying goods for their own purposes or simply to show others that, by reason of your possession of them, you are indeed worthy of their admiration?

In what ways can you use your skills and financial assets to demonstrate your identity in Jesus Christ and not your financial situation or any other temporal earthly position?

LESSON TWO
Trustee

Manage God's assets as a trustee for eternal, spiritual, and godly outcomes.

The most expensive public works project in the State of Minnesota is taking shape within a mile of my house. The third leg of the Minneapolis and St. Paul light rail system is being built from downtown Minneapolis to the southwestern suburbs of the city. The 14.5-mile extension of the city's existing light rail system is now projected to cost taxpayers approximately $2.75 billion dollars.[1] The project has been pushed out another four years, with more cost overruns anticipated. From the perspective of a traditional cost-benefit analysis, this building project will never make economic sense.

The "shareholder primacy" theory of legal obligations requires a company's board of directors and its managers to make financial decisions to maximize a profit for the shareholders of a for-profit company. Traditionally, board members or managers who made decisions contrary to the objective of maximizing shareholder return could be subject to a lawsuit for a breach of a legal duty to maximize the shareholder profitability. More companies are now trumpeting business decisions based, at least ostensibly, on the factors known as "Environmental, Social and Governance factors" (or "ESG factors").

---

1 Peter Callaghan, "Southwest light rail, a project left for dead, is 25 percent complete." August 26, 2020. *Minn Post.*

According to the ESG Global Study in 2022, 26% of global investors indicated that these "ESG" concerns are central to how these investors make investment decisions.[2] More shareholders are looking at factors beyond shareholder investment returns. Shareholders are reviewing a company's records to ascertain the company's history related to environmental impact, the implication on social outcomes, and the company's governance structures before making decisions as to whether to invest in the company.

As a society and as a community, we have made decisions that elevate certain values above others, perhaps at staggering financial costs. If secular leaders chose to elevate these ESG factors above financial factors, Christians must likewise elevate biblical factors above strict financial cost-benefit factors. Rather than being tied to a strict cost-benefit analysis of our decisions—whether investment, charitable giving, or employment decisions—our decisions must elevate biblical principles above secular ones. *If our society is willing to pay billions of dollars for environmentally friendly modes of transportation, Christians should be even more willing to pay billions of dollars to achieve spiritual benefits for our children and our churches.* As Christians implementing a biblical estate plan, we should elevate the significance of a different type of ESG-based decisions, those being *eternal, spiritual, and godly* factors.

Conspicuous Consumption for the Glory of God

A few short days before His death and resurrection, Jesus was anointed by Mary in the town of Bethany. Matthew tells us that Mary's gift of perfume was "lavish."[3] According to commentators, the perfume was worth a year of wages as measured by a day-laborer's daily wage rate. The value of the perfume was three times the amount Judas would receive for betraying Jesus, an indication of the relative value that Mary and Judas each placed on their relationship with Jesus. When Judas and the other disciples heard about the anointing, they were indignant at this seeming "waste" of assets. *"Why this waste? For this could have been sold for a large sum and given to the poor."* But Jesus, aware of their attitude, said to them, *"Why do you trouble the woman? For she has done a beautiful thing to me…Truly, I say to you, wherever this gospel is proclaimed in the whole world, what she has done will also be told in memory of her."*[4]

---

2 https://www.capitalgroup.com/eacg/esg/global-study.html.
3 Mathew 26:6–13.
4 Matthew 26:9–12.

One can imagine the angst as Judas' quill hits the papyrus scrolls to conduct some quick calculations. Not just Judas, but likely the other disciples as well. "Does Jesus know how many mouths that this could have fed had it been sold?" Jesus' answer is unsettling to spreadsheet-producing misers like me who want a neat and clean cost-benefit analysis for the use of financial assets. But instead of a quantitative analysis of financial decisions, Jesus' teachings direct that our financial decisions must be made to lavish worship and praise on Jesus. A secular approach dictates that we own everything, including our own bodies, our life stories, and our finances. But under a biblical approach, we worship Jesus through the management of our finances, our life narratives, and even our bodies.

A Trust Relationship with God's Possessions

"To a man whose only tool is a hammer, everything looks like a nail." When I read Scripture, I feel like a carpenter, with hammer in hand, standing in a semi-finished room with nails protruding everywhere. As a trust attorney, I see Jesus' teachings about money to be a forerunner of modern American trust law. I therefore wish to apply the basic principles of modern American trust law to decisions about how God calls us to use everything placed in our care, especially our financial assets. *God's provisions of our life narrative, our finances, and our very bodies is akin to a modern trust legal relationship in that God is the creator, and we are His trustees to achieve His purposes.* In this chapter, I describe the basics of the trust as a legal relationship. I hope to frame our estate-planning decisions as a trustee of assets owned by God. In this way, we might develop a deeper appreciation for our stewardship honors as well as our duties.

A trust is a legal relationship in which:

The owner of an asset, called the *"grantor,"* appoints a *"trustee,"* who holds legal authority, subject to duties, to administer assets for the *purposes dictated* by the grantor.[5]

GOD AS THE GRANTOR

First, God is the "grantor" or "creator" of the trust. The *grantor* is the owner of the assets, establishing the trust as a legal arrangement

---

5 See American College of Trust and Estates Counsel, "What It Means to Be A Trustee: A Guide for Clients." 2005.

to achieve purposes that are either written in a trust agreement or provided verbally to a trustee. The grantor is not necessarily legally obligated to create the trust but is creating a trust out of love and affection for the "beneficiary." It is important to note that the grantor was the original owner of the assets of the trust. God is the owner of everything you consider to be "yours."

- God owns all the physical assets of the world.

"The Earth is the Lord's, and everything in it, the world, and all who live in it." Psalm 24:1

- God owns the means of producing all wealth, including the wealth in your business and retirement accounts.

"For every beast of the forest is Mine, the cattle on a thousand hills." Psalm 50:10

"Remember the Lord your God, for it is he who gives you the ability to produce wealth." Deuteronomy 8:18

"…all that is in the heavens and in the earth is yours. Yours is the kingdom, O Lord, and you are exalted as head above all Both riches and honor come from you, and you rule over all. In your hand are power and might, and in your hand it is to make great and to give strength to all." 1 Chronicles 29:11–12

- God owns the narrative of your life story.

"I have been crucified with Christ. It is no longer I who live, but Christ who lives in me. And the life I now live in the flesh I live by faith I the Son of God, who loved me and gave himself for me." Galatians 2:20

- God owns your very physical body—to use as He determines.

"…In your book were written, every one of them, the days that were formed for me, when as yet there was none of them." Psalm 139:16

"You are not your own; you were bought at a price." 1 Corinthians 6:19–20

Our Role as Trustee

God owns all assets but appoints us as His trustees. In general, the **trustee** can be an individual or an institution, such as a bank.[6] The

---

6 In most cases, the trustee is an individual who is a different person than the grantor. In some

trustee takes physical possession of the valuable item (the "asset") conditional upon obligations to follow through with the stated objectives of the grantor. The trustee has no legal right apart from his role as trustee; that is, the trustee holds physical possession of the asset only at the direction of the grantor.[7] In the biblical metanarrative of creation and redemption, God has called us into stewarding His assets as trustee.[8]

In three of Jesus' parables, the parable of the talents (Matthew 25:14–30), the unforgiving servant (Matthew 18:23–35) and the dishonest manager (Luke 16:1–9), Jesus describes how certain individuals are placed in the position of a servant, also known as a steward or manager, to manage the master/owner's assets. Each of the servants, also known as trustees, are required to manage assets for the benefit of the master/grantor.

As trustees of God's assets, we have an obligation, as fiduciaries, to follow His directions to achieve His purposes. In the law, a **"fiduciary relationship"** is a relationship in which the "fiduciary," also known as the trustee, manages something of value for the benefit of the persons named as the "beneficiaries." I advise my clients who are acting as fiduciaries that they must effectively "forget" their own self-interested desires and goals with respect to the assets of the trust and make decisions solely and exclusively for the benefit of the beneficiaries. According to Randy Alcorn, "Whenever we think like owners, it's a red flag. We should be thinking like stewards, investment managers, always looking for the best place to invest the Owner's money."[9] Let's consider ourselves as God's trustees of God's assets rather than owners of assets as we look to Scripture to determine how to achieve His purposes.

Our Purpose: To Seek an Eternal Return

God's Word directs that we administer assets under our care for a different purpose than our secular neighbors do. The parable of the dishonest manager found in Luke 16 turns assumptions about financial management on their head. In this parable, Jesus endorses a type of behavior that attorneys would argue creates a lawsuit—what the law

cases, such as with a "revocable trust," the grantor is the trustee during his lifetime.

7 In a trust relationship, the grantor/owner generally has the legal right to pull assets out of the trust relationship with the trustee, thereby terminating the legal agreement, the legal relationship, that exists with the trustee.

8 And God said to them, "Be fruitful and multiply and fill the earth and subdue it." Genesis 1:28

9 Randy Alcorn, *The Treasure Principle* (Sisters, OR, Multnomah, 2001), 123.

would describe as a "breach of a fiduciary duty." Especially for a trust attorney like me who counsels my trustee clients to abide by their legal obligations, the parable is unsettling and worthy of meditation.

The servant in the parable, whom I will refer to as the "trustee," was charged by the owner/grantor with "wasting" the possessions of the trust. We are not told how the trustee wasted the assets, but apparently the trustee recognized the charges as valid. The trustee knew that his time as a trustee was at an end. In clear violation of legal duties to the owner, the trustee contacts the grantor's debtors, whom the trustee knows owe the grantor a substantial sum. The trustee acts for his own personal benefit, to the detriment of the trust and its owner, by agreeing to "write off" a portion of the debt. This was a clear violation of the trustee's legal "fiduciary" duty to his master.

At this point in the story, Jesus pulls the rug from underneath the trust attorney. The master *commends* the fired trustee for his shrewdness. "For the sons of this world are more shrewd in dealing with their own generation than the sons of light. And I tell you, make friends for yourselves by means of unrighteous wealth, so that when it fails they may receive you into the eternal dwellings."[10] The trustee/servant is commended for his shrewdness not because the trustee used his position to improve *the condition of the trust* but to improve his *personal situation* after the end of this particular trusteeship. The servant/trustee leveraged his current opportunities for his next personal opportunity.[11]

The point of the parable is that Jesus calls us to use our temporal financial wealth not to better our own personal financial situation in this life, but to improve our situation in the next life. We should use the financial assets we have on earth to better our situation in heaven— that is, to seek an eternal "return on investment." Our calling as God's trustee with His assets is not to maximize personal consumption and seek a financial return on our *earthly investments*. We are called to leverage our earthly financial assets to maximize an eternal "return on investment" for ourselves, our families, and our communities.

Christians should take a page from the ESG playbook. To correlate

---

10 Luke 16:8–9.

11 Some Biblical scholars argue that the reason for the master's commendation was a self-interest; that by reducing the amount of the debt outstanding, he would be more likely to collect something. But no indication is given in the text that the amounts owed would eventually be collected. More importantly, the justification given by Jesus for the servant's shrewdness was not to improve the condition of the trust, but simply to improve the personal situation of the trustee.

a biblical approach to a secular modern-day approach, we might say that a biblical ESG framework should be one in which we focus on **eternal, spiritual, and godly** outcomes. Jesus' point in the parable of the dishonest manager is to use our trust assets **in our lives, and in the lives of those around us, to worship the living Christ.** Jesus goes on to preach that we can either hold eternity in our hearts as our ultimate objective, or earthly financial gain, but not both. The love of money is so strong that it will, if left unchecked, overwhelm our love for God's kingdom. Jesus teaches us, *"And if you have not been faithful in that which is another's, who will give you that which is your own? No servant can serve two masters, for either he will hate the one and love the other, or he will be devoted to the one and despise the other. You cannot serve God and money."*[12]

Rather than worship money, Jesus invites us to take all we have gathered and "spend" it for the sake of our joy in Jesus. "The kingdom of heaven is like treasure hidden in a field. When a man found it, he hid it again, and then in his joy went and sold all he had and bought that field."*[13]* From an eternal perspective, we would waste financial assets if we did not use them for eternal gain. The question for a Christian, then, is not seeking an optimal financial "return on investment," ("ROI") for its own sake. We are instead called to optimize the opportunities presented to us for the purpose of maximizing an eternal return on God's investment, an "eternal ROI."

Applying ESG Decision Framework Under American Law

As residents of the United States, we are blessed to have the legal freedom to use our financial assets. The laws of the United States codify the American individualistic mentality of doing as we please and even to make decisions that others find unreasonable. We have the legal right to *"waste"* our own financial assets. We also have the legal right to "waste" professional advancement opportunities for the sake of the gospel when a secular approach would dictate taking full advantage of such opportunities. **Let us therefore take advantage of these legal opportunities to waste our financial assets when we see the opportunity to increase joy in God and to the glory of God.**

This framework has several important practical applications to our estate-planning decisions.

---

12 Luke 16:12–13.
13 Matthew 13:44.

Consumption for God's Glory

We are one of the beneficiaries of the trust that God calls us to manage. God is glorified when we consume the assets under our trusteeship to increase our enjoyment in Him. Paul writes, *"So whether you eat or drink, or whatever you do, do all for the glory of God."*[14] Our chief goal, as stated in the Westminster Confession, is to glorify God and enjoy Him forever.[15] Mary and the friends surrounding Jesus and Mary would have enjoyed the pleasant aromas of the anointing, especially in hot and dusty Judea. The disciples surely enjoyed many good lunches of fish and loaves over the fire or reclining at table with their Savior and Friend. Jesus did not end the wedding party at Cana on account of the cost of the festivities. By turning the water into the choicest of wines, Jesus encouraged the continuation of the wedding feast and all related festivities. In each of these cases, the sensory pleasures experienced by each of the disciples and by Mary must be considered part of the act of worship.

If we consume assets without concern for the giver, or if we consume assets for the sake of consuming more than our neighbor, we are not stewarding those assets for eternal glory. If we refuse to use financial assets to support our spouse or our children because we misperceive that it is up to us to provide for their future needs, we demonstrate a lack of trust in God's future provision for us. We also lose the opportunity to consume those assets to God's glory during our lifetime. Consumption within a marriage, family, and ministry are certain to honor God. Jesus calls us now to enjoy consumption of His gifts now, just as Jesus did with His disciples.

There may be points in life where we are called to go "all in" on a particular decision because it will lead to eternally significant purposes. In 1519, a Spanish army invaded and ultimately conquered Mexico. As the Spanish disembarked from their ships, the Spanish commander, Herman Cortes, ordered that his own ships be burned as his men disembarked. Cortes' men understood that they had come to the point of no return. The Spanish invaders were committed to winning the battle at all costs. Perhaps God will call you and your family at various times to "burn all your financial ships," and go "all in" to attempt to achieve a particular biblical ESG outcome.

---

14 1 Corinthians 10:31.
15 Westminster Shorter Catechism #1: "What is the chief end of man? A: Man's chief end is to glorify God and enjoy him forever."

You might be called on to make sacrificial financial transfers. If we are certain that decisions yield ES-positive outcomes, Jesus makes it clear that we can and should "waste" the assets under our care—that is, to burn the ships, for that purpose. Jesus calls us to a life of sacrificial giving, even while living free from anxiety over future provision for our needs. *"But seek first the Kingdom of God and his righteousness, and all these things will be added to you."*[16] As trustees, we are not called to know the future or even how God will provide financially for us and others in the future. We are called to make the best decisions we can with our limited knowledge of current affairs and no knowledge of the future to achieve an optimal eternal return.

Leveraging Human Capital for Godly Gain

In his first letter to Timothy, Paul admonishes wealthier members of the church to personally enjoy the assets they owned. However, he also encourages them to not only share their financial wealth, as one would expect, but also to leverage their financial position to do good works. Paul writes, *"As for the rich in this present age, charge them not to be haughty, nor to set their hopes on the uncertainty of riches, but on God, who richly provides us with everything to enjoy. They are to do good, to be rich in good works, to be generous and ready to share, thus storing up treasure for themselves as a good foundation for the future, so that they may take hold of that which is truly life."*[17] Our human capital should be utilized for the sake of the church even when it yields no personal financial benefit.

From a secular perspective, you are wasting your human capital if you do not employ your services for maximum financial return. One is "wasting" time if not accumulated human capital to create a bigger nest egg. In contrast, some I know who employ a biblical view of their time *have become rich in good works* by devoting themselves to various ministries. Some are tutoring inner-city kids in South Minneapolis or children in one-parent homes; others are overseeing building projects for international missions organizations. These clients are using their own personal retirement accounts to meet their personal financial needs so that they can spend themselves—that is, spend the human capital that God has given to them to steward—for God's glory. I know many friends who become full-time stay-at-home parents or leave their higher-paying professional careers to increase ministry opportunities.

16 Matthew 6:30–33.
17 1 Timothy 17–19.

In each of these cases, the believer has not only "wasted" the human capital opportunity to maximize a financial return, but also wasted the opportunity for a larger financial inheritance for their children. The eternal, spiritual, and godly purposes are elevated above a personal financial return.

Make Sacrificial Financial Gifts

"You know, you don't have to give away so much money to charity." I am privy to conversations occurring between Christian clients and financial advisors operating from a secular perspective. From that perspective, making charitable gifts is a nice gesture…but only up to a point. An advisor operating from a secular approach would throw up significant cautions when you give to the point of detrimentally impacting your financial future. If you hire a professional financial advisor who operates from this perspective, be ready to receive a scolding like the one that Judas gave Jesus about the use of the assets for the anointing at Bethany. From a secular perspective, you should keep your assets for your own future needs; otherwise, you are "wasting" your assets by making sacrificial charitable gifts.

Along similar lines, a secular plan would not permit an inexperienced adult child to make critical business decision when the decision could be readily made by the senior generation. Imagine a member of a varsity sports team sitting out an important varsity game to let a member of the junior varsity team play and thereby gain experience. Your children will make mistakes, and you will pay for those mistakes. As we will discuss in subsequent chapters, providing your children with the opportunity to experience failure will likely lead to long-term eternal, spiritual, and godly benefits. If we make decisions based solely upon financial profit maximization, we will retain control of our most productive assets and just let our children glean the harvest. But if we place them in positions of authority during our lifetime, we are more likely to see that they succeed to wisdom, and therefore earthly and eternal wealth. Applying an ESG framework to these asset transfer decisions, you might look for judicious opportunity to implement a gifting strategy.

Retaining Financial Assets for a Specific Future Outcome

Finally, we might save financial resources to achieve future ESG benefits. Too often, I see clients saving assets without any specific purpose. The goal is simply to maximize a return on the investment, but not necessarily apply those savings towards any laudable goal. In the parable of the rich fool, Jesus emphasizes the folly of accumulating worldly wealth and relying on the uncertainty of worldly wealth at the cost of relying upon God.[18] The rich fool had no specific aim for accumulating his own assets, other than to consume as much of his savings for as long as possible. Instead of accumulating assets for no purpose other than personal consumption, our goal in accumulating assets should be structured to achieve specific and discernible purposes. Astute professional financial planners can assist us with an investment portfolio with a risk tolerance specifically tailored to meet our objectives. Unlike the rich fool, we should maximize financial return not for its own sake but to achieve a specific and discernible purpose for us or even the beneficiaries of our legal estate plan after our deaths.

Specific future purposes might include:

- living expenses during the "doing good works" retirement.

- the future educational costs of children or grandchildren.

- a 50th wedding anniversary trip, short-term missions trip, or even a car maintenance fund.

In the parable of the rich fool, it turned out that most of the rich fool's accumulated wealth was enjoyed by others once he died. This transfer to others was then, quite obviously, outside of his direction. We must be certain to utilize the earthly legal rights we have during our lifetime to control the post-death distribution plan, and thereby implement a post-death plan to achieve specific ESG purposes. We are called to wisely implement worldly tools to "waste" financial resources for eternal, spiritual, and godly outcomes.

THE TRUSTEE'S DUTY

In each of Jesus' three "manager" or "steward" parables,[19] the manager had an obligation to the original owner of the assets. Each of the servants, also known as trustees, were accountable for their performance to the original owner. If we agree that our situation is akin to the managers in those biblical parables, it logically follows that we owe a duty to God, and not to anyone else. We will ultimately be called

---

18 Luke 12:13–21.
19 These parables are the talents (Matthew 25:14–30), the unforgiving servant (Matthew 18:23–35) and the dishonest manager (Luke 16:1–9).

to account to God for how we managed the financial assets under our care.

In subsequent chapters, we will address the relational and spiritual dimensions of providing for our children. We may ultimately decide to distribute most or all of our financial assets at our death to our children to honor them through an unmerited inheritance. In doing so, our objective ought to be to fulfill our duty to God in achieving an eternal outcome in the life of our children, not because we owe any duty to our children. *Our duty is to please God, not appease our children.* As you make your personal estate-planning decisions, make decisions to abide by your fiduciary duty to God, the owner of all.

ILLUSTRATIONS FOR APPLICATION

The following real-world illustrations may be helpful for you as you address how to use your trust assets for an eternal, spiritual, and godly outcome.

Wasting Business Capital to Transfer Wisdom

Years before I began representing Bob and Sara, they gifted each of their four children an ownership interest in the family business. Each child was also provided a leadership position commensurate with their skills. Two of the children made costly management mistakes that ultimately set Bob and Sara back several years in their plans to retire from company management. At personal financial cost, Bob and Sara allowed their children to learn from costly mistakes. Bob told me, "We gave each of our kids significant opportunities, and at various points, each of them blew it."

When I commenced legal work for Bob, Sara, and the rest of their family, their adult children had turned the corner on the wisdom spectrum. Each child had leveraged past mistakes into capabilities in various ministry and business pursuits. Under Sara and Bob's tutelage, each of their children has developed a degree of wisdom over worldly wealth. This wisdom might not have been possible in the absence of the opportunities that Sara and Bob as parents presented to them. While it seemed at the time that the financial decisions were a "waste" to Sarah and Bob, this financial waste was well worth the benefit of instilling wisdom in their children.

Wasting A Child's Future Consumption Standards

Mark and JoAnne are successful real estate developers who met in college through the Campus Crusade for Christ ministry (now called "CRU"). Mark and JoAnne continue to be involved in CRU and have already set a financial "finish" line for their consumption standards such that a significant portion of their total annual income is directed to CRU and other ministry causes.

Mark and JoAnne recently completed an estate plan with me in which they provide for their seventeen-year old daughter, Sophia by creating a testamentary trust to provide for Sophia's needs in a way that honors her as their daughter, but without negatively impacting Sophia's own faith journey.[20] Their legal plan says that if both Mark and JoAnne die before Sophia is reaches the age of thirty, a specific and limited amount of assets is allocated to a legal testamentary trust for Sophia's needs.[21] Any other remaining assets pass to CRU and other ministries.

Mark and JoAnne have determined that they owe a duty to God to achieve eternal purposes. If the Lord calls both Mark and JoAnne to heaven and significant assets are released to the CRU ministry, two important ESG benefits are achieved: (1) the CRU ministry's needs would be met with substantial financial assets and (2) Sophia's future consumption standards are held in check by receiving a limited financial inheritance.

Wasting Human Capital for International Missions Opportunities

Bart is a semi-retired banker with business interests in various international agricultural companies. Bart has an extensive professional network of key players in the industry. Bart became involved in a missions organization focusing on alleviating starvation and increasing food security in the developing world. Rather than fully leveraging his time and extensive professional contacts to increase his own personal holdings and business opportunities, Bart made the decision to "waste" these professional contacts to leverage the contacts for the benefit of the organization. While Bart's decision was a "waste" when it came to his personal financial situation, his human capital investment undoubtedly exceeded any financial return.

---

20 I will explain the use of a testamentary trust in Section 8 of the book.
21 In this case, the total amount of assets allocated to Sophia's Trust is the product of $100,000 times the number of years between the second death between Mark and Joanne and Sophia's reaching age 30. As will be discussed in subsequent chapters, the "cap amount" assures Mark and Joanne that Sophia will seek the Lord's leading in finding gainful employment.

The Challenge of an ESG Approach

If I had been present at the anointing at Bethany, I would have joined Judas in objecting to the waste of the money. But Jesus appointed Judas as the group's trustee to be responsible for the group's finances. Jesus did so even with the knowledge of Judas' eventual breaches of his legal duties to the group as the trustee of the group's expense account. If Jesus had greater objectives in mind than financial management, shall we not also look to great purposes for our meager life savings? As trustees, we have an obligation to make good financial stewardship decisions, both during our lifetime as we "spend" financial and human capital and through a legal estate plan for how assets are handled following death. May we make decisions with Philippians 3:8 in mind, which reads, *"Indeed, I count everything as a loss because of the surpassing worth of knowing Christ Jesus my Lord."*

REFLECTIONS
On Our Roll as Trustee

Reflect on your role as trustee of everything of value in your possession as assets that are owned by God for which you owe Him a duty. May you prayerfully integrate your role as trustee of God's assets into your personal estate-planning decisions.

If you were present with Jesus at Bethany, would you have responded in the same manner as the disciples did in objecting to the "waste" of financial assets?

Have you made estate-planning decisions because you feel you must abide by the wishes of your children or your friends? Is it more important to you that you please your children, or please the Lord in your estate-planning decisions?

Is it more important to you that you be liked by your children, or that you attempt to steward their growth in wisdom?

Have your financial decisions been driven by pure earthly financial cost-benefit analysis rather than an eternal cost-benefit analysis?

In what ways could you waste your financial assets for the purpose of achieving eternally-significant outcomes?

Are there assets currently in your possession that are better placed in the hands of others to optimize ESG outcomes?

Integration Worksheet

The following ESG Decision Matrix, below, is intended to organize your priorities in decision-making. . For a particular decision, prioritize the eternal, spiritual, and godly outcome of that decision. Secondarily, address the temporal and financial implications. The Decision Matrix might be used to make decisions about consumption, saving, career, and human capital decisions.

E-S-G DECISION MATRIX

Decision to be made:

	A	B	C
Possible Outcomes			
Likelihood of Outcome [%]			
Spiritual Impact to Recipient			
Spiritual Impact to Me			
Financial or Tax Result to Recipient			
Financial or Tax Result to Me			

LESSON THREE
Story

Sharing your stories of past sufferings, successes, and stewardship setbacks brings clarity to your personal estate plan.

In July of 2009, I experienced a type of suffering that I wouldn't wish upon anyone—the death of our oldest son. Little Micah, nine months of age, was in perfect health. A few days earlier, Micah had fallen out of his highchair while reaching for his toes. While he sustained a black eye from his fall, no one felt that his condition was serious, much less life-threatening. On each of the next two days, various pediatric doctors saw Micah because he developed a fever and an unusual cough.

On Sunday morning, July 26, I drove to the local Target to fill a prescription. When I arrived home, my wife came running out of our house screaming at me, "Micah has stopped breathing! Micah has stopped breathing!" The EMTs arrived within two minutes, and the ambulance just a few minutes after. But no one could revive Micah.

The grave reality of out loss hit my wife first, then it hit me. I held my wife in my arms on our kitchen floor as we screamed and cried together, praying as earnestly as we could that God would allow our little son to take a breath and come back to us. But God did not answer our prayer, and we never heard Micah cry again.

Over the next twenty-four hours, Micah was kept alive by a ventilator. But by reason of the oxygen loss to his brain, we were told there was no possibility that Micah would ever regain consciousness. We determined that we had to let him go. Heather, deciding that she could not be in the room when Micah's ventilator was removed, said her final goodbye by encouraging Micah to, "Run to Jesus, sweetie, run to Jesus." A few minutes later, I held my son in my arms as the doctors removed the ventilator. In just a few minutes, my son's little heart stopped beating.

Following Micah's death, doctors determined that Micah had aspirated a pea when he had fallen from his highchair. The following Sunday morning, when trying to cough up the pea, the pea became lodged in his windpipe. According to pediatricians, the chances of the pea becoming lodged in the windpipe are infinitely small.

For Heather and me, Micah's unexpected death has had lifelong implications in how we view God's sovereignty, our sin, our work, our parenting, and even our financial decisions. All of us have a story that shapes how we view ourselves, our life circumstances, and, most significantly for purposes of estate planning, our worldly wealth. Likewise, each of us has various explanations we give ourselves for how we have experienced professional or financial success. This personal narrative must be shared with family and friends to allow them to fully leverage your experiences. *By sharing with others how we believe God has used our past sufferings, successes, and stewardship setbacks, we can bring focus to our estate planning and encourage our children and church with how God will work in their own lives.*

A biblical estate plan properly contextualizes your personal suffering and successes in the broader redemptive purposes of God's plan. God authors our story, not us. Therefore, Christians should be more willing than our secular neighbors to share narratives of our life events because we believe that God ultimately gets the glory. While I am not suggesting we must write a 500-page memoir, I believe in the importance of sharing how certain significant life events impacted you. In a later chapter, we will address how to prepare written letters of instruction, commonly referred to as either ethical wills or legacy letters, to encourage others or bring clarity to estate planning issues. Before turning to those directions, however, we should first consider how your past impacts your estate-planning decisions. To that end, you might consider how you have been impacted by the following:

- seasons of suffering

- successes

- stewardship setbacks

It is my hope that these topics will prompt conversation with your family so that you can marvel together about God's **past provision.** These stories of past provision might also help you make **current stewardship decisions,** and then create a plan for the how remaining financial assets you hold should be allocated **following your death**.

Our Personal Suffering Narrative

From a secular perspective, suffering is the worst-case scenario. Whether in our own lives or in the lives of our children, suffering is to be avoided at all costs. For that reason, the secular world attempts to accumulate a limitless amount of assets by reason of the pervasive assumption that money is a savior, a salve for all wounds. Some have even allocated resources for the cryogenic freezing of their body at death. The secular world places its hope in the possibility that financial assets and human ingenuity will be sufficient to live forever, and to do so without God. In Psalm 10, the Psalmist writes about the arrogant.

"In the pride of his face the wicked does not seek him;

All his thoughts are, 'There is no God'…

He says in his heart, I shall not be moved;

Throughout all generations, I shall not meet adversity."[1]

As Christians, we place faith in the God of suffering, the God who allowed His Son to go to the cross for us. The Apostle Paul promises that we will endure suffering to showcase God's power. *"For we who live are always being given over to death for Jesus' sake, so that the life of Jesus also may be manifested in our mortal flesh."*[2] For Christians, the question is not whether we will experience suffering, but how we will respond to those sufferings.

The biblical patriarch Joseph experienced tremendous, undeserved suffering, and yet did not lose trust in God. First sold into slavery by his brothers, he was presumed dead by his own family. Once in Egypt, he successfully interpreted dreams, only to be forgotten by those he

1 Psalm 10:4, 6.
2 2 Corinthians 4:11.

helped. When Joseph reveals himself to his brothers, it is clear that Joseph understood how God used suffering in his life to accomplish great things not only for his immediate family, but to fulfill the covenant made to his great grandfather Abraham. To his brothers' utter amazement, Joseph tells them that their previous egregious behavior was part of God's plan to save their entire nation. *"And now do not be distressed or angry with yourselves because you sold me here… so it was not you who sent me here, but God."*[3] Joseph was able to contextualize his suffering in the scope of God's broader purpose. *"As for you, you meant evil against me, but God meant it for good."*[4]

In many of our sufferings, we can start to see a light ahead through the heavy fog of grief, sickness, financial setback, or other sufferings. We can see the form of some specific purposes taking shape. In my case, I do not know all the purposes that God accomplished in allowing Micah to die, or even enough to yet justify his death in my mind. But we can point to good and noble benefits in our lives and the lives of others from our suffering. The further away in time we are from those dark days of July 2009, the more we grasp the spiritual and relational benefits of what God was able to accomplish.[5]

In a like manner, the story of your personal sufferings are not for your edification only. Rather, the story of your sufferings are for those around you. Paul tells the Corinthian church in 2 Corinthians that the suffering that has occurred to him is of particular benefit to the church in Corinth. Paul writes, "If we are afflicted, it is for your comfort and salvation; and if were are comforted, it is for your comfort, which you experience when you patiently endure the same sufferings that we suffer."[6] Paul felt that it was critical that the church know about the extent of sufferings in Asia *("we were so utterly burdened beyond our strength that we despaired of life itself")* so that the church could be encouraged by what God had done in their lives and in the church.[7] ***God allows suffering in our lives not just for our own benefit, but as the very means by which others are encouraged in Christlikeness.***

Sharing your suffering narrative yields numerous benefits.

✓ Our stories of suffering impact how our children view their

---

3 Genesis 45:5, 7–8.
4 Genesis 50:20.
5 Heather and I are involved in grief support ministry, including through the ministry we started called Hope for the Mourning.
6 2 Corinthians 1:6.
7 2 Corinthians 1:8.

own sufferings. Your children will have an example to follow as they encounter hardships in life. Through better understanding your suffering stories, they will understand that God has a unique narrative for each of them.

✓ A reflection on your own suffering narratives might cause you to change your ministry participation. You will have the most credibility and effectiveness among those who have suffered as you have. You might fully leverage the platform afforded by your narrative of suffering to encourage others enduring a similar suffering.

✓ You might focus additional financial giving to those ministries helping those enduring suffering that you experienced. Your joy in giving will be increased on account of the coordination of your stories of God's provision in suffering with your stewardship decisions.

✓ Sharing your stories of suffering remind your children to look to God for sustaining grace, not to a sizable financial inheritance they might receive from you. Our children should be reminded that money is not to be used to head off any possible suffering. Instead, our stories of suffering and God's sustaining grace remind our children to look to God for provision.

Our Personal Success Narrative

"So that's how I was able to double the profitability of that division when I took over." My client Joe finally pauses for a breath after providing me with a long summary of his myriad professional career successes. "If it was not for my leadership, we never would have made it as a company." I laughed aloud in response to his comments, believing his comments to be in jest. I realized by the annoyed look on his face that he was serious…and I was fired.

Some successful people need a dose of humility to go along with their generous heaps of self-aggrandizement. In contrast, I am blessed to work with some Christian clients who are happy to credit God for professional and financial successes. These stories of success have the effect of encouraging all of us to live in the assurance that He will meet our future needs. We can attribute the circumstances of successes— being in the right place at the right time, having the right market conditions, or the right professional relationships as being the work of a good and loving God. While the world might call it "lucky," we know God has a purpose in our financial successes. Christian clients who reflect on their own personal successes tend to loosen control over the professional decisions being made by their adult children, knowing that the same God who provided for them previously will likewise provide for their children.

My friend Tim was employed early in his career by a New York investment firm. During this time, he became an expert in the financial products associated with the sub-prime mortgage industry and mortgage products. When Tim was forced out of this job, his career looked a bit uncertain. At his subsequent investment firm, however, Tim became convinced of the problems associated with the sub-prime mortgage industry. By the time of the 2008 sub-prime mortgage crises, Tim had positioned investments for his new firm to profit his company to a far greater degree than anyone could have imagined. If Tim had not been forced to move companies, he would not have been able to make this large investment and bring a great profit for his new company. Looking back, Tim can see the hand of God in his departure from his first investment firm. Tim is glad to have changed investment firms, and so was the new firm.

In a biblical estate plan, the hand of God is the narrative of your success. God used many factors outside your control to cause you to succeed. These might have included your education, your professional relationships, and even the macroeconomic conditions He permitted to occur. By recognizing the factors that impacted your own successes, you can loosen any grip on the narrative of success you may have created for your own children. Your story should glorify God as your provider, and you can let go of any perception that a child's financial successes, and your future successes, will be accomplished only in the manner that you have determined.

Personal Stewardship Setbacks

The biographies of successful leaders demonstrate that success comes only after numerous setbacks and, in some cases, perhaps conspicuously costly failures. For most, success is at the apex of a learning curve that was many years in the making. Your story of success must include the lower points on that same learning curve.

The Assurance of God's Future Blessings

From a secular perspective, it is reasonable to hoard financial assets.

With no promises of sustained financial success, it is reasonable to accumulate assets to guarantee future provision. By contrast, a biblical narrative of success points to God's future provision for us despite our past mistakes. God blesses us even though, in the words of Paul in 1 Corinthians, *"not many of us were wise according to worldly standards, not many were powerful, not many were of noble birth."* [8] God blesses us because of who God is, not because we have somehow earned success. As a result, we can recount our past stewardship setbacks to our family because it brings glory to God for His provision for us.

Being Relatable to Our Children

The narrative of our past failures provides the proper context for our own children's inevitable failures. In Chapter 1 ("Identity"), I applied Jesus' teaching in the parable of the unforgiving servant to our estate-planning decisions.[9] There, Jesus shares the parable in response to the question posed by Peter, "How many times should I forgive my brother who sinned against us?" If our heart has been truly changed by the gospel, our attitude towards our children will be different from the attitude of our secular neighbors.

Parents operating under a secular mindset view a child's stewardship skills as a simple binomial fork in the road—do they have what it takes, or not? These parents view their children's behavior as if the child were trying out for the sports team or performance team in school. These parents then stop continuing stewardship mentorship. Just as with the unforgiving servant in Jesus' parable, the parents forget their own past personal stewardship failures.

A biblical approach, in contrast, considers our greater forgiveness from Christ as the fuel for a forgiving heart towards our children. Additionally, the act of sharing our stories allows our children to learn from our mistakes, as well as their own.

A Family's Past Stewardship Setbacks

The power of narrative over our estate-planning decisions can be seen in my law office every day. With each client or client family, there is a story behind how the family received my name, and how they came to believe that they needed legal assistance. In cases where the senior generation had little to no professional guidance, the administration

---

8 1 Corinthians 1:27.
9 Matthew 18:21–35.

of the assets following their death is generally more cumbersome and taxing, literally and figuratively, than it should have been. When the junior generation family members initiate conversations about their own planning, they often indicate that, because of these headaches, they wish to receive my counsel to avoid making the same mistakes. Notably, however, as the second-generation clients are posed questions requiring decisions about their own planning, *the default answer is to mirror the ill-conceived estate planning of the parents. The narrative of family wealth is so powerful that one generation's sins are often visited on the next generation.*

The estate planning mistakes could be relationally substantive or simply by reason of ignorance of the law. There may have been favoritism regarding the amount or percentage of financial assets. Most commonly, however, the senior generation made one of the following errors:

(a) a genuine misunderstanding about how estate planning law works,

(b) a failure to communicate the identity of the fiduciaries and beneficiaries, and/or

(c) a failure to communicate a desired family legacy of use of assets to the children.

Identify the errors you perceive that were made by your parents or other family. Address any further resentment you still might harbor about those errors. If your parents failed to understand the legal significance of a planning decision to your detriment, make it a point to avoid replication of those errors in your own plan. Likewise, any failure to communicate fiduciary or beneficiary appointments by your parents need not be repeated by you. If you were left with a significant financial inheritance but no real vision for how to use the inheritance, don't repeat the same error into the next generation. Instead, start a new family legacy by creating a narrative for your family on your desired use of the assets following your death.

ILLUSTRATIONS FOR APPLICATION

Support Ministries Consistent with Your Story

I became friends with Andrew and then his wife, Lori, through a men's Bible study group for local attorneys. We struggled in prayer with

Andrew and Lori as they first endured years of infertility and then, later, the emotional and legal difficulties associated with adoption. At a date past the time when Andrew and Lori had originally hoped to become parents, our prayers were answered when they became parents through the legal adoption of two children from Brazil.

Andrew and Lori were able to leverage their story as they sought to minister to other parents seeking international adoptions. Their suffering story was closely intertwined with the mission of the particular adoption ministry. As their friends, we have been blessed in the joy of their adoption and by seeing how Andrew and Lori have leveraged that joy into their missional work. In your case, you might use your suffering narratives as a means of ministry to encourage others who are enduring the same suffering. Just as Andrew and Lori make financial and human capital contributions to international adoptions organizations, you might seek opportunities to intertwine your stewardship decisions with your suffering narrative.

Use Your Success to Achieve Eternal Returns

My friend Tim, whom I profiled previously, is mindful of his narrative of success. Tim's narrative of success has freed him from what would otherwise have been bondage to a secular definition of success—seeking greater and greater financial returns. Tim has shepherded the use of his own success narrative to encourage others in the private equity industry, especially younger businesspeople. Tim has also used his financial skills in leadership to assist international missions organizations. You might decide that you should use your financial resources or your time and talent to likewise invest in the success stories of others so that God's grace to you in your success might overflow into the success stories of others.[10]

Learn from Past Stewardship Errors

Shortly before I met them, Janice and Allan were the beneficiaries of the estate of Allan's late father. Unfortunately, Allan's father had failed to plan his affairs, and the legal and tax issues related to the transition of his business and real estate assets were a mess. From the outset of my relationship with Janice and Allan, the theme was to not let the "sins of the father" be revisited upon the next generation—that is, Janice and Allan's children. Allan's father had not only failed to

10 2 Corinthians 9:13.

understand the legal and tax decisions he should have made as the owner of significant assets but also to provide a narrative of the wealth itself. Janice and Allan, in contrast, were able to make the necessary legal decisions as well as provide their children with what elements of the narrative they could gather from previous interactions with Allan's father. If your parents have failed to plan, you need not revisit that sin upon your children. You can implement a plan to benefit the next generation through a well-designed estate plan.

REFLECTIONS
On Our Life Stories

Reflect on your personal stories of suffering, success, and stewardship setbacks. Subsequent chapters will address how to integrate these narratives into specific estate-planning decisions. May you prayerfully integrate God's provision for you in these stories into your personal estate-planning decisions.

Suffering

What were the three most significant points of suffering in your life, whether specific events or even seasons of suffering?

How has your perspective on a period of suffering changed since that suffering first occurred?

How has your view of God's provision for you in suffering changed since the suffering first occurred?

If you were to endure this suffering again, what would you have done differently? If your children will be called to endure this suffering, how would you advise them to endure the suffering in light of your own experience?

What individuals or ministries assisted you in these times of suffering? What were the specific ways in which they assisted you?

Do you have friends, neighbors or others enduring a similar suffering now? What existing ministries or churches are meeting their needs right now? What resources could you give to support these ministries who are supporting those enduring these sufferings?

Success

What were the three most significant successes that you achieved in your life? These successes could be personal, professional, or financial.

What past mistakes or missteps placed you in a position to achieve these successes? If you were to provide your children with a full picture of everything that went into your success, what background information should they have about the setbacks you experienced prior to those successes?

What outside forces beyond your control were involved in your achieving each success?

For any professional success achieved, what relationship or financial costs did this success entail?

What organizations or individuals could most use your personal mentorship right now?

If you could do it over again, what would you have done differently? If your children were seeking to achieve the same outcome, how would you encourage them in their personal endeavors?

Is there a way to use your personal success stories as reminders that each of your children must find their own way consistent with God's narrative for their lives?

Past Stewardship Setbacks

Family Stewardship Mistakes

Were you negatively impacted, either financially or emotionally, by the planning decisions of your parents or grandparents?

Was there, or has there been, adequate communication of the estate-planning decisions made by your parents?

Have you been treated fairly by your parents? If not, do you have any continuing resentments about their planning decisions?

What poor decisions were made by you or your family that you can learn from in implementing your own estate plan?

Personal Stewardship Mistakes

What were the three most significant financial or career decisions you made in your life?

What lessons were learned from these mistakes?

What outside forces or influences were present when you made these decisions?

How did each mistake impact subsequent decisions?

What do you hope your children will learn from your stewardship mistakes?

LESSON FOUR
Communicate

Read your own will during your lifetime by properly communicating your estate plan.

From a secular perspective, creating ambiguity and uncertainty about your personal estate plan could serve useful purposes. If you want to fully leverage your wealth to extract desired behavior, allowing for ambiguity about your estate planning would require your children to pay attention to your needs and desires. Likewise, you could keep your church or favorite ministries at your beck and call by not only conditioning your gifts upon certain behavior but also being vague with your commitments.

Christians, in contrast, have a set eternal inheritance; therefore, the earthly inheritance we leave for our children and churches should be unconditional, certain and stable. Under a biblical estate plan, ambiguity offers no benefit. A Christian should therefore take on the task of properly planning and communicating an estate plan for the benefit of family and charitable organizations without any uncertainty or drama.

This section outlines the proper communication of a biblical estate plan in three sections, as follows:

- *Disclose:* Share critical information about your assets and digital activity with your spouse and advisors.

- *Plan:* Inventory your plan and create a legally binding estate plan.

- *Blessing:* Bless your children through the ceremonial disclosure of your plan.

At our law firm, our mantra is this: "You are not done planning until you are dead." While this is true of all the decisions discussed throughout this book, this is particularly true of the ongoing efforts to keep track of your assets, liabilities, and online presence. I hope you can use this section on a regular basis to make sure that you have adequately communicated your plan to your family.

4A: *Disclose*

Share critical information about your assets and your digital activity with your spouse and advisors.

"Ananias, why has Satan filled your heart to lie to the Holy Spirit and to keep back for yourself part of the proceeds of the land? While it remained unsold, did it not remain your own? And after it was sold, was it not at your disposal? Why was it that you have contrived this deed in your heart? You have not lied to men but to God."[1] Ananias and Sapphira were members of the early church who sold personal real estate, apparently turning a nice profit. The couple then lied to the church about the full extent of those personal earnings. By reason of that dishonesty, the couple was struck dead. The Lord's swift and unapologetic staunching of the potential negative implications of the fraud of Ananias and Sapphira is a sobering reminder of the importance of honesty in our own personal financial affairs.

From a secular perspective, it makes sense to hide embarrassing information about current or past failures. If there is no ultimate authority, we should take steps to keep secret all our sins—or at least the sins of which our friends would disapprove. But Jesus promised that, at the end of days, all our thoughts, words, and actions will be made fully known. *"For nothing is hidden that will not be made manifest, nor is anything secret that will not be known and come to light."*[2] As Christians, we understand what is at stake when it comes to the disclosure of our assets, our plans, and even our online accounts. To live in Christian integrity is to be accountable to select individuals who know about our private lives, including everything from our finances to our electronic footprints. This integrity between word and deed has spiritual benefits to us and our community, to be sure, but it also creates a far more efficient estate plan for our named successors. *The full disclosure of our assets, our legal plan, and our online presence keeps us accountable during our lifetime and creates an efficient transfer plan at death.*

1 Acts 5:3–4.
2 Luke 8:17.

Disclosure to Your Spouse

"*I don't want my wife to know about that bank account.*" A client of my law firm, whom we shall call "Lonny," called my law partner in a panic ahead of a joint meeting involving himself, his wife, and our firm. "I wanted to let you know ahead of our meeting about this additional account that isn't included on the financial statement we previously provided. But please don't tell my wife about that account during our meeting."

When questioned about the purpose of the account, Lonny indicated that the account is what he referred to as his "WAM" account, an acronym for his "Walking Around Money." Lonny's wife kept them on a limited budget. Lonny and his wife so frequently disagreed about how to use assets that Lonny had created an arrangement in which an individually owned account (the "WAM" account) received a portion of his monthly pension distribution before the rest of the pension went into the account that his wife managed.

In a recent survey conducted by Fidelity, 39% of married couples indicated that they did not know how much their spouse makes. When asked to guess, 9% were off by more than $25,000.[3] Likewise, an American Express study found that nine of ten couples "actively avoid" talking about money, and a 2018 study conducted by Dave Ramsey found that money is the single largest source of stress in a marriage, and the second-leading cause of divorce. Hiding the existence of any assets or liabilities with your spouse will not solve your marriage problems during your lifetime. Disclosing your assets and liabilities to your spouse should not be perceived as an implicit suggestion to your spouse that your spouse should take certain actions with assets if you died. The disclosure of the assets will serve to protect him or her from any misperceptions about the extent of your assets and where those assets are located. Whether any omission on your part is intentional or negligent, any omission would wreak havoc on the administration of your assets following death. You must honor your spouse by disclosing all your assets and liabilities to your spouse during your lifetime.

Professional Advisors and Trusted Contacts
Inasmuch as I respect my mechanic and my dentist, neither of these professionals need to have a full disclosure of my assets to complete

---

3 https://www.fa-mag.com/news/many-couples-clueless-on-what-partner-earns--fidelity-says-63126.html.

their job adequately. This is not true, however, for your attorney, CPA, and financial advisor. These professionals can provide you with appropriate advice only if they have a complete picture of your financial situation. Full disclosure of your current assets and liabilities to these professionals increases the likelihood that you achieve your financial goals. The full disclosure to your professionals *now* also arms them with information that they can use *later* to assist your family once you have died.

Some clients are "Do-It-Yourselfers" in making investment decisions and/or preparing personal income tax returns.[4] Some DIY'ers want to avoid paying professional fees, others don't want to be pressured by sales pitches. Regardless of the reasons for "going it alone," I advise our DIY clients to have a plan in place now for hiring help for your spouse and family when the DIY'er has D-I-E-D.

A full list of your assets and liabilities must be provided to not only your spouse, but at least one other party. This third party "trusted contact" could be some combination of your professional advisors, your named fiduciaries, a friend, or your adult children. In some instances, it might be appropriate to provide your adult children with full knowledge of assets and the terms of an estate plan.[5] Keep in mind that the disclosure of the existence of your account assets does not in itself provide the person with either ongoing access to current information on the account or to control of the account in any way. Likewise, knowledge about the existence of your estate plan does not provide the person with any legal authority.

Once you decide who should receive it, the following information should be provided to your trusted contacts:

- Financial statement
- Legal documents; and
- Legacy letters, if any.[6]

---

4 The disclosure of additional asset information to your professional advisors is likely to lead to a net cost savings to you and your family, even after taking fees into account. Your advisors are in a position to give your surviving family members the professional assistance they need if you have fully disclosed your objectives, your plan, and your assets to them during your lifetime.

5 Protecting this information from your children would be appropriate (i) when your children are minors, (ii) when the disclosure of that information would adversely impact incentive to seek the Lord's professional calling or (iii) when you have made provisions that would, on balance, embarrass them or potentially make sibling relationships more difficult. Especially in those instances, you should provide full disclosure to at least one other person besides your spouse and your professional advisor.

6 In Section 8, I cover non-binding legal directions called Legacy Letters.

Disclosure of Online Accounts

"*I want my information kept private*," a client tells me. When pressed about the information that should be kept private, and the information that should be public, clients generally respond that they wish for their online lives to be private, and their generous charitable giving to be public. From a secular perspective, there is no standard outside of ourselves by which our outward "good works" are judged. If we can trick everyone into thinking we are as moral and upright as our last financial contribution, we will, like the Pharisees, be able to justify ourselves in our own minds and perhaps trick a few of our like-minded Pharisaical friends.

All of us want to put our best foot forward. We want to receive the appreciation for charitable contributions and to have our personal shortfalls excused by circumstantial evidence. The secular worldview emphasizes the degree to which the law allows for the protection of "private" information and the trumpeting of our "good works" in public. The secular approach directs us to keep our digital footprint private. We can engage in online pornography, or perhaps even illicit relationships, and keep the knowledge of such activities away from family. The secular approach is to put our best foot forward and hide the ugly warts.

But Scripture emphasizes that God knows everyone, and all of our deeds, good and bad, will be judged at the Bema Seat—at the judgment day of Christ. "Nothing in all creation is hidden from God's sight. Everything is uncovered and laid bare before the eyes of him to whom we must give account."[7] "So whether we are at home or away, we make it our aim to please him. For we must all appear before the judgment seat of Christ so that each one may receive what is due for what he has done in the body, whether good or evil."[8]

While our identity in Christ is certain, the health of our long-term legacy could be tarnished by what happened during our lifetime on our web browser. Many of us benefited greatly from the work and ministry of Ravi Zacharias and his apologetics ministry. With great sadness, we learned, following his death, that the sexual abuse claims made in the final years of his life were true. By reason of Zacharias' improper online activity, culminating in illicit sexual behavior, his legacy as a zealous defender of the faith is now tarnished.

7 Hebrews 4:13.
8 2 Corinthians 5:10

As opposed to how Zacharias took steps to assure he had absolute privacy in his communications with women other than his wife, no digital communications should be "off limits" to those closest to us. Christians know that all will be disclosed at the end of time. John Stevens writes, "God will ultimately judge us on the basis of his perfect knowledge of our private lives, not just the public reputation that we have been able to construct. A day will come when everything that that has been hidden will be revealed, and every work that has been spoken will be judged." [9]

To avoid the tragedy of a duplicitous life, Christians should seek integrity in all their dealings by creating the appropriate accountability structures so that a spouse or trusted contact has access to our online accounts. In this regard, Christians implementing an estate plan from a biblical worldview will create efficiency advantages for those who follow them at their death vis-à-vis our secular neighbors. If you maintain a desire for privacy above accountability and do not provide others access during your lifetime, then following death, your surviving friends or family members must muddle through legal account authorizations, perhaps even court authorizations, to access online accounts. In contrast, the disclosure of online accounts and assets during your lifetime has two related and important benefits for Christians: (1) lifetime accountability for online media sites, and (2) the transfer of knowledge and financial wealth following death.

Disclosure of Digital Assets and Accounts, Generally

A "digital asset" or "digital account" is anything of value, or any mode of communication, which can be accessed using a computer, smart phone, or other digital device and that is being stored for your use and benefit by a third-party service provider. Unlike tangible personal property that is immediately accessible to those in possession of it, a digital account or digital asset is maintained on a third-party platform, such that the owner can access such accounts or assets only through third-party service providers. Types of digital assets or accounts include:

- Online bank and financial accounts;

- Online shopping accounts;

---

9 Blog post "Right to Privacy: Are Christians Entitled to a Private Life," April 15, 2016. Right to Privacy: Are Christians Entitled to a Private Life? Blog post, "Dissenting Opinions," located at www.John-Stevens.com, citing Luke 8:17 and Matthew 12:36.

- Cloud-stored intellectual property, such as photos and other creative work;

- PayPal, Venmo, and other direct payment accounts;

- Social media, such as Facebook, Instagram, Twitter;

- Digital music and movie inventory (e.g., Apple); or

- Your cryptocurrency assets, if you are savvy enough to hold them.

Any American operating in contemporary society must have access to these accounts. As a result, in order to create an efficient transfer of knowledge, it is critical to have a plan in place for these digital assets and accounts.

Your Authority Under Current Law

Under the "Uniform Fiduciary Access to Digital Assets Act," a uniform set of legislation that has been passed into law in most states,[10] you have the authority to provide your designated fiduciary, under the terms of your estate planning documents, with legal authority to deal with your digital assets in the event of death or incapacity. Your estate-planning documents should include specific provisions to name one or more key individuals with the authority to access and administer your digital accounts and assets. As with many estate-planning issues, however, it is not as simple as just signing a document with certain provisions. Rather, as summarized below, we should carefully consider their options and, where appropriate, reach out to the service providers to achieve the clarity and accountability consistent with a biblical worldview.

A Service Provider's Online Tools

A service provider may, but is not required to, provide a user with the right to designate a successor decision-maker in the event of death or incapacity. Certain service providers (most notably, Apple), take the legal position that you do not possess the rights to transfer the digital asset in question (e.g., your Apple music and movie collection) to your designated beneficiaries. In these cases, it is not a matter of whether your fiduciary has access; it is simply that the asset in question cannot legally be transferred to anyone else. In some cases, the authorized person (sometimes called a "Trusted Contact") would have access to

10 Minnesota's law is MN Stat. §521A and was enacted in 2016.

your accounts during your lifetime. In other cases, the Trusted Contact would be the person contacted by the service provider when the service provider is made aware of your death. If the service provider offers this as an option, you should take steps to name a spouse and/or close friend as your "Trusted Contact" with the service provider.

If you fail to designate a Trusted Contact in accordance with a service provider's online tools, and if you have not included provisions in your estate-planning documents, the service provider's terms of service will legally control. Depending upon the service provider, it may be unclear whether anyone has any authority over your digital account assets following your death. Based upon these rules, I encourage you to use the template spreadsheets included in the exhibits within this book to provide your spouse and your "Trusted Contact" with the information necessary to allow your spouse and Trusted Contact to administer these accounts, both during your lifetime and following your death.

Bank, Retirement Accounts, Credit Card Accounts, and Online Shopping Accounts

For online banking, investment, and other financial transaction accounts, create a list of accounts that are current, and perhaps a list of accounts now closed. You save your family and your fiduciaries tremendous time and headache by clearly specifying those accounts that have already been closed or that you simply don't use anymore. For those accounts that are currently in use, you should specify whether you have an authorized user already named.

Social Media

If a tree falls in the forest and no one is in the forest to see it or hear it, did it actually fall? I've likewise wondered, if you died at the height of the pandemic, would the service provider and your "online friends" ever know? Those who have a significant social media presence should consider what should be stated on their Facebook and Twitter accounts following death. For example, you might consider what your Trusted Contact will say on your account at your death. You could go so far as to decide whether your Trusted Contact should extend an invitation to a memorial. For those who have prepared a legacy letter, you can decide whether the legacy letter will be shared via social media.

Passwords

I once dated a girl who, when she broke up with me, told me I belonged in the 1950s. Not surprising is that my password storage system has been straight out of the 1950s—that is, written in pencil on (yes, you guessed it) yellow legal paper. With some service providers, such as financial institutions, your agents would eventually gain access to your accounts even if agents don't still have your password following death. In other cases (most notably, with your Apple ID and password), not having a plan for the transmission of your ID and password may result in the loss of information or files unless your family obtains a court order following death.

It is critical from an estate-planning perspective that family be aware of all accounts and digital assets. I include in this chapter a 1950s-style template for your use in storing this information. Regardless of whether you use my 1950s-style record keeping system for IDs and passwords, or modern-day password storage services (e.g., LastPass or 1Password), create a plan for those accounts and passwords. For accountability reasons, Christians should be providing a spouse and/or Trusted Contact with access to those accounts anyway. The provision of that information should cause neither additional hardship nor potential embarrassment.

ILLUSTRATIONS FOR APPLICATION

The following real-world illustrations demonstrate the importance of fully disclosing your assets and online presence during your lifetime.

Disclosure of Accounts and Assets

A few months after Jim's death, I met Jim's surviving wife, Juanita, and their close friend, Sean. Jim was a well-respected anthropology professor who, we believe, did very well as a do-it-yourselfer in the stock market. Juanita, in contrast, is a delightful and intelligent salesperson but has had no interest in financial matters. According to Juanita, Jim made no disclosures to her about the extent of his investments generally, or the location of his accounts in particular.

As Jim was dying of cancer, he made Sean promise to look after Juanita's financial affairs. Unfortunately for Sean and Juanita, Jim left no financial records for Sean. As of the date of this writing, we have been able to locate some, but not all, of the accounts that Juanita believes were being managed by Jim. Had Jim disclosed the accounts to either Juanita or Sean, Sean would have been able to fulfill the deathbed promise he made to his friend. The last time I spoke with Sean, Sean continues to feel (false) guilt about his inability to fulfill his promise to his dying friend. If Sean had been provided with adequate disclosure of Jim's assets, Jim would have allowed Sean to fulfill his promise.

Online Accounts & Mental Health

Sharon came to our firm for our assistance a few months after the death of her young adult daughter, Andrea. Andrea had experienced health issues and professional setbacks in the past, but no one expected that she would take her own life. With our assistance, Sharon was able to obtain a court order to direct Apple to unlock her daughter's cell phone, thereby granting Sharon access to Andrea's communications. While the court order was necessary in this case, a court order would not have been necessary in other cases had the account owner shared information about the account with at least one other trusted individual. In this case, Sharon was able to access Andrea's history, information that helped Sharon in her own grief journey. In your case, be sure to make your spouse or at least one other individual aware of the existence of all your accounts and how to access them.

Professional Expertise, at the Last Moment

My late client, Phil, held his assets and decisions close to the vest. Some individuals like Phil are incentivized by the joy of being part of the deal. Unfortunately, it seems they can never slow down long enough to keep their family, fiduciaries, or advisors up on the status of the planning, or even where assets are located.

Just a few months before he died, Phil disclosed he held properties in several other states, including a horse farm as well as several investment properties in another state. Shortly before Phil died, we were able to obtain local professional assistance to plan for these assets not previously disclosed. Had Phil not finally understood the importance of disclosing assets to his advisors, and introducing his advisors to one another, it would not have been possible to conduct this end-of-life tax planning. Phil finally told me, "I recently realized, Cory, that unless I share with you the accounts I hold, my business interests, and the relative value, no one, not even my wife, will know where all my assets are located."

In these two previous examples, Jim and Phil both made incorrect assumptions about what others would know. Don't make the same mistake; disclose the nature of your assets to your spouse and professional advisors.

REFLECTIONS

On the Disclosure of Your Assets & Digital Activity

Reflect on how you have disclosed the nature of your assets and digital activity to your spouse and advisors. To avoid any unnecessary drama following your death, it is critical that you disclose the existence of both to the appropriate people.

Your Assets:

To communicate your plan to your family, it is critically important that you provide your spouse, your designated fiduciaries, and your advisors with a full and complete summary of all your assets and all your liabilities. Either complete your own personal financial statement or use the Financial Inventory template at the end of the next chapter.

Your Electronic Footprint:

You should provide access to your electronic footprint.

Who has access to digital accounts?

Does your spouse have access to all digital accounts?

Would you consider asking another individual in your life to access your accounts periodically?

Is there anything in your communications history that you do not wish for your spouse or family to see?

What is the main purpose of your digital communications? Is the means of your communications allowing you to communicate in any disingenuous manner?

Would you like your death to be communicated to others through your social media channels?

Have you established a will or trust providing your spouse the complete authority to access your communications following your death?

Do you have a plan in place for the storage of information (including IDs and passwords) for your accounts and digital assets?

Credit Card, Banking, Brokerage & Other Financial Accounts

For your credit card, banking, investment, savings, and other financial institutions, list the financial institution, your username, and password.

FINANCIAL INSTITUTION	USERNAME	PASSWORD	COMMENTS

Online Purchasing, Sales, & Retail Accounts

For your online purchasing accounts (e.g., Amazon, Target, eBay, etc.), list the website, username and password.

WEBSITE	USERNAME	PASSWORD

Digital Photo, Music, and eBook Libraries & Entertainment Accounts

For your online photo, eBook, and music storage websites, list the website, username and password. Likewise, list the site name and login information for any entertainment accounts, such as Netflix, Hulu, etc.

WEBSITE	USERNAME	PASSWORD

Email Accounts

List all email addresses, together with passwords.

EMAIL ADDRESS	TYPE OF ACCOUNT	PASSWORD	COMMENTS

Social Media Accounts

List the usernames and passwords for social media sites, such as Facebook, LinkedIn, YouTube, etc. Provide your wishes for the use (or disabling) of such accounts in the event of your death or disability. Indicate whether you have provided a named contact (e.g., "Legacy Contact" on Facebook) to be responsible for those accounts in the event of your disability or death.

SOCIAL MEDIA ACCOUNT	USERNAME	PASSWORD	COMMENTS

4B: *Plan*

Inventory your assets and implement a legally binding estate plan.

I am frequently called by the surviving family members of a deceased loved one to **read the will**. Some families are dismayed to learn that a will is not necessarily definitive. The distribution of your assets at your death has more to do with the legal ownership of your assets than about what your will says. If your assumptions about the legal structure of your estate plan turn out to be erroneous, your family may face any number of unwelcome surprises.

Here, as in other aspects of our estate planning, we must be no less wise and learned than our secular neighbors. If we are to steward God's financial assets well, we must educate ourselves on some basic legal principles for how assets pass at death.[1] As a trustee of God's assets, it is incumbent upon us to take inventory of our trust assets and implement a plan for the efficient transfer of our assets in accordance with our trustee duty to implement eternal, spiritual, and godly objectives. In this chapter, we will focus on taking an inventory of financial assets, categorizing those financial assets into one of five categories, and then taking steps to assure ourselves, our family, and our supported ministries that our legal estate plan will accomplish our objectives.

Understand the Law and Plan Accordingly

As Christians, we must follow Jesus' teaching "to be as wise as serpents and as innocent as doves" when it comes to understanding the means of commerce. Let us therefore exercise worldly wisdom in order to achieve optimal outcomes for our family.

Your Legal Debts & Expenses

"Son, I have good news and bad news." The son is startled by this interesting beginning to his phone conversation with his dad.

---

1 While our biblical trust arrangement also includes our human capital and our bodies, in this chapter I will focus exclusively on financial assets.

"Okay," responds the son, "what's the bad news?"

"The bad news, son, is that you will not be receiving an inheritance."

"Oh," the son responds. "But what is the good news?"

"The good news," the father responds, "…is that I am not moving in with you."

Following your death, your assets must be used to pay any outstanding legal obligations and debts. Perhaps by reason of significant end-of-life health care costs and other living expenses, the extent of your financial assets will be reduced in your final days. You are "on the hook"—legally obligated—to pay for your own expenses, including medical and health expenses not covered by insurance. However, it is critical to note that should you hold an insufficient amount of assets at your death to pay for those expenses, your children are not *legally required* to pay them. It is critical to keep in mind that, in these United States, your children do not inherit your debt.

Your Family & Ministry Support Obligations

At your death, you would hold legal obligations to provide for your surviving spouse with a certain portion of your remaining legal assets. If you died with minor children, you would likewise hold legal obligations to support those minor children. Such legal obligations are consistent with a biblical directive to provide for one's household and, so long as you implement a biblical plan, will have no impact on Christians who have already taken steps to provide for their family.

If you have made commitments to ministry organizations during your lifetime and die with such commitment unfulfilled, there is likely no legal obligation for your family to fulfill that pledge.[2] However, you might rightfully feel a moral obligation to be certain that pledge will be fulfilled if you die before it is completed. Not only should you adequately communicate what ministries should be supported in the event of your death, but you should also educate yourself on the most tax efficient means of fulfilling these commitments.

American Legal Freedoms to Transfer Assets at Death

Aside from the legal obligations noted, American law provides the

---

2 If the charity acted in reliance on that pledge (e.g., built a new sanctuary because of your pledge), the charity could bring suit against your estate on legal grounds called "promissory estoppel." I address this in greater detail in Section 11.

owner of an asset with full legal rights over his assets, both during lifetime and then at death. In my experience and observation, many of my clients and their adult children suffer from a misunderstanding that their assets must legally be distributed to their children once both parents die. Indeed, under a secular estate plan, clients will often succumb to the pressures, both from within the family and even one's social community, to maximize the financial size of the inheritance to children. A biblical estate plan, on the other hand, accounts for God's rightful claims over our assets and supersedes not just all claims we have on our worldly wealth, but over the rights, expectations, and entitlements that others might have as well. The key question for most of my clients, then, is not what they are obligated to do from a legal perspective, or what secular culture expects of them, but what is most appropriate from an eternal perspective.

The Five Legal Means of Asset Transfers

At your death, the ownership of your assets will transfer by one of five (5) legal means. I have included one illustration for each of the five legal means of transfer.

1. *Jointly Owned Assets*

First, if assets are jointly owned with another person, the surviving co-owner becomes the new owner at death.

Jointly owned assets can be likened to a child's teeter-totter; it is a "winner take all" arrangement. Whoever falls off the teeter-totter first loses the right to control the assets at death, and the entire value of the assets fall to the survivor. The deceased co-owner's legal estate plan has no relevance in these arrangements. Instead, the assets become owned by the surviving owner, and are subject to the surviving owner's own financial situation, family situation, contractual obligations, and even tax liabilities.[3]

This legal structure is particularly difficult for surviving families to accept if they believed that it was mom's intention that mom's assets jointly owned with one of her children be used for the payment of end-of-life and post-death expenses. The family is often surprised to discover that the surviving co-owner child is legally entitled to

---

3 If your co-owner has creditor issues or is involved in divorce proceedings, a creditor or divorcing spouse may seek to compel you to sell the property, even if the property was only transferred to the co-owner to achieve estate planning objectives.

the entire account, without having to pay for any of those expenses.[4] In many instances, joint ownership of assets with one's spouse is ideal and appropriate. For the reasons stated, carefully consider the implications of this form of ownership with anyone other than your spouse.

2. *Beneficiary-Designated Assets*

Second, assets passing by a beneficiary designation are distributed by a legal contract to the charities or individuals named under the beneficiary designation. Assets passing by a beneficiary designation are like a pre-programmed elevator. The rider of the elevator is brought to the designated floor, even if the rider has no idea what is on the floor, how long it will take, or what will appear on the other side of the elevator door once the doors open. The elevator is simply set to deliver the rider to the designated floor.

It is important to note that these types of assets are legally directed to the named beneficiaries independent of the participation of the named fiduciaries. These types of assets typically include tax-deferred qualified accounts, such as 401K, Roth IRA and IRA plans, as well as life insurance policies and annuity accounts. The administrators of these types of assets, such as the IRA custodian or the life insurance companies, will respond to information inquiries only from those individuals or charities the decedent listed as beneficiaries; also, they will share only the information necessary to allow the beneficiary to receive the designated share of the assets. Anyone other than the named beneficiaries, when inquiring about valuation or status, will be told to, "Get lost; it's none of your business."

3. *Trust Assets*

Third, assets owned in trust are distributed according to the terms of a trust created by the deceased during that person's lifetime. While living, the deceased owned, controlled, and benefited from the trust assets. Following that person's death, assets transferred through a trust can be compared to an Amazon delivery.

An Amazon delivery vehicle (the trust) does not own the item being delivered (the assets); the vehicle (the trust) is simply the means of delivery. If the delivery driver (the trustee) knows where she is going, does not encounter delays due to poor weather or road construction,

---

4 In these instances, the family also loses the full benefit of a tax benefit, called the "step-up" in cost basis that would be the case if an asset was owned individually or in a revocable trust.

and does not consume the perishable package or otherwise destroy it in transit, the package (the assets) will be safely delivered.

When someone with a trust dies, as long as the directions are clear and the delivery driver (trustee) is competent and trustworthy, the deceased's trust will efficiently deliver that person's assets to the new owner. The delivery driver (the trustee) is not supposed to share with neighbors any information about the contents of the package (assets), and the delivery driver (trustee) doesn't need permission to proceed with the delivery of the package (the assets) from any outside third party.

Following the death of the trust creator, the trustee must make the beneficiaries named in the trust aware of the existence of the trust, the fact that he or she is named as a trust beneficiary, and the current assets of the trust. As the trust is subsequently administered, the trustee must keep the beneficiaries reasonably informed of the status of the trust administration. Note that the trustee is authorized to share information about the trust only with the beneficiaries.

4. *Probate Transfer That Is Subject to a Will*

Fourth, if assets do not fall under one of the three categories mentioned above, the assets become part of your estate at death. If you have a last will in place at your death, the terms of your will are then read and legally applied to assets in this category.

Transferring assets through a probate proceeding according to a will is akin to the tardy student who must stop at the principal's office to obtain a tardy excuse slip before attending class. Just like the student will still be able to attend class for the rest of the day, the beneficiaries of an estate will ultimately benefit from the assets subject to the probate. However, like the student who experiences a delay on the way to class, beneficiaries experience a delay in asset distribution. Just as tardiness may even involve future ramifications, probate can also cause problems down the road. And finally, like a student's tardiness is announced by a late arrival to class, probate requires that the deceased's death be announced in the newspaper.

If you die and your assets are subject to probate, your family will need to obtain the approval of a court or court-supervised agent before proceeding with asset transfers. Probate is the branch of the state court system that oversees the legal transfer of certain types of assets you owned at the time of your death. If you die with probate assets, a court will require family members to (1) submit your will to the court to confirm that your will was properly signed, (2) provide public notice of your death through the relevant legal newspaper, (3) allow your creditors a certain amount of time to make claims for unpaid debts or expenses, (4) take steps to make sure that the directions given under your will are carried out.

As opposed to assets that pass through one of the previously referenced categories, the nature and extent of probate assets are subject to full public record. The legal newspaper for your county "broadcasts" the fact that you died and advertises the opportunity for your creditors to come forward to have bills you owe them paid through the probate process. If probate proceedings are necessary by reason of the title to assets, then certain family members must be notified of the existence of the probate proceedings, even if these family members are not named as beneficiaries. Especially in instances in which charitable beneficiaries are named in a plan, the effect of these communication requirements on surviving family can cause unnecessary hassle and, in some instances, difficult relationship dynamics. In most instances, therefore, it is wise to attempt to avoid any probate proceedings.

5. *Probate Transfer That Is Subject to Intestacy*

Fifth, if assets are not in one of the first three categories mentioned above, and if you had no will in place at death, then not only do the assets become part of your estate at death, and thereby subject to probate, but the beneficiaries of your estate are dictated by state law. These state rules are called "rules of intestacy."

Transferring assets through an intestacy probate proceeding is akin to a school uniform policy where everyone has the same fashion plan, with no allowed departures. Similarly, everyone who dies and leaves a surviving spouse has the same plan; everyone who dies with no surviving spouse but surviving children has the same plan. The public policy behind these rules is to provide our society some direction on what the deceased individual *would have wanted* had the deceased owner decided. For many of us, the state default rules happen to be what we want, but this is simply a matter of happenstance.

In general, assets pass by rules of intestacy in the following order:

1. A surviving spouse, if any;

2. The children of the deceased, equally, with any share for a deceased child allocated among that person's children;

3. If no spouse or children, then equally among parents, if living; and

4. If none of the above, then equally to the deceased's siblings.[5]

In such instances, not only are these assets subject to the same probate court process as noted above, but the family has no choice but to implement the state's intestacy rules for the transfer of assets at death. While your assets might be allocated to your desired loved ones (e.g., your spouse or your children), it is best to provide explicit direction in that regard, so your family is not left to the "school uniform policy" to obtain permission to transfer assets.

In conclusion, we should have a basic understanding of how assets are allocated after death since the law sometimes leads to unexpected results. *Christians should have a general sense for how our assets will pass at death so we can be sure our plan is implemented.*

ILLUSTRATIONS FOR APPLICATION

Most of the post-death difficulties that arise among family members following death occur because of a failure to communicate the nature of one's assets and to marry up the assets with actual, not perceived, legal rules for transfer of assets. The following three situations* arose by reason of lack of clarity around the parent's intentions and what the parent did or did not understand about the law.

Unclear Intentions about a Loan

Stephanie and her daughter Laura had a tumultuous relationship. They had first been in business together, then, as a result of that business arrangement, went through family counseling together. Their relationship was a roller coaster. At one point, Laura sued her own mother, Stephanie, over ambiguities in business debts. Stephanie's other two children generally steered clear of getting involved between them. A month before Stephanie died, Laura wrote a $20,000 check to Stephanie that Stephanie deposited. Stephanie left no record of how she characterized the transfer. It was not clear whether this was a gift, a loan from Laura to Stephanie, or a payment on one of the past loans that Stephanie had made to Laura but Laura never repaid. Following

---

5 Uniform Probate Code Section 2-103.

death, Laura claimed that the $20,000 was a loan to her mother that must now be repaid. While the facts appear to suggest that it was a payment on a past loan owed by Laura, nothing could be shown definitively. Had Stephanie completed an asset inventory or other asset summary in the years before her death, this ambiguity would certainly have been avoided.

Unclear Intentions about Life Insurance

Just a few months after he retired, Dean died unexpectedly in his sleep. Following Dean's death, his wife Deidre discovered that Dean had designated his two children as the recipients of $50,000 of life insurance policy proceeds directly through a beneficiary designation on file with the life insurance company. Dean had designated Deidre as the beneficiary of all remaining assets.

This came as a surprise because Dean's trust agreement directed that each of his two adult sons should receive $100,000 at his death, with his wife Deidre receiving all remaining assets. In Dean and Deidre's case, all assets except for the life insurance policy were jointly owned. Since there were no assets allocated to Dean's trust, no assets could fulfill the gift of $100,000 to his sons. As a result, the gift of $100,000 to each of his sons was not legally effective.

No one really knows for certain whether Dean intended for his sons to receive just the $50,000 of life insurance proceeds, the $100,000 designated from the trust, or perhaps even the life insurance proceeds plus the $100,000 from the trust. Dean is not the first, nor will he be the last, to misunderstand the legal significance of beneficiary designations and how those designations may not only confuse surviving family members, but perhaps even thwart one's own estate planning objectives.

Unclear Intentions about Charity

We did not represent Sue during her lifetime, but apparently Sue was a faithful and generous donor to various ministries, and an organization she had supported contacted us following Sue's death. Sue had previously disclosed to the ministry organization that she would be naming the charity in her will to receive a significant gift following her death. However, no gift was ever received by the ministry following her demise. When we contacted Sue's family, we were told that all her assets and accounts were moved into joint ownership before death to avoid probate court proceedings.

According to one family member, Sue told her family that they should give the promised charitable gift "only if they wanted to." When we contacted the family, they responded, quite predictably, that "they didn't want" to follow through on Sue's commitment. In this case, since the assets were in joint ownership at Sue's death, Sue's will did not legally direct the transfer of any assets, including those to the ministry. Unless the ministry uncovers facts suggesting undue influence or fraud as to the transfer of assets to the joint ownership account, the charity has no legal right to bring a suit to recover the promised gift.

In cases like this, joint ownership is not likely to achieve your estate-planning objectives. While individual ownership might create a need for probate proceedings at death, the benefit of probate court administration is that it assures the promised beneficiaries that the deceased loved one's planning objectives are carried out.

REFLECTIONS
On Your Legal Plan

Reflect on your own personal legal plan if any. Have you abided by your duty to God, as the owner of your assets, to create a legally binding estate plan at your death? To properly steward the assets under your care, it is imperative that you create a legal plan consistent with your objectives.

Do you understand the legal implications of owning assets?

Who can help you understand the legal implications of how you own your assets currently?

What legal debts do you have to others currently, and what legal obligations for ongoing support do you have to spouse and children?

Will you leave behind adequate financial resources to pay for legal obligations of support and expected expenses and debts?

I recommend you use the following inventory table in two steps. First, use it to take stock of your current assets and how those assets would pass at your death under your current plan. Second, after reading the sections of this book that apply to your situation, prayerfully complete the inventory according to your intended or desired outcome.[1]

---

1 The completion of this section is a necessary, but not sufficient, legal condition to achieve your estate-planning objectives. You should be sure to consult with legal counsel to obtain legal advice.

FINANCIAL INVENTORY

ASSET	HUSBAND*		WIFE*		JOINT*
	INDIVIDUAL	IN-TRUST	INDIVIDUAL	IN-TRUST	
Primary Residence					
Other Real Estate					
Checking, Savings & Money Market Accounts					
Stocks, Bonds & Other Taxable Investments					
Closely Held Business Interest					

*Only write the amount of the asset in one of the appropriate columns

RETIREMENT ACCOUNT	NAME OF ACCOUNT	OWNER	VALUE	PRIMARY BENEFICIARY	SECONDARY BENEFICIARY
IRA/401K					
Roth IRA					

LIABILITIES	HUSBAND	WIFE	JOINT
Home Mortgage			
Other Debts (Describe)			

LIFE INSURANCE POLICIES (CO. & POLICY #)	FACE VALUE	OWNERS	INSURED	BENEFICIARIES
IRA/401K				
Roth IRA				

4C: *Blessing*

Communicate your love to your children through the ceremonial disclosure of your plan.

As far as drama and intrigue, nothing currently streaming on Netflix can beat it. The story of Isaac, Rebecca, Jacob and Esau and the misplaced blessing on Jacob is the classic tale of family strife, intrigue, and deception. Among other lessons, this story shows us that family disharmony and dysfunction related to a family inheritance has existed for thousands of years.

In the ancient Middle East, it was customary for only one of an Israelite's children, usually the oldest son, to receive the "birthright."[1] This birthright provided the recipient with a double portion of the divided inheritance. In that agrarian culture, it was critical that the landholdings, the herds of sheep and cattle, and other assets be preserved through concentrated holdings for the benefit of the entire family clan. As we see throughout the rest of Genesis, the intrigues initiated by family members to secure the sought-after inheritance rights created a family rift that lasted throughout multiple generations.

In Genesis 27, Rebecca somehow learns of Isaac's plan to bless Esau with the ceremonial birthright pronouncement. She therefore devises a plan to deceive the elderly Isaac by dressing Jacob in Esau's clothing and scents or perfumes (as they would consider perfume) to disguise Jacob as Esau. By reason of Isaac's old age and poor vision, Rebecca helps her favored son Jacob trick Isaac into blessing Jacob rather than Esau.

Our law firm periodically receives calls from adult children of our clients that go something like this: "My dad has told me that he wants me, not my siblings, to receive the entire inheritance once he dies. Can you make arrangements to revise his will to name me as the sole beneficiary?"

---

1 Deuteronomy 21:17.

These adult children have the same mentality as Jacob. These children use the self-justifications of, "I respond to requests for help from my mother," or "My siblings are not present in my father's life." Just as Jacob felt the ever-present desire to feel loved by his parents, we see this dynamic play out frequently in estate-planning conversations. Even when adult children are hard-pressed by their own financial struggles, I believe the desire is the same felt by Jacob towards Isaac—a desire to receive the blessing of a parent, even under false pretenses. Even in the days of Isaac, each of the children could also be provided a unique blessing by the patriarch independent of the birthright.[2]

Christian parents should boldly proclaim that the blessing they bestow upon their children is independent of the financial and legal fiduciary appointment decisions made by them. If you are successful in continually encouraging your children through words and deeds regarding your love for them, you will have pronounced a blessing over your children far greater than a financial gift. The most enduring family pronouncement is when we are healthy and cognizant, when our kids can see the brightness of our eyes, the warmth of our hug, and the emotion in our full-throated voice of affection as we tell them, if not repeatedly then regularly, how much we love them. Depending on the suffering we endure between now and our last days, we may not leave our children with as large a financial inheritance as we would like. But your unconditional blessings of them during your lifetime will leave an indelible mark far more important than the extent of any financial inheritance.

Information to Be Shared with Your Children:

A public pronouncement of blessing to your child should include the adequate communication to them of your estate plan. The extent of the disclosure will depend upon a number of factors, including the maturity of your children and your own financial and health situation. In general, however, I recommend that the following information be provided to adult children:

- **Your Narrative Story.** Ideally, you should have a written description of your story—that is, how you inherited assets, how the Lord allowed you to gather assets, and what you learned through your mistakes. You should share your desires for a long-term legacy for them, generally, and articulate the use of any financial assets left behind.

---

2 See Genesis 27:36, where Esau states that Jacob took his birthright as well as his blessing.

- **Fiduciaries.** You should let your children know who you have chosen as your "fiduciaries" under the terms of your estate plan. If you have chosen a professional trustee or fiduciary, that person should be introduced to your adult children.

- **Key Advisors.** You should introduce your children to your professional advisors and provide your children with their contact information.

- **Individual Beneficiaries.** You should let your family know the general plan for the disposition of your remaining assets. If you own unique or "indivisible" assets (*e.g.,* land or even sentimental family heirlooms), you should communicate the plan to your children for the distribution of these assets. Please note that the disclosure to your children of who will benefit is a separate question of knowing how much the beneficiaries will receive.

- **Charitable Planning.** If you decide to make charitable gifts at death, you should inform your children of these gifts so that, unlike in the movies, there are no surprises. If there are ongoing lifetime charitable gifts that you are currently making that you would like your children to continue, you should inform them of those gifts.

- **Brief Legal Overview.** You should provide a brief one-page summary of the legal structure(s) involved in your plan, such as beneficiary designations, trusts, or business entities, and how those planning structures achieve your overall legacy objectives.

- **Family Vision Statement.** Finally, some clients are blessed to have children or other family members who share faith in Christ. Children might have indicated a desire to "marry up" their own personal goals for stewarding God's resources for eternal purposes, so you could invite them to work together with you on a financial vision statement.

We generally advise against providing full disclosure of current balance sheets, both because it may lead to unconscious expectations on the part of a child regarding a future inheritance, and because your financial situation will certainly change, to some degree, between your sharing the information and the time of your death.

Ceremonial Family Meetings

Before the days of the written word, the verbal blessing of the patriarch to his family was the legally binding act by which the appointed individual would be officially introduced as the next in line. At the end of his life, Jacob called his sons together for a public pronouncement of blessings.[3] In Jacob's case, he blessed Judah and Joseph, but also called out Reuben's outrageous behavior, and likened his son Benjamin to "ravenous wolves.[4]" While we need not follow Jacob's lead in laying bare all of family dirty laundry, there is value in following his lead of a public family blessing.

While oral pronouncements are no longer legally binding, they leave a far more indelible imprint on the family's collective memory than a stale legal document. I have had the privilege of participating in client family meetings, and I can attest to the emotional and relational benefits of such meetings. If you have not already done so, you should plan a ceremonial family meeting to disclose your legal estate plan. You might keep the following factors in mind in planning the meeting.

Context of Ceremony. First, you should conduct the meeting in a context of ceremony. If adult children are multi-tasking with childcare issues or work issues, or even trying to catch up on the sports game on television, it would detract from the ceremonial effect of the information being disclosed. You are looking not only to communicate the information itself, but also emphasize how important these legacy planning discussions are to you, even if they don't quite (yet) grasp the relative degree of importance. Let your children know the subject of the meeting ahead of time, both so that they are not blindsided by the subject of the gathering, and so that they can address the subject with some degree of ceremony.

Constituents. Second, if you are disclosing decisions about the allocation of unique assets or your decisions on asset distributions, include only your children in the meetings. While there is a place for grandchildren and your sons-in-law and daughters-in-law, it is not in these most significant discussions or disclosures. My own experience is that when it comes to discussions about the family cabin or other unique asset divisions, it is best to include only children and not their spouses. Children are more likely to have emotional ties

---

3 Genesis 49. In Jacob's case, his blessing takes the form of predicting future outcomes, particularly for his sons Judah and Joseph and their respective lineages.
4 Genesis 49:27.

to the unique assets in question, and they are more willing to accept sibling unanimity as a goal. A child's spouse, in contrast, is more apt to look at discussions through the lens of maximizing receipt of total financial value. In the context of discussions between adult children about the family cabin, the adult children, not the spouses, are seeking to reach an amicable solution to preserving ongoing family ownership. Excluding spouses tends to turn down the potential emotional temperature in the room. Including children also increases the perceived sense of ceremony by including only the direct-line beneficiaries in these discussions.

Clarity. Finally, you should be as clear and straightforward as possible with your plan. If you decide to incorporate any written summary, keep it simple (one-page outline); this would certainly not be the time to provide any legal documents. If you decide to provide your adult children with the details about your current net worth, you should be very clear that this amount is subject to a number of factors, including fluctuations in the market and your own future living expenses.

The Benefits of Full Family Disclosure

According to a 2018 survey of high net-worth households, only one-third of families surveyed indicated that they had discussed their estate plan with their children. When questioned, most of those who had not yet shared any information about their plan cited the difficulty in making decisions.[5] Among other reasons, the survey cited a "high degree of confidence in one's own ability to make decisions as the reason for not disclosing the estate plan." While the secular approach is to kick the can down the road and thereby avoid making difficult decisions, not to mention disclose those decisions to others, Christians are called to disclose these decisions.

Even secular professionals are coming around to these traditional biblical principles. In a new academic study entitled, "The Better-Than-Expected Consequences of Asking Sensitive Questions," authors Hart, Schweitzer and Ven Epps found that most assumptions about asking sensitive questions are unfounded. According to the authors, "individuals make a potentially costly mistake when they avoid asking sensitive questions, as they overestimate the interpersonal

5 Merrill Lynch Private Wealth Survey through Phoenix Marketing International Survey, cited in thinkadvisor.com.

costs of asking sensitive questions." [6] We avoid asking difficult or sensitive questions to friends, family and strangers alike because we assume that initiating difficult conversations will be considered offensive. Surprisingly, the study showed that rather than creating relationship harm between the conversation participants, the questions actually improved the relationship. The difficult questions create the opportunity to allow the respondent to share thoughts, beliefs or feelings of more significant importance than those one might typically discuss with others in our current culture of hundreds of "surface" relationships. N." If we don't ask important questions to friends and family members, we miss out on the opportunity to deepen a relationship with them.

If you are able to communicate your plan to your family, you will reap at least three benefits.

Legal Certainty

First, you would achieve legal certainty that your wishes will be carried out following your death. An estate plan can be legally overturned by a court after your death only if the circumstances surrounding the execution of your legal documents demonstrate either (1) that you were "unduly influenced" by someone into signing the documents or (2) you did not have sufficient mental capacity to understand what you were signing. Therefore, if you have open communications with all your children at the same time during such time as there is no evidence of dementia, you will have a "bulletproof" plan from a legacy perspective.

Desired Asset Distribution Format Among Children

Second, adequate communication might allow for a more desirous format of distribution following your death. When I perceive that a client has an extreme case of the "Minnesota nice" syndrome with her adult children, I try to remind her that she is the "boss;" that is, the ultimate decision maker. That being the case, if a client or client couple has articulated a plan for the division of assets that does not appear to truly benefit one or more adult children, communicating the plan allows for the child or children to provide the client with the necessary feedback on the plan in order to reconsider. For example, many of my

6 "The Better Than Expected Consequences of Asking Sensitive Questions," authors Hart, Schweitzer and Ven Epps found that our assumptions about asking sensitive questions are unfounded. https://knowledge.wharton.upenn.edu/article/why-you-shouldnt-be-afraid-to-ask-sensitive-questions/

clients create a plan for the allocation of the ownership of the family cabin among some or all children. However, when an adult daughter moves to the opposite coast, or marries into a family with a separate family cabin, the adult daughter can express an issue with the format. At that time, the plan can be reconsidered.

Clearance of Emotional Baggage

Third, open dialogue creates an opening for children to respond to you, now, over the coffee or conference table instead of responding with animus toward their siblings over your coffin. Once parents tell their children of the plan, an aggrieved daughter or son can deal directly to mother and/or father during their lifetime instead of making their disagreement a source of contention among their siblings following their parents' death. In many cases, these responses are the result of longstanding emotional obstacles that exist between parents and their adult children. Financial advisor Ross Levin writes about the benefit of family meetings, even meetings that, "…degenerate quickly because someone says something that causes feelings to get hurt." Levin emphasizes the benefits of even those meetings that lead to disorder because of the long-term planning benefits to the family. "Rather than wonder what people are feeling, disclosure leads to a better understanding of various viewpoints and therefore helps alleviate the unsolved mysteries after death that occur in families that don't talk about challenging things."[7] Once both parents are gone, no one is present to mediate the emotional baggage that still exists in the mind and heart of a sixty-something-year-old daughter over the fact that her siblings had better dental work or nicer sandbox toys than she did as a child. Unbelievably, both situations have existed among our clients in two different families.

When it comes to the relationship between attorneys and clients, or between clients and their children, if we don't take the opportunity to ask important questions or raise difficult topics, we miss out on the opportunity to deepen a relationship with them. In turn, these deeper relationships may actually prove to be beneficial when it comes to managing estate-planning matters.

If Isaac and Rebecca had conducted open and honest conversations with their children, much family strife could have been avoided . Some clients don't want to bear bad news to potential beneficiaries

---

7 Ross Levin, "Spend Your Life Wisely," Star Tribune, February 28, 2021.

about an inheritance. These clients, whom we in Minnesota sometimes refer to as our "Minnesota nice" clients, would rather maintain a comfortable ambiguity rather than face the disappointment of potential beneficiaries. We communicate our love for them as well as a true blessing through the honest disclosure of information. In Isaac's case, he should have approached both Esau and Jacob with words of encouragement and acts of love, even while making his intentions clear at the same time that Esau was the recipient of the birthright.

"Jacob, I am going to publicly announce your brother Esau as the recipient of the birthright. This is not because he and I are hunting partners, or that we share other interests. I am providing your brother with the birthright simply because it is our custom to do it this way, not because of anything you did wrong. We have found special ways to bless you and honor you, as our beloved second son, and we will continue to find additional ways to demonstrate to you how much we love you and wish to honor you as our second son."

ILLUSTRATIONS FOR APPLICATION

If you are blessed to have adult children, I encourage you and your spouse to bless your children through communicating your plan to them. I offer three illustrations from my law practice to apply to your own unique situation.

Blessing Your Children with the Closing Dinner

Ryan was an accomplished attorney specializing in buying and selling businesses. Before he retired, Ryan often participated in "closing dinners" with his clients—meals at fine restaurants scheduled with his business clients after the successful close of a deal. When Ryan and his wife Kelly finalized their plan, Ryan and Kelly proposed that we schedule a closing dinner.

Ryan, Kelly and I hosted a meeting at my office that included their entire family as well as their CPA and financial advisor. Dinner reservations for the family were made down the street for the post-meeting festivities. Ryan, Kelly and their family marked the ceremonial significance of the decisions made through the "closing" meeting with their attorney and advisory team, and then with a memorable meal. Through this closing dinner, Ryan and his wife impressed upon their children the importance of the disclosures made and the blessing of being part of the family. In your case, you might consider a ceremonial closing dinner, which might include renting a vacation home for a long weekend, attending a musical performance or sporting event, or taking a family trip together.

Blessing Your Children By Naming a Professional Trustee

Dr. Jill was a well-respected physician. She and her late husband were the parents of four sons, all four of whom became respected and established physicians. From infancy and into adulthood, these sons were in perpetual competition with one another. Dr. Jill determined that she could not bear to choose one son over another, and so determined that she would name all four of her sons as co-trustees at her death.

The result of this decision was predictable—lots of contention and even litigation. The four sons were constantly trying to "one-up" each other, creating a nightmare for the trust administration. Had I been the attorney representing Dr. Jill during her lifetime, I hope that I could have convinced her to ceremonially bless each of her children through means separate from naming all four of them as co-trustees. By naming a professional trustee, each of the sons would have been spared the outcome of years of hard feelings and large legal fees. I encourage you to avoid the same mistake as Dr. Jill by ceremoniously blessing each of your children in a manner other than naming all of them as trustees.

Introducing Charitable Endeavors

Ted transformed the fledgling company he inherited from his father into an established, multistate operation. Ted and his wife Bev have three adult children, each of whom demonstrated differing aptitudes and capabilities. Their oldest son was becoming increasingly involved in the family business and demonstrated an aptitude and ability to eventually lead the family companies. Their middle child had struggled through various professional endeavors. She did, however, appreciate the opportunity to be involved in community charitable work. Their youngest daughter was determined to be a homemaker and to spend as much time as possible with her husband and their children at Ted and Bev's lake property.

Bev, Ted and I determined it appropriate to convene a family meeting. Bev and Ted blessed each of their children and legally designated each of them in ways that were unique to the child's particular situation and calling. One child would take over the family business, although not necessarily receive the entire company as a gift. The second child would be responsible for the family charitable foundation, while the third child would receive a cash gift as well as ownership in the family cabin. As far as we know, each of the children appreciated the disclosure of the plan and appeared to be honored by the blessing.

REFLECTIONS
On Family Blessings

Reflect on how you might ceremoniously bless your children. Have you adequately communicated your plan to them during your lifetime—that is, "read your own will"?

What specific steps have you taken to disclose your plan to your family?

Have you disclosed to your adult children the critical elements of your estate plan?

Given your particular family situation, what would be the best context to conduct a family meeting?

Who should be invited to the meeting, and what should be shared with them?

Have you introduced your key advisors to your children?

Have you pronounced a blessing upon each of your children in the presence of others?

Have you shared your narratives of suffering, success and stewardship setbacks with them?

LESSON FIVE
Fiduciaries

Appoint those individuals or institutions who are in the best position to execute your plan.

As a man who loves a good meal, I have always been honored to be part of an Anlauf family dinner. Most of the members of my wife Heather's family, the Anlauf family, have strong views on how meals should be properly prepared. Another brother-in-law, who also came to the Anlauf family by marriage, provided me this sage advice before we were married: "Whatever you do, enjoy the great food, but stay out of the Anlauf family kitchen." While I am honored to be part of the family meal, I am not qualified to cook, and given the abundance of good cooks, there is no need for me to be in the kitchen and otherwise pretend that I am a cook.

Just as the Anlauf family can have too many cooks in the kitchen, an estate plan should not only have ***the right number of cooks in the kitchen, but the right cooks completing the right tasks***. Some well-meaning parents, to avoid the possibility of disappointment among children, effectively ask all of their children to bake the ham, or all of their children to mash the potatoes, and all of their children to make the dessert. They name ***all*** of their adult children in ***all*** "key individual" or "fiduciary" roles. In such an event, all the children would need to participate and agree upon all fiduciary decisions, large and small. In addition to the very real possibility of disagreement over even relatively minor matters, naming more than one individual presents tremendous logistical hurdles. Among other tasks, all the named children would be required to attend real closings, review account statements, and sign tax returns.

In the age of the Old Testament patriarchy, it would have been a significant dishonor, if you were the eldest son, to have someone else named in your place. In addition to receiving a financial blessing, the birthright recipient had a pseudo-fiduciary duty to oversee the family's asset holdings. The honorary nature of being appointed as a key individual continues to this day, as so many of my clients place themselves in a position within their family in which they are forced, from a relationship perspective, to name a child as a fiduciary. But as we will see in examples from the Old Testament, appointing the wrong individual in a fiduciary role will have disastrous consequences.

For the reasons stated in subsequent chapters, we must follow the example of the Old Testament patriarchs by honoring our children. ***Honoring your children through a well-designed estate plan does not require you to appoint your children as legal fiduciaries; in fact, in might be best to name someone other than your children to assure the proper execution of the plan.*** The appointment of the appropriate fiduciaries is among the most critical decisions of your estate plan, as even the best-laid legal plans can be shipwrecked by a nefarious fiduciary. In this chapter, I summarize the fiduciary appointments you must make, then provide five biblical principles to consider in making proper appointments.

Universal Fiduciary Appointments

By law, each of us has the legal authority to name individuals to make decisions for us, either during our lifetime or following our death. Regardless of our specific circumstances, every adult in the United States has no less than three important decisions to be made regarding key individual or fiduciary appointments, as follows:

- **Power of Attorney:** The individual(s) named under your power of attorney designation, who are called your "attorneys-in-fact," have the legal authority to make *financial decisions* for you *during your lifetime*. This is of critical importance if you become unable to make your own decision, such as by reason of dementia, a brain injury or another mental deficit.

- **Health Care Agent**: The individual(s) named under your health care directive, called your "health care agent," has the legal authority to make ***health care decisions*** for you if your medical care provider determines that, by reason of poor health, you are unable to make your own health care decisions.

- **Personal Representative/Executor:** The individual named as your "personal representative" holds legal authority to implement your directions *following death*.

Additional Fiduciary Appointments

In addition to these universal fiduciary designations, your circumstances may require you to make two additional appointments:

- **Guardians:** The individual or couple named by you who would hold all parenting authority for any surviving minor child until the child reaches adulthood.

- **Trustee:** The individual or institution named by you would have the legal authority to manage trusts created by you.

I have included a summary at the end of this chapter as a means for you and your spouse to consider who you would designate for these positions.

Five Lessons from Ancient Israel

Examining the lives of the Israelite kings in the Old Testament provides us with some key insights for making our own fiduciary appointments. Wisely consider the effect of defaulting to children or others who are "owed" the role, but instead consider who is in the best position to wisely steward the plan.

1. Decide now, knowing that you can change your appointments as circumstances change.

First, appoint a trusted friend or family member while you are in good health, and let your decision be known among your friends and family. If you have studied King David's life, you know that while David was known as "a man after God's heart," David made many mistakes, especially in marriage and parenting. Perhaps by reason of the intra-family political pressures that arose because of his polygamous marriages, it appears that King David spoiled his many children and was an emotionally distant father. David sought to avoid becoming involved in the inter-family disputes that arose in his household. Toward the end of his life, David was so ill and infirm that a beautiful young woman, Abishag the Shunammite, was brought to lie with the old King at night to keep him warm.[1]

While King David was facing these infirmities, King David's oldest living son, Adonijah, appears to have positioned himself to become the presumptive heir to the throne. In a set of circumstances that only a trust and estate litigator would love, one of King David's wives, Bathsheba, came to remind King David of a promise that he previously made; that is, that Solomon, who was David's son by Bathsheba, would be King David's successor. At the very moment that Adonijah was using taxpayer dollars to celebrate his succession to the throne, King David openly pronounced that Solomon, not Adonijah, would occupy David's throne. Can you imagine the "Breaking News" headlines for these events on one of today's modern cable news networks?

While none of us is currently leading a nation of millions, you or your clients should not make the same mistake as King David. Many of my clients, not wanting to stir the pot among family, will punt on making important fiduciary decisions. By not deciding, they are only increasing the likelihood that strife and animosity will occur among family members after their death. It is always better to tactfully articulate your fiduciary decisions while you are healthy, even if you have no reason to believe that a fiduciary role will be utilized. The chances of you and your spouse both dying before your children reach adulthood is very small. However, the negative ramifications of failing to direct the appropriate guardianship appointment could be disastrous if no designation is made. You must therefore make the relevant fiduciary designations immediately, knowing that you will always have the legal right to change your designations as life changes.

2. Consider the relationship dynamics among your family.

Second, avoid appointing an adult child in any legal position of discretionary authority over financial assets earmarked specifically for his or her sibling/s. If you establish a testamentary trust for the benefit of a child or grandchild, you will also need to name a trustee for that trust. As demonstrated by the long history of difficult sibling relationships, attempt to avoid naming the beneficiary/child's sibling as the trustee, as the relationship will not likely flourish on account of the obligations placed on the trustee/child. Within our legal system, legal remedies are the only recompense for bad actors. Court

---

1 1 Kings 1.

injunctions, financial compensation, or both, are the sole means of legally enforcing a person's legally binding estate plan. These legal remedies, however, cannot adequately address the emotional turmoil and relationship wreckage that can result from the enforcement of a plan. The law simply does not care about the painful animosity that often arises where one sibling becomes the legal "gatekeeper" of another child's financial inheritance. A biblical estate plan, therefore, should incorporate the relationships that currently exist between and among family, and work to implement a plan that alleviates, rather than aggravates, any existing intra-family relationship strains.

After King David died and Solomon succeeded him to the throne, Adonijah was left as a son without a kingdom, a child without a meaningful financial inheritance of his own.[2] In a move that signaled his desire to establish a symbolic kingship in the name of his father, Adonijah asked Solomon for permission to marry Abishag. After Adonijah's first failed attempt to capture the throne, Solomon rightly viewed Adonijah as a continued threat to his own throne. Rather than let this threat continue, Solomon put Adonijah to the sword.

While your kids are not fighting to the death over middle eastern kingdoms, neither logic nor significant attorney's fees tends to be a barrier to hotheaded siblings using whatever means necessary to get their way with their parents' money. Our children might feel aggrieved if a sibling is named as a trustee of their portion of a substantial inheritance following death.[3] Rather than place a child in a no-win decision over the management of a sibling's inheritance, you should consider alternatives to naming a related trustee, such as a professional or independent trustee. The professional trustee is not coming to Thanksgiving dinner. While a professional trustee is certainly far costlier to the trust, given the necessity of the trustee fees charged to the trust, this fee is far less significant than the emotional and relationship damage that could result from siblings being at odds with one another.

When considering your options for trustee, consider the following list of advantages and disadvantages associated with each type of trustee:

2 1 Kings 2
3 According to Proverbs 18:19, "A brother offended is more unyielding than a strong city, and quarreling is like the bars of a castle."

A. Beneficiary/Family Member

Advantages:

- Knowledge of your unique asset situation and planning objectives
- Cost savings

Disadvantages:

- Lack of Experience
- Potential pressures related to good faith and impartiality duties

B. Non-Professional Individual(s)

Advantages:

- Knowledge of your unique asset situation and planning objectives
- Cost savings

Disadvantages:

- Lack of Experience
- Lack of incentive to administer the estate in a timely manner

C. Independent Professional Trustee

Advantage:

- Professional expertise in trust administration

Disadvantages:

- Lack of prior knowledge of your unique asset situation and planning objectives
- Higher fees

D. Attorney, CPA or Financial Advisor

Advantages:

- Professional expertise in administration, including reduced need for obtaining professional assistance. If professional assistance is required, assurance of finding good legal help.

- Knowledge of your unique asset situation and planning objectives

Disadvantage:

- Potential conflict of interest related to attorney's fees
- Higher fees

3. Consider the candidates personal and professional advisors.

Third, consider who the potential fiduciary will turn to for advice.
Whether or not a potential fiduciary will make good decisions can
be often predicted by the identity of the individuals from whom
they currently obtain advice. Following the death of King Solomon,
King Rehoboam succeeded him to the throne. Immediately upon his
accession to the throne, Rehoboam was confronted with conflicting
counsel.[4] One set of advisors, who had been his father's advisors,
counseled in favor of reducing the severe tax burden that King
Solomon had imposed. A second and younger set of advisors advised
Rehoboam to increase the tax burden. Rehoboam ultimately chose to
follow the advice of the younger set of advisors, and the result of the
increased tax burden was a revolt and a splintering of the nation of
Israel.

By reason of his ascendancy to the throne, Rehoboam had the right
to choose his key advisors. As with the case of King Rehoboam, I
have seen fiduciaries choose a new set of "younger" advisors who are
arguably not really advisors at all, but just friends who will tell the
fiduciary what the fiduciary wants to hear. I wonder how much King
Solomon knew about Rehoboam's two sets of advisors ahead of his
own death. I wonder if he chose to turn a blind eye to the fact that his
son Rehoboam might choose a saltier set of advisors than his own.

The most difficult fiduciaries to work with are those who think they
know it all. Some of my fiduciary clients seem intent on reinventing
the wheel, acting litigious toward third parties, and even seeking ways
to overrule the intentions of the original legal owner and trust grantor.
If your fiduciary candidate would take the approach of "I don't know
what I don't know," that person has sufficient humility to ask for, and
receive, professional advice from those who have been there before.
The individual trustee candidate should be coachable; that person
needs a healthy dose of humility about his or her own limitations and

4 2 Chronicles 10:8.

a willingness to seek the necessary investment, tax, and legal counsel. Be wary of those who want to be the star of the show and who would refuse outside help because of it. In sporting terms, we would say it is better to choose a *role player* trustee than a *star player* trustee.

While the stakes are not as high for us as they were for King Solomon and King Rehoboam, it is nonetheless important to consider the variables that impact the appropriateness of fiduciary designations.

> **Personal Relationships.** With what type of "characters" do your candidates currently associate? What life choices have those characters made? Do your candidates speak in glowing terms about friends who skirted the law? Would the candidate and his friends "do it their way" rather than the legal way? Does your candidate have a strong marriage in the sense that he or she will be able to take good counsel and assistance from a spouse? Would a spouse or family member pressure the trustee to act in a manner other than what the trustee has been asked to do? Would these individuals pressure the trustee in a way that would adversely impact that person's ability to follow through with both the letter of the law as well as the spirit of your estate plan?

> **Professional Relationships.** If the type of assets owned by you requires professional legal or tax advice, do your candidates have professional relationships already in place to assist them with key tax, accounting and perhaps business or legal decisions? If those people are not the same as your professional relationships, are you content with the choices made by the candidate regarding professional advisory relationships?

4. Consider the character attributes of the candidates.

Fourth, consider how the character attributes of the candidates would be implemented in executing the necessary tasks. King David's appointment of King Solomon started out well for the nation of Israel. Ultimately, however, it resulted in disaster for the nation of Israel. As we examine candidates to name in various fiduciary roles, we should look for candidates who fit the description of King Solomon in the first part of his reign ("Solomon 1.0") rather than the second part of his reign ("Solomon 2.0").

During the first part of his reign, King Solomon was considered the wisest man to have lived up to that time. "And God gave Solomon wisdom and understanding beyond measure, and breadth of mind like the sand on the seashore, so that Solomon's wisdom surpassed the wisdom of all the people of the east and all the wisdom of Egypt... And people of all nations came to hear the wisdom of Solomon, and from all the kings of the earth, who had heard of his wisdom."[5] But Solomon ignored the Lord's direction to walk in the ways of the Lord when Solomon's 700 wives, princesses, and 300 concubines turned Solomon's heart away from the Lord.[6] "So Solomon did wat was evil in the sight of the Lord and did not wholly follow the Lord, as David his father had done."[7] While none of your candidates could be as wise as Solomon 1.0, you should consider the character attributes of individual candidates for each of the roles you need to fill. Following are additional considerations for naming fiduciaries:

Guardians and Trustees: The Importance of Godly Character

Your guardian will fill the role of the stand-in parent in place of you and your spouse. The designation of the proper guardian might have eternal, spiritual, and godly benefits to your children if both you and your spouse die before your children reach adulthood. Christian parents should consider the following factors for their guardianship designations:

- **Disciples of Jesus.** Based upon your observation of the faith walk of the candidates, do they have the ability and willingness to disciple your children in the gospel of Jesus Christ?

- **Uniformity of Core Beliefs.** Could the candidates manage the spiritual and educational opportunities for the children consistent with the parenting goals you have established for your children?

- **Capacity.** Does the candidate have the current physical and emotional capacity to parent your children in addition to any of their own?

- **Marriage.** Do the candidates have a healthy marriage? I generally recommend clients name a husband and wife to act jointly as guardians. If they divorce, or if either of them is unable to act, your named successors would serve as

5 1 Kings 4:29–30, 34.
6 1 Kings 11:3.
7 1 Kings 11:6.

guardians.

- **Personal Financial Stability.** What is the financial situation of the candidates? The children of the candidates should be raised with a standard of living consistent with the standard of living provided for by you through the trust(s) established for the benefit of your children.

- **Relationships with Surviving Family and Church**. Do the candidates have the ability and willingness to maintain relationships with your surviving family members, especially grandparents, as well as members of your church and other supportive friends.

Bear in mind that all of us are imperfect, and so you must make the best choice possible. If you waited for the perfect candidate to be your minor child's guardian, you would never name anyone. You and your spouse must therefore come to a negotiated settlement as to who would be in the best position to act.

Diligence and Advocacy

Your candidate for each of these fiduciary roles should be diligent about gathering information about your situation, being timely in decision-making and, when appropriate, advocate on your behalf. We are told that King Solomon 1.0 learned so much about the natural world that people came from around the world to hear him speak. King Solomon was clearly blessed with the ability to gain knowledge and wisdom.[8] Like Solomon version 1.0, a fiduciary should be willing to press into the knowledge of the chosen professional advisors and medical professionals for information about your situation. Your fiduciary must be willing to use this information gained and advocate your desires on your behalf. Especially in the health care context, a health care agent should be willing to diligently gather information about your care and advocate on your behalf.

Capacity and Proximity

Your candidate must have the capacity to take on the tasks, and the physical ability to do so, given his or her current life situation. Solomon 2.0 could not, and did not, attend to his own soul and

8 1 Kings 4:31–34.

worship the Lord as his father David had done. How would Solomon have had time to worship the Lord while appeasing his 700 wives and the "gods" that these wives followed? If you can envision the life your candidates currently lead, and then add into that life mix the obligations you would be asking them to fulfill, consider the likelihood that they can successfully manage your situation.

5. Consider the Number of Cooks in the Kitchen

Fifth and finally, name the fewest number of individuals necessary to successfully complete the duties required of the position. In the case of Solomon and Adonijah, an office sharing agreement was workable between them. There would be no "Kingship Sharing" in the nation of Israel. George Washington, who knew something about how to manage important tasks, once said, "My observation is that whenever one person is found adequate to the discharge of a duty…it is worse executed by two persons, and scarcely done at all if three or more are employed therein." There may be good reasons to name more than one decision-maker, but clients should be advised of the gains in efficiency earned by naming as few individuals as possible.

If an adult child is receiving good help and advice from professional or non-professional advisors, no one is in a better position to act for you than a member of your immediate family. In those situations in which more than one adult child meets all of the qualifications specified in this chapter, it is best to "divide and conquer" rather than have too many cooks in the kitchen. If three children are all equally qualified, a widow or widower could name one child as personal representative, a second child as power of attorney, and a third child as health care agent. Each child, while keeping the two others reasonably informed of his or her decisions, does not need to physically involve his or her two siblings to make decisions.

In subsequent chapters, we will consider various means of honoring your children. However, because of the risks associated with improper or inefficient implementation if the tasks are left to the wrong individual, it is better to separate the tasks of honoring each of your children from naming a fiduciary. In fact, if you have concerns about one of your children, you might elect to name **none of your children in any role** to avoid the perception of dishonor directed towards the non-elected child or children. Instead, consider each of the candidates for your fiduciary roles from a more disinterested approach, knowing that other opportunities exist for you to honor each of your children.

Christians should appoint the most appropriate individuals or institutions to achieve the tasks necessary for the successful completion of a biblical estate plan. We should name as few individuals as necessary to achieve the objectives. In those instances in which we are concerned about "offending" others, we might create new jobs so that everyone can be a "cook in the kitchen." Even if means that we risk offending one or more people who feel entitled to act, we must carry out our obligations to the Lord as His trustee to appoint the most qualified candidate. As we consider the management of the assets which God has given us, we might carefully consider who will "carry on" the objectives to which God has called us.

ILLUSTRATIONS FOR APPLICATION

The following client illustrations emphasize the importance of appointing the appropriate fiduciaries in your estate plan.

Appointing a Professional Trustee

While Elizabeth had no children of her own, Elizabeth was a matriarchal influence in the lives of her ten nieces and nephews. Elizabeth's plan directed that, at her death, each of the ten nieces and nephews would receive a generous specific gift, with all remaining assets passing to her church. Originally, Elizabeth had designated three of the ten nieces and nephews as the trustees and personal representatives. However, when Elizabeth and I met a few years before her death, it became clear that the designation of these nieces and nephews would place a burden on each of them. Each of these nieces and nephews had numerous work and family obligations and would have little capacity to serve. Instead, Elizabeth appropriately decided that a professional trustee would be in a better position to handle her investment assets at death.

Following Elizabeth's death, the professional trustee was able to attend to the trust administration without burdening any of the family members. By naming a professional trustee, the family benefited from the inheritance, but without the legal tasks associated with post-death trust administration. In Elizabeth's case, the church was effectively paying for the professional trustee, as Elizabeth named the church as the recipient of remaining assets. In your case, you might likewise consider naming a professional trustee to manage the administration of your estate or trust if the nature of your assets are not unique and such an appointment would free family from the burden of the work.

The Nephew with Unique Asset Knowledge

In contrast to Elizabeth's unique family situation is the family and business situation of my client, Dave. Like Elizabeth, Dave has no children of his own, but is very close to his four nieces and nephews. As in Elizabeth's case, Dave named his nieces and nephews as beneficiaries of his remaining assets, which include business interests in various technology companies. One of Dave's nephews, Todd, has been active with Dave in Dave's technology businesses. While Dave could appoint a professional trustee to act when he dies, we agreed that it was appropriate for Todd to act as trustee. Dave has taken it upon himself to schedule meetings with Todd twice a year to provide Todd with ongoing updates on his businesses. In Dave's case, the appointment of Todd is ideal, given Todd's personal business acumen and his knowledge of Dave's business matters. In your case, consider whether you have anyone in your life who has a unique knowledge of your situation or whose skill set would be useful to administer your assets following your death.

Inventing New Jobs

Marlene simply cannot bring herself to not name all five of her children to have some role following her death. Marlene and I have therefore invented new roles for three of the children so that, in addition to the child named as Personal Representative and the child named as successor Trustee, the other three also have roles. Although these roles would be only "honorary" in nature, as ultimately the trustee (following death) or attorney-in-fact (during lifetime) has the legal authority over these matters, naming someone will at least ostensibly provide additional people with additional tasks. By "creating a job" for all family members, the family has the benefit of taking on a task in a time of grief, and Marlene feels good about the fact that no one in the family is excluded. By way of example, and by no means is this list exhaustive, here are some "created" jobs that could be assigned by those who don't wish to exclude anyone:

o   Family Heirloom Coordinator

o   Digital Accounts & Social Media Accounts Director

o   Family Gathering Coordinator

o   Memorial Fund Collaboration Specialist

Alas, attorneys are not very creative, so I'll leave it to you to create additional jobs unique to your family should you feel an obligation to give each of your "cooks" a job in the kitchen.

REFLECTIONS
On Your Fiduciaries

If you have not already named your key individuals, **now is the time to do so**. Reflect on the attributes necessary to administer your legal matters after your death. Identify which of the five legal roles summarized at the beginning of this chapter apply to you. If you are married, you will need to discuss the pros and cons of various candidates with your spouse and come to a mutual agreement. Once you have identified all the roles you need, review the attributes summarized in this chapter to identify your best options. For each identified role, choose both a primary as well as a secondary agent. Your secondary agent would act only if your primary agent were unable or unwilling to act.

Financial Power of Attorney: Lifetime Financial Decisions

- Capacity to take on organizational and bookkeeping tasks

- Existing personal and professional relationships

- Physical proximity to you

>   Primary: _____

>   Secondary: _____

Health Care Directive: Lifetime Health Care Decisions

- Demonstrated capability of making difficult decisions under emotional stress

- Ability to advocate your desires with health care professionals

- Physical proximity to you

>   Primary: _____

>   Secondary: _____

Guardians: Parents for Minor Children

- Followers of Jesus; uniformity of core beliefs; capacity; marital status; financial situation

- Current residence, or ability to move to your current residence

    Primary Couple: _____

    Secondary Couple: _____

Personal Representative: Post-Death Administration of Assets

- Demonstrated ability to seek and obtain good advice
- Capacity and physical proximity

    Primary: _____

    Secondary: _____

Trustee: Administration of a Child's Inheritance

- Demonstrated ability to seek and obtain good advice
- Capacity to take on asset management tasks; good health and longevity
- Wisdom in discerning needs of a child or other beneficiaries

    Primary: _____

    Secondary: _____

LESSON SIX
Memorial Stones

Memorialize God's enduring faithfulness by articulating the true value of unique assets.

After forty years of wandering in the desert, Israel is finally able to cross over the river Jordan and enter into the Promised Land. As the nation crosses the Jordan, Joshua directs a representative of each of the twelve tribes of Israel to carry a stone on his shoulder. The stone is intended to memorialize, for the ages to come, God's faithfulness to the Israelites.[1] "When your children ask their fathers in times to come, 'What do these stones mean?' Then you shall let your children know, Israel passed over this Jordan on dry ground. For the Lord your God dried up the waters of the Jordan for you until you passed over, as the Lord your God did to the Red Sea, which he dried up for us until we passed over, so that all the peoples of the earth may know that the hand of the Lord is mighty, that you may fear the Lord your God forever."[2]

A biblical estate plan should utilize tangible property as "memorials stones" of God's faithfulness. When my children were in first grade, they would take various items to school to describe to their classmates during "show and tell." We might "show and tell" the family items in our possession that are of significant sentimental value to us because of how the item demonstrates God's enduring faithfulness. Your family

1 Joshua Chapter 4.
2 Joshua 4:21–24.

would benefit from knowing the items that you have in your life right now that help you remember God's enduring faithfulness to you. These memorial stones could then be used as a means, following your death, to encourage others with the fulfillment of God's promises. As part of a comprehensive biblical estate plan, identify sentimental items, why they are sentimental, and how those sentimental items demonstrate God's enduring faithfulness to you and your family.

A client of mine has in his possession World War II memorabilia. This memorabilia was obtained by his late grandfather during his tours of combat. Included in this collection are pictures taken from the body of a deceased German fighter pilot who died after a dogfight with Allied fighters in North Africa. The pictures of the deceased German's own family members are a grim reminder of "what could have been." The physical possession of the now-brittle photographs are an ongoing memorial stone of God's sovereign purposes for the surviving soldier's family.

You have possessions unique to your family because the possessions tell a story about God's enduring faithfulness. These might include:

o   A family business

o   A family cabin or home

o   Family photographs

o   Jewelry, artwork, or hand-made household items

These types of "memorial stone" assets have narratives that ought to accompany the planning for the transfer of these assets. In many cases, these memorial stones, these unique family assets, are "indivisible" assets in the sense that these items cannot be divided across multiple beneficiaries. *A good estate plan needs to direct how to distribute unique assets, including "indivisible" assets.* We should not only have a general sense for how the law would work to distribute unique or indivisible assets, but also be mindful of the relationship dynamics between our children resulting from the allocation among our family of unique and indivisible assets.

Unique assets can be categorized in one or both of two broad categories based upon their primary use. An asset could be (1) a nostalgic/sentimental asset, and/or (2) a utilitarian/service asset.

A **sentimental asset** is being retained mainly because of some connection the item has to the past, whereas a **service asset** is being retained mainly because of some expected future use it provides you and your family. Within each of these two categories, we should identify the forms of value within each of these indivisible assets. An asset is likely to have some **inherent value**, which is value that is clearly identifiable. In contrast, assets may have undisclosed value, which is value that I refer to as "**stealth value**." In creating a plan for distribution, we should create a plan for the distribution of each of these types of unique family assets.

Sentimental Assets: Sharing Stories of God's Faithfulness

Even if you have never considered yourself a hoarder, you might have more in common with hoarders than you think. It has been commonly believed that hoarders are driven by fears of unforeseen events occurring in the future that will require the use of some item they are keeping. However, recent academic research has shown that accumulating "stuff" is driven by pleasure sensory triggers, not fears of catastrophic events.[3] Researchers discovered that hoarders keep an item around the house to create a memory prompt for a pleasant memory of the past, not out of a fear of catastrophic events in the future. If you own items that create a memory prompt for you, don't endure false guilt about how the item creates a memory prompt. Instead, use the item as a "memorial stone"—a means of sharing the narrative of God's faithfulness to you and your family.

Your Narrative of the Item. Take some time to inventory items that have sentimental value to you. Whether in writing or over dinner with family, take the opportunity to share the narrative behind each item. If you can share a full narrative of the item, you might uncover a certain "stealth value" to the item. Your family may not realize that the jewelry you have in your closest holds some third-party as well as sentimental value. In the absence of a background narrative, both the stealth value as well as the sentimental value of the asset would be lost to others. Even for assets that have only sentimental value, you can at least use the opportunity presented by your possession of the item to draw attention to some element of your life story that can bring praise to God.

Whether Others Have Sentimental Connections. Your family might hold "memory prompt" benefits, or sentimental connections, to your possessions as well. You may hold possessions that hold sentimental

---

3 Randy Frost and Gail Stekettee, *Stuff; Compulsive Hoarding and the Meaning of Things*, (Mariner, 2011). The "Proust Phenomenon," or "Proust Effect" is used by academics to describe how the senses can be powerful triggers for memory.

benefits for a child or grandchild to some event in the past, an event that leads to a narrative of God's faithfulness to you through a particular season of your life. Perhaps certain items document a shared suffering or success, an item that is just as much a memorial stone to the family member's narrative story as it is to your own. Clients are often surprised to learn which assets create a memory prompt for family.

We should share the reasons why an item constitutes a memorial stone, even if our memorial stories are not sentimental to others or used by others after our death. If you identify items that have no effect on anyone besides you, then you can direct that those items should be destroyed in the event of your death. In the process of identifying the items that have a memory prompt for others, you can be assured that your surviving family members who would benefit from using such items as memory prompts will be able to receive it following death.

Do not be disheartened if none of your sentimental items provide memory prompts for others. You can glorify God for the wonderful memories occasioned by those items for the rest of your lifetime, and your joy in recounting God's provision for you need not be lost simply because your children do not share the same memory prompts in the same manner.

Service Assets: Maximizing the Transfer Value to Family

While some of your possessions hold only sentimental value, most items will have utilitarian or "service" value. In maximizing the value of the transfer of your unique assets to children or other beneficiaries, attempt to quantify the various ways in which a service possession holds value. Determine why the item holds value and in whose hands the item would be most valuable.

Determine Any Sweat Equity Value. If you own an asset that has any service value by reason of the contribution by others, some portion of the value would be "sweat equity." This commonly arises in the context of a family farm, business, or cabin when one or more of your children have contributed human capital or financial value to your unique item. A portion of the value is attributable to a child's intellectual or professional expertise, financial contribution, or their literal sweat in the form of manual labor. In these cases, it is imperative to attempt to quantify the sweat equity. It is never possible to get it exactly right, but you should nonetheless attempt to quantify that value.

Determining Third-Party Value. If you own an asset that an unrelated party would pay money to own, then you have an item with "third-party value." The tax code calls this value the "fair market value" of a possession. For unique and individual assets, you should inventory such items by providing family with any background as to fair market value. Just as sentimental assets might have previously unknown "stealth" value to your family, providing your family with a full history of your service value assets may likewise uncover stealth third-party value. Even if you can't identify fair market value yourself, you are likely in a better position than your family to identify a trustworthy professional who could value the item. This commonly occurs with various unique collections, such as works of arts, jewelry, and sports memorabilia. Your narrative history of possession, passed along to others, will allow subsequent owners to maximize the third-party value.

Determining a "Family Member Ownership Premium." Finally, certain family members may find an item more valuable than others because of the life situation of the family members. Certain family members might derive even more value from the possession than a next-door neighbor who would pay only the "third-party value." Examples of this premium to a family member, from least significant to most significant, might include the following examples:

- The gas grill at your cabin. If your estate plan directs that your cabin will be distributed to your daughter at your death, your daughter should likewise receive the gas grill. The location of the grill at the cabin results in the grill holding more value to your daughter than any third party, accounting for the hassle of moving a gas grill.

- Mother and daughter both enjoy a particular artist's work, and each of them own pieces of the artist's work. If kept together, ownership of the entire collection would be greater than the sum of its parts. Since the daughter has some pieces already, allocating those items to her, through lifetime gift or post-death transfers, would maximize the value of the collection.

- A son's employment in his father's business has allowed the son to forge business relationships with many of the key clients. At death, the son's business connections within the business would make the business more valuable to the son than to any third party who would be in a position to buy the business. In these instances, the son could receive the business while other children receive other assets equal to the third-party value.

Communicating the Value to Your Children

Trust law generally provides the trustee with the discretion to sell any trust-owned assets if, by reason of a change of circumstances, the sale and subsequent reinvestment is in the best interests of the beneficiaries. In some states, it is now possible to create "purpose trusts," a type of trust that elevates the health of an animal or inanimate object above a human individual beneficiary. The trust must be funded with additional assets to use for the care, protection, and preservation of the asset. These types of trusts have been used to provide for the ongoing care of pets (pets with apparently expensive tastes), the costs associated with "cryonic suspension" of human family members, the costs associated with cryonic suspension of the pets, and other unique and special "purposes."[4]

For secular clients, I can understand the desire to keep a tight grip on one's financial and life circumstances when all is well. From their view, there is no certainty that the future will be any better for them or their children. With special purpose trusts, it is possible to legally direct that the specified asset must be retained and not sold. In the context of a farm or a cabin, such a special purpose trust would serve to make sure that the asset itself is preserved, regardless of the life circumstances of the surviving family members. In Minnesota, it is not uncommon for my cabin owner clients to create a special purpose trust to hold the cabin. These trusts hold ownership of the cabin and liquid assets to cover the carrying costs associated with continued ownership and retention of these expensive properties. In some cases, the "cabin trust" plan is implemented even with known opposition of the next generation, the beneficiaries whom the plan is supposed to benefit.

A special purpose trust is often implemented when clients are stuck in the past—whether because they believe that their children must be tied to the family narrative of cooperating in the use of a family cabin, or because the family previously benefited from farming or business income. I have been privy to special-purpose planning discussions in which the patriarch father, having a history with a family farm, is providing the following message:

"Son, we have created a trust to retain the farm in trust indefinitely, for your continued benefit. You will benefit from this farm lease income,

---

4 A.W. King III, *Trust Planning in Unprecedented Times*, Wealth Management, Jan 10, 2022.

because I am certain that equity markets are fraught with risks, even a well-diversified portfolio of stocks and bonds. We have created a plan so that you can never sell the farmland. I am certain that no other asset that you invest in will provide any return. In any event, I would rather you receive the income from the land for sentimental reasons, even though you will never set foot on the farm property after my death. I understand you will only resent me for not allowing you to achieve higher rates of return on other investment opportunities."

Likewise, a special purpose trust could be created to own a family cabin and administer the family cabin regardless of the needs of the child. Here, the fictional narrative would be construed as follows:

"Daughter, we have decided to create a special purpose trust to retain the family cabin that we received from my parents. By this plan, you are missing out on a larger financial inheritance, one which you and your siblings could have used to create an annual memory-making trip together at a VRBO rental that would have been convenient for you. I am instead requiring you to use the property that we enjoyed back in the 1950s, though this is now completely unmanageable for you and your siblings, and it is highly unlikely you will visit the property because of the distance from your current residences."

From a biblical perspective, we can have a loose grip on the passage of time, even time spent on a beautiful summer day at a glorious northern Minnesota lake cabin. We trust that God will provide us, in the passage of time, with his sustaining grace in our lives and in the lives of our children. The life narratives of our children will be different than ours, and we must be ready to accept that difference in narrative. While we should provide our children with the story of how God used a cabin or other unique asset to bless our family time together, we cannot impose our past narrative on God's plan for our children. Rather than requiring them to enjoy God's assets in the same manner we enjoyed God's assets, we ought to provide our children with the assets with an open view towards their life situation, goals, spouses, and respective callings. We should instead be open-handed with unique assets, encouraging our children to form a narrative consistent with their respective life callings. *"No eye has seen nor ear heard, nor the heart imagined, what God has prepared for those who love him."*[5] Rather than a closefisted special purpose trust, the message sent to your family about your unique asset might sound something like the following:

5 1 Corinthians 2:9.

"Grandson, we are giving you our family cabin. We enjoyed many years of fishing, swimming, and sunsets on the beach and dock. But we know that your life will change, and you might not be able to use this exact cabin. God may call you elsewhere. If so, we want you to sell the cabin without giving it a second thought. Then, use the proceeds to create family memories for yourself and your family."

LEGAL PROCESS:

Once you have identified the unique assets and indivisible assets you own, you should create a legal plan that incorporates a God-honoring plan for the transfer of sentimental and service items at your death.

Conduct a Swedish Death Cleaning

Many possessions in the modern American home are in the category of neither serviceable nor sentimental. With these items, loosen the ties that bind these items to your home, as well as your closets and storage facilities. Estate planning attorneys universally advise their clients that estate sales net far less than most clients expect they will. Instead of relying on an estate sale, implement the Swedish tradition known as *dostadning,* which is Swedish for *death cleaning.*[6] Swedish death cleaning is not about cleaning up *after* your death; rather, it is about your efforts, in your *own lifetime*, to rid yourself of unnecessary clutter to minimize the work imposed upon others following your death. If you are able to conduct a periodic *dostadning,* your children will have a far smaller expense (*e.g.,* a "junk luggers" bill) once you and your spouse are gone.

Communicate Value to Your Children

Memories fade, and documents are lost. You should therefore take steps to convey to your family, in writing, information about unique items in your possession so that the value is known and fully appreciated. I recommend you give special consideration to each of the types of value noted above. You should document the sentimental value, the sweat equity value, and any family ownership premium. The information provided should include:

- *Financial history:* This might include the appraised value of the family artwork, the appraised value of the jewelry, and a complete list of the sports memorabilia collection. Include the cost basis of the item and other relevant financial information.

6 See Margareta Magnuson, *The Gentle Art of Swedish Death Cleaning* (Scribener, 2018).

For cabin properties, having the original purchase price and the record of subsequent improvements might save significant capital gains taxes for heirs.

- *Narrative history:* The narrative history of the item, particularly for sentimental items that have no historian outside of yourself. How did the item come to have sentimental value? Are there other sentimental items that should be paired with these items?

- *Family discussions & decisions.* The communication of value to your children should prompt conversations with your children about how they value those items. In generations past, grandmother's dinner plate might have had not only some collector or antique value to a third party ("third party value"), but also sentimental value. In most cases, the comment I hear from my clients is not, "Well, we talked to our kids, and they don't want anything." Once the value is conveyed to your children, you should document plans for the transfer of assets, either during lifetime or following death.

No two memorial stones that crossed the Jordan with the Israelites were alike. Your life situation is unique to you, so you should look for those stones that memorialize God's faithfulness to you. We are often like the Israelites, periodically forgetting the ways in which God continually renews and strengthens us. If we can use possessions to serve as memorial stones to God's enduring faithfulness, we will have stewarded our stuff and our stories well, and perhaps encouraged our children to do likewise.

ILLUSTRATIONS FOR APPLICATION

The following three illustrations serve as examples for how you might use your possessions as memorial stones to God's goodness and faithfulness.

Allow Others to Establish a New Memory Prompt

Over a recent holiday family dinner, my client Sharon took the opportunity to share with her children and grandchildren the sentimental significance of her jewelry collection. Perhaps to her disappointment, Sharon learned that no one in the family had the same sentimental connection. No one wants the jewelry. As a result, Sharon contacted me to update her legal documents so that, at her death, her jewelry collection will be sold and the proceeds allocated to each of her grandchildren. The grandchildren will then be requested, but not legally directed, to use their portion of the cash to purchase one or more new items of durable nature (*e.g.,* artwork, household furniture) to serve as a memorial stone to God's faithfulness in Sharon's life. In many cases, the most significant memorial stones owned by the surviving children of deceased parents were items that the children purchased in honor of their parents with inherited assets following death. In death, just as in life, do not assume that you can monopolize how your remaining assets will be used to glorify God through your life and legacy. You may take Sharon's approach, which is to provide an open hand to your children and grandchildren to determine how to make memorial stones to your life.

Dual Sentimental and Service Value Items

To the untrained eye, the desk that sits in my home office appears to be simply a sturdy piece of home furniture, well-built but not especially aesthetically pleasing. The desk has always had sentimental value to me because it was received as a gift from my grandfather. Since my grandfather used the same desk to prepare his Sunday school Bible lessons, the desk serves as a memorial stone to a Christian heritage.

In addition to having sentimental value, I only recently discovered that the desk also has stealth third-party value. A recent visitor to my home is an antique furniture expert and happened to notice the table. According to this visitor, the desk is an early 1900s "library table" that holds some collector value.

I have therefore shared the value of the table to my family—both the sentimental value as well as the service (third party) value. After my death, my family can use the item to reflect on the blessing of my Christian heritage. However, if none of my children wants to keep the item, we will at least have passed along the narrative, thereby honoring the Lord and the legacy of my late grandfather. The knowledge I have shared regarding its service value will (hopefully) ensure that they also contact an antique dealer when they are ready to get rid of the table rather than taking it to Goodwill!

The Family Home

Tanner and Ruth purchased their family residence about thirty-five years ago. The area has grown in popularity, such that the family residence is now worth four times what Tanner and Ruth originally paid for the property. However, property taxes and maintenance expenses have also grown significantly. Between Tanner and Ruth's current medical and care expenses, expected future care expenses, and all costs associated with maintaining the family home, it is not likely that Tanner and Ruth can continue to own and manage the property. Tanner and Ruth's five children all desire for the family home to be retained in the family. In fact, all five of the children have agreed that the sentimental value of the residence is so high that each of them would prefer to receive a lesser financial inheritance if they can be assured that the family home would be retained by someone in the family.

One of the five children, Levi, works just a few miles from the residence. After several years of communicating about various planning options, Levi and his family sold their home, and moved into Tanner and Ruth's residence. Using a legal structure called a limited liability company ("LLC"), Tanner, Ruth, and Levi each determined an ownership percentage in not just the family residence owned by the family's LLC, but also the cash accounts held by the LLC used to pay for the costs of upkeep at the residence. As of right now, Tanner, Ruth, Levi and Levi's family all reside in the residence. However, after the death of Tanner and Ruth, the portion of the LLC attributable to Tanner and Ruth's ownership can be allocated equally among all five children, and Levi can continue to reside in the residence. This planning was possible only because all seven of the family members agreed that the residence had unique sentimental value, agreed upon a value for the residence, and created a plan to preserve that value.

REFLECTIONS
On Your Memorial Stones

Reflect on what items in your possession serve as memorial stones to God's sustaining provision for you and your family. For each of those items, determine how the item should be valued and how you will disclose the nature of that value to your family.

Using the table on the following page, organize assets that you consider to be unique. By way of example, this list might include jewelry, artwork, collectibles, firearms, and other unique and indivisible assets. You don't necessarily need to include items with overt value, but perhaps include assets with unknown and underlying stealth value. For each item, provide a summary of the item, where it is located, information that would distinguish it from other assets, and any narrative background history. If appropriate, you should record any previous valuations of the asset, and disclose anyone that a fiduciary or family member could ask for assistance in valuing the asset, such as an appraiser or trusted business contact (a "trusted contact").

UNIQUE ASSETS ORGANIZER

ASSET & DESCRIPTION	LOCATION & OTHER IDENTIFYING INFORMATION	NARRATIVE BACKGROUND	TRUSTED CONTACT & VALUATION INFORMATION

LESSON SEVEN
Children

We design a wealth transfer plan to achieve eternal outcomes in the lives of our children.

"Well…. at least Dad made us a lot of money." At the funeral of a deceased business owner, the son's eulogy was brief, emotionless, and shockingly honest. Nothing more could be said other than he left his kids a big inheritance. In this instance, the son's eulogy was the honest outcome of dad's lifelong pursuit of the almighty dollar. The eulogy documented his dad's core identity.

In Luke 16, Jesus provides a grim picture for those whose core identity has been based solely on the pursuit of worldly wealth. In that parable, Jesus shares the story of Lazarus, a poor beggar, as well as an unnamed rich man ("Rich.[1]") In Jesus' parable, Rich and Lazarus both die and are then sent to differing eternal homes—Lazarus is sent to heaven, to the side of Abraham, while Rich is sent to Hades to receive eternal torment.

In Luke 12, Jesus shares the parable of a different man, a man sometimes referred to by Bible commentators as the "rich fool." The rich fool decides that, because of his wealth, he can "build bigger barns" and "take life easy."[2] As with "Rich" in the parable of Luke

---

1 According to Tim Keller, it was remarkably countercultural for Jesus to provide us with the name of Lazarus, the beggar, without providing us with the name of the "rich man."
2 Luke 12:16–20.

16, we are not told the actual name of Mr. Rich Fool in Luke 12. In each parable, the identity of wealth was such a part of these characters that, once they died and left their source of identity behind on earth, there was no means to identity them in eternity. Each of these fictional characters in these parables had, at their death, no true heritage or identity, nothing with which to identify themselves other than a financial inheritance.

In his classic 2014 book, *Zero to One,* billionaire investor Peter Thiel criticizes a pervasive approach to planning. Rather than planning for a definite future, our modern culture too often plans for an "indefinite" future. Thiel writes,

"If you treat the future as something definite, it makes sense to understand it in advance and to work to shape it. But if you expect an indefinite future ruled by randomness, you'll give up on trying to master it. Indefinite attitudes in the future explain what's most dysfunctional in our world today. Process trumps substance: when people lack concrete plans to carry out, they use formal rules to assemble a portfolio of various options. This describes Americans today." [3]

The secular estate-planning perspective is based on the assumption that the accumulation of a greater and greater level of assets is in everyone's best interests. Moreover, a secular mindset generally follows an indefinite future mindset—that is, not knowing what the future holds. Therefore, the accumulation of money becomes the end in itself. In an indefinite world, Thiel says, "…people actually prefer unlimited optionality; money is more valuable than anything you could possibly do with it. Only in a definite future is money a means to an end, not an end itself."[4]

Unlike those whose life is complicated by heading into an indefinite future, Christians can plan for a definite future. For Christians, the most important point of departure from a secular estate plan is the role of purpose in the planning for our children. Rather than planning as if the future is uncertain, we can plan for a certain future, a future that is certain to include setbacks, sufferings, and successes in the lives of our children. The financial resources that are in our hands can be used to achieve definite purposes.

3 Peter Thiel, *Zero to One.* Crown Business Publishing, p. 61–62.
4 Id. at 71.

We have the legal right to direct how assets are to be distributed to our children, both during our lifetime and at death. We must therefore take steps to create a purposeful plan. We must avoid the "rich fool" mentality of "building bigger barns" for ourselves and our children. We must take steps to avoid making the accumulation of money an end in itself, with the end result being that our children are left with worldly wealth but no eternal wisdom, rudderless and self-absorbed, a modern-day version of a "rich young ruler." We must wisely transfer assets to our children during lifetime, and then legally direct where assets are to be distributed with a sufficient degree of specificity that, at no point, is there too large of a "left over" amount for children or grandchildren.

In this lesson, I address how to design a purposeful wealth transfer plan for your children based on these five guiding factors:

Honor: Honor our children through an unconditional financial inheritance properly ordered in the context of the child's personal obligations and calling.

Equity: Provide equitably for our children by promoting a multiplicative mindset.

> **Wisdom:** Make lifetime gifts to develop wisdom among our children.

> **Limit:** Knowing that worldly riches impede spiritual vitality, establish limits to the worldly wealth transferred to our children.

> **Trust:** Create the appropriate legal means to accomplish specific goals for our children.

If our future is secure in Christ, why plan as if the future is indefinite? Instead of accumulating assets for the sake of accumulating assets, let's create a purposeful plan for the transfer of wisdom and wealth to our children. If our kids spoke at your funeral today, what words would they use to encapsulate the significance of time and attention? Let us be cautious to avoid falling into the ways of the world and have no separate defining characteristic other than our salary, job title, or the extent of the worldly wealth we leave behind. Instead, let us use our opportunities wisely to leverage worldly wealth for eternal gain.

7A: *Honor*

Honor our children through an unconditional financial inheritance properly ordered in the context of the child's personal obligations and calling.

"Earn This." In the climactic scene of the World War II film, "Saving Private Ryan," the company commander, played by the actor Tom Hanks, utters his dying words in the ear of the young Private Ryan. Hanks' character charges the young Private Ryan to "Earn this!" Fast forwarding to the present day, the elderly Private Ryan is shown visiting the cemetery where his fallen comrades were laid to rest years before. There, the aged veteran Ryan weeps over the tombs of the men who gave their lives for his. Private Ryan was left in a state of ongoing existential angst. As the aged Private Ryan stands among the graves, he makes a statement that ought to haunt all those who are not saved by grace, which is "I hope I have lived my life well enough to earn it!"

If I were Private Ryan's shoes, I would have reacted in the same way that I respond to God now—nothing I could have done, over the balance of my life, would have earned my right to live. Just as we cannot earn our way back to God, we cannot expect our kids to live a perfect life. We didn't ***earn*** our own heirship into God's family; it was given to us. If we are to demonstrate the same Christ-like attitude towards our children, we cannot expect our children to *earn* an inheritance. We cannot expect our children to follow our directions perfectly or to somehow deserve an inheritance.

Under a secular approach, we could require that of our offspring. Utilizing this approach, some of my clients are *frequent flyer* visitors to our office, amending and revising the amounts or percentages to their children based upon a "what have you done for me lately" measuring stick. In contrast, a biblical estate plan recognizes that just as God brought us into heirship through no merit of our own, we likewise honor our children in an unmerited fashion. A financial inheritance to our children must be an unconditional gift, appropriately ordered within the context of a child's obligations to the critical

Christian institutions of family, marriage, and society. In this chapter, I summarize how to honor a child through an unconditional inheritance while also recognizing the centrality of these institutions in the life of the child and the child's own family.

The Symbolic Blessing of an Unconditional Inheritance

We must provide an unconditional financial inheritance to our children because God calls us to symbolically honor our children as members of our family, and our role as our child's parent. An inheritance is, at its very heart, a symbolic demonstration to our children and to the outside world of their status as our children. The Holy Spirit is the demonstration of our new status as an heir of God's family.[1] Paul writes, "The Spirit Himself bears witness with our spirit that we are children of God, and if children, then heirs—heirs of God and fellow heirs with Christ…"[2] We have the symbolic blessing of the Holy Spirit throughout our earthly lifetime to demonstrate God's adoption of us as His sons and daughters. In a similar fashion, an inheritance is a symbolic demonstration of their status as our treasured children.

In the Sermon on the Mount, Jesus references how parents are naturally inclined to give good gifts to our children.

"…Which one of you, if his son asks him bread, will give him a stone? Or if he asks for a fish, will give him a serpent?" If you then, who are evil, know how to give good gifts to your children, how much more will your Father who is in heaven give good things to those who ask him!"[3]

In admonishing us to turn to God in prayer for good gifts, Jesus assumes that we have a good and natural inclination towards providing good gifts to our children. God's generous treatment of us makes sense because of what each of us parents already intuitively understand—that God provides a common grace to all parents, Christian and secular alike, of a desire to provide good gifts to our children.

Throughout Scripture, we observe that God honors the parent-child relationship. God honors the symbolic meaning of an inheritance to a child. After God promised Abram that he would become the father of many nations, God not only blessed Abraham through Isaac and Isaac's offspring, but even blessed Abram through his son, Ishmael.

1 Romans 8:15.
2 Romans 8:16–17.
3 Matthew 7:9–11.

Even though Ishmael himself was not the progeny through whom the promise of the favored nation status would be fulfilled, God honored the parent-son relationship between Abram and Ishmael by blessing Ishmael as the father of another nation.[4]

The Pentateuch includes inheritance rules that demonstrate how God honors the parent-child relationship in the context of an inheritance. A child is required to receive an inheritance regardless of the longevity of his or her parents. When Zelophehad died with no living male heirs, the Lord directed that his daughters receive an equal share of the remaining assets.[5] Under the law of primogeniture, the oldest son born was to receive a "double portion." In order to illustrate the importance of the relationship between the father and son regardless of the relationship between the father and the son's mother, the Lord directed that this oldest son receive the double portion even if, and perhaps in spite of, the fact that this son was the son of the "unloved" wife.[6] The inheritance was made to these "heirs" not because of their behavior or the behavior of their parents, but because God honors the symbolic impact of an inheritance as an attribute of family heirship of the family.

Blessing the Lost Sheep in Your Family

Some of my clients seem genuinely surprised when their young adult children make financial mistakes. Following the startling discovery that these children are imperfect, significant family drama ensues, including the possibility of reducing a share to the child or even eliminating the child's share altogether. The narrative within these "successful" families might sound something like a mantra from a professional athlete's autobiography:

"….kids, our family name and business is success. If you don't make good decisions, you are not really part of the family. Our family is built on success. If you can't cut it in sports, school, or business, you are out. Your share in this family and in our successes must be reduced or removed."

In creating an estate plan for their children, the secular approach is a Darwinian conditional approach—either get on board or get out of the house. According to this mantra, "to the mighty go the spoils."

God honors the significance of the parent-child relationship when it

---

4 Genesis 16.
5 Numbers 27:5–11.
6 Deuteronomy 21:15–17.

comes to an inheritance. When it comes to God's love for us, there is never any "exception" to these relationships or condition upon which God's love for us is based. Our relationship with our children is likewise to be one of unconditional love. If the Spirit Himself bears witness to our being children of God and heirs of all that God has promised, how can we act towards our own children in a manner any different than how God treats us as co-heirs with Christ?[7] In Jesus' parable of the two sons, Jesus illustrates God's unconditional love for us, even at great cost to Himself. In the parable, consider the heart of the father in paying any financial cost for the purpose of obtaining the re-entrance of his younger son back into the family. Our provision to our children of an inheritance is likewise not a return of any degree of affection exhibited by them toward us, but an application of our gratitude in Christ's free gift of salvation to us.

The receipt by adult children of a proportionate share of a surviving parent's assets is so deeply rooted in today's entitlement culture that, in the absence of an alternative plan effectively communicated during lifetime, you run the great risk of creating significant resentments between you and your children if you don't provide for them. In my experience from observing these situations following death, if your children are at the time of your death not friendly toward the gospel, your children will associate your act of disinheritance with your Christian faith. The very legal means you would use to "punish" your non-Christian children would be the additional fuel to the fire of animosity the child already holds towards the faith. Just as with the younger prodigal son who received his inheritance upon returning home, the provision of an equal inheritance for a comparatively undeserving child will serve as an incalculable source of encouragement to the wayward son or daughter. *Let us undertake, at perhaps great financial cost, that our love for our children is unconditional and not based upon the child's acceptance of the faith, their own personal behavior, or their perceived needs.* If we are invited by Jesus to use whatever financial means we have in this life to leverage those assets into eternally significant outcomes, we ought to take every available opportunity, even unlikely ones, when it comes to "winning back" a wayward child.

Honoring Your Obligation to Your Own Children

We honor our children because it is God's plan for those of us who

7 Romans 8:14–15.

are able to earn a living to first provide for our own dependents. In 1 Timothy 5:8, Paul writes to Timothy about the obligations of families in the early church, "But if anyone does not provide for his relatives, and especially for members of his household, he has denied the faith and is worse than an unbeliever." A biblical estate plan requires that we recognize the needs of those who live with us and plan for the needs of these family members who are dependent on our income for their ongoing living expenses.

For those of us who still have children under our care, we have the obligation to make every effort to leave behind a sufficient financial inheritance to meet their financial needs through a period of dependency. Many of my Christian clients in their forties to sixties are currently providing for their aging parents as well. It is also noteworthy, in this regard, that Paul admonishes the members of the early church to provide for their own parents who are "truly widows" in the sense that such widows need financial support.[8] In prioritizing the needs of widows who don't have family on whom they rely, we see Paul's assumption that family members, and not the church itself, should be the primary means of support for children and adults who have no means of making a self-sufficient living.

You hold biblical obligations of support to those in your household who are currently dependent upon your income and assets. Create a plan to meet those needs through a sufficient period that would allow them to become self-sufficient (such as children) or locate other means of support (such as a non-working spouse or parents). As we have already noted, Christians must plan as though we will not live to see tomorrow. We must therefore prepare a legal estate plan as if we will die today, considering the current needs of our dependent family members.

The Use of Life Insurance

If you have children, you should endeavor to calculate the total costs of raising dependent children and make arrangements for your children as if you were going to die today. As of August 2022, the cost of raising two children in a two-parent family totals $310,605 from birth through the age of seventeen. Annually, raising a child costs about $18,271 per year.[9] As of 2018, the average four-year college costs were $194,040

---

8 1 Timothy 5:3. See also James 1:27.
9 Brookings Institution Study, as cited in *Child-Rearing Expenses Soar Amid Inflation, Wall Street Journal, Saturday, August 20, 2022.* Experts reviewing these reports believe that, depending

for private school, and \$85,480 for in-state tuition.[10] In total, the cost of raising two children is approximately \$900,000 from birth through age seventeen. Additional considerations would be cost of living differences in your particular region, whether other family members are dependent upon you, and what impact your death would have on your surviving spouse's employment situation.

While these figures appear staggering, a healthy working-age parent could use a life insurance company's actuarial tables to his advantage. For those of us who are healthy and possess a long life expectancy, a life insurance policy is relatively cheap. If the Lord calls you home before the life insurance company's actuarial tables so dictate, your family benefits. What a good deal—you get to go to heaven, your family will benefit financially from the fact that, at least from the perspective of the actuarial tables, you were a "curve breaker." For health reasons, not everyone is able to obtain health insurance. In that event, you would likely structure an estate plan so that all of your remaining assets are allocated for the benefit of your dependents at death.

Elevating Eternity in the Hearts of Our Children

While we must honor our children as our children through an unmerited inheritance, wisdom dictates how the receipt of your child's inheritance would support more important callings in your child's life. An inheritance would impact the following areas of a child's life: (1) the child's relationship with a spouse, (2) the child's relationship with siblings, (3) and the child's own professional or ministry callings from the Lord. From my own law practice experience, I wish to provide some encouragement and insight on how to best provide a meritless financial gift to your children without negatively impacting these more significant relationships that exist in their lives.

(1) Honor the Child's Marriage Covenant.

We should honor a child's marriage by elevating the institution of marriage above the protection of a child's financial inheritance.

"Well, that was a son-in-law." So exclaimed my golfing partner as he hit his drive deep into the woods off the tee, with no likelihood that the

---

upon the specific cost of living in your city, the true cost might be even more, especially with single-parents who need to pay additional costs for child care. *Child-Cost Estimates Mask Wide Disparity. Wall Street Journal, Saturday, August 21, 2022.*
10 From a 2018 study called "Trends in College Pricing."

golf ball would be found.

"What do you mean, 'son-in-law,'" I asked?

"Not what I had in mind," he replied!

If you have a son-in-law, you can relate to the disappointment faced by my own father-in-law when I asked him permission to marry my wife. God works in mysterious ways, perhaps most notably through ne'er-do-well sons-in-law like me. Fairly frequently, my wealthier clients will ask me to meet with their adult children who are engaged to be married. The client states that the purpose of the meeting is to "discuss the possibility" of creating a prenuptial agreement, which sends an implicit message to the child that the meeting with the family attorney to create an prenuptial agreement is for the purpose of protecting inherited family wealth from a divorcing spouse.

In the event of a divorce, a court reviews all assets owned by the couple. Assets characterized as "marital" assets are split in an equitable fashion between the divorcing parties, while assets that are characterized as "non-marital" assets are allocated to the spouse owning the asset. While a gift or inheritance is initially a "non-marital" asset, that attribute can be lost through actions taken during the marriage. A prenuptial agreement, also known as an antenuptial agreement, allows a couple to legally contract with one another over how assets they bring into the marriage are characterized as "marital" or "non-marital" assets and thereby divided in the case of a divorce or death. In 2018, a Minnesota court case created legal precedent making the enforcement of prenuptial agreements even more difficult than such agreements had been previously. [11] By reason of this precedent, our law firm has recently decided to cease representing families in preparing prenuptial agreements, as we believe such agreements will with increasing frequency be viewed as unenforceable.

From a biblical perspective, the more important reason for not advocating an antenuptial agreement is the relationship wedge driven between the spouses entering into such an agreement. Based upon divorce statistics, there is good possibility that the marriage of one

---

11 The court case in Minnesota was *Kremer v. Kremer,* 912 N.W.2d 617 (Minn. 2018). An antenuptial agreement must be "substantively fair" to both parties both at the time the agreement is entered into, as well as at the time that it is enforced. Divorce proceedings are subject to a type of "spare no legal expense" or "scorched earth" litigation in which litigants attempt to "win" at all costs. It is highly likely that the "substantive fairness" question will be litigated, thereby minimizing the likelihood of enforcement of an antenuptial agreement.

or more of your children will end in divorce. If you require a child to create a prenuptial agreement, the implicit message sent to your child and the child's intended is that your money is more important than their marriage. As it is, marriage is difficult enough even before you introduce the influence of a strong-willed mother- or father-in-law. From the perspective of your adult children, consider the biblical admonition of leaving one's parents and cleaving to one's spouse.[12]

By requiring a prenuptial agreement that maintains gifted or inherited assets as "separate property," the implicit message sent from the family is that the financial inheritance is more important that the health of the marriage itself. You are discouraging the child from valuing a spouse as a partner in all elements of the marriage. Instead of falling into the same camp as our secular neighbors, let us encourage our adult children to enter the marital union unbounded by our own expectations related to worldly wealth.

(2) Honor Each Child as an Equal Heir.

We should honor each of our children equitably, and not using the promise or threat of a disproportionate inheritance to leverage our children into desired behavior.

From a secular perspective, the opportunity presented by the inheritance question among multiple children is a golden opportunity to leverage your children into desired behavior. By either promising a greater percentage, or else threatening a lower percentage, a parent can use estate-planning discussions to achieve certain behavior on the part of their children. As a parent, you could use the possibility of an unequal inheritance to manipulate your children into the following types of desired behavior:

- To increase time and attention given to the aging parent, perhaps to the detriment of the child's relationship with the child's spouse and children;

- To provide personal care and/or cohabitation with the child and the child's family;

- To influence the child's religious, moral or political views;

- To require a child to enter into a prenuptial agreement with a fiancé/fiancée; or

---

12 Genesis 2:24.

- To simply create drama around your desired plan following for the purpose of keeping your memory alive following the death of the aging parent.

From a secular perspective, it seems entirely logical to implement a plan by which to avail oneself of the power provided by your financial wealth to leverage your children into desired behavior. While you may want them to get along with one another, this is likely less significant than a desire to influence their behavior. By creating the possibility of an unequal inheritance, you would create a spirit of intrigue and distrust among your children, one that would last even past your death.

Under a biblical framework, we ought to respect the unique family, professional, and ministry callings of each of our children. In a subsequent chapter, we will explore how to best manage the equities of disproportionate distributions between children based upon the circumstances that are occurring in their lives independent of your involvement. Too many of my clients take it upon themselves, in an effort to achieve a certain desired outcome, to drive a wedge between their children. From a biblical perspective, we should be aware of the allure of using financial wealth to create adverse sibling relationship. Rather than driving our children apart from one another, we should use the financial assets in our care to drive them closer together.

(3) Honor the Child's Professional Calling.

We should honor our children through encouraging each of them to find their unique calling.

"I don't want my daughter to become a social worker; she cannot make a living that way." If you take a self-centered, self-absorbed narrative of personal wealth creation, you are more likely to believe that your children must follow a career path you set out for them, including perhaps the same path that made you successful. It's difficult for the world to recognize God's call on the lives of our children, especially when their callings depart from the success of the parents. A secular estate plan is therefore generally focused on the outcome of a career decision as measured by dollars and living expenses, rather than how children might be called to a lesser-paying ministry or profession.

Under a secular approach, incentive structures can be created to encourage a child to attain to certain levels of achievement. A common planning strategy is to use a trust to create a set of incentives for the ostensible purpose of creating self-sufficiency. In reality, however, financial incentives like these will often stifle a child's incentive to follow God's leading in life. An "incentive trust" is a type of trust that distributes assets only upon demonstration by the child of earning a particular degree, a certain amount of income, or longevity in a certain job, program, or industry. Other structures, called "pot trusts," allow for distributions to be made among a certain group of named beneficiaries, typically children or grandchildren, to meet certain expenses, such as educational expenses. However, both the incentive trust structure and the pot trust structure create the possibility that a family member will make professional decisions to maximize the receipt of trust assets, not necessarily following God's call in their lives. These structures could:

- Increase the living standards of an able-bodied and capable adult children so that they can consume more for the sake of consuming more, and even conspicuously more;

- Manipulate children toward careers that require income to meet a standard of living that reflects well upon the parents;

- Causes the children to "chase after" the receipt of the trust distributions in a god-like fashion, supplanting the role of God's provision for calling and career in the lives of the adult children; or

- Create an incentive for children to follow the career paths dictated by parents instead of by God.

From a biblical perspective, we recognize that each of our children will develop their own narrative, and that the financial inheritance should encourage them along that narrative. While we recognize that our narrative will overlap with each of our children, we recognize that each child's narrative is personal, and that each child is called to fulfill God's narrative in his or her own life. In contrast to our secular neighbors, a biblical estate plan for our children recognizes the degree to which the desire for an ever-increasing consumption standard pushes out a desire for godliness in the lives of our children. A biblical estate plan will therefore consider how to provide each child with a grace-based financial inheritance, to encourage each of our children to pursue God above money.

We can be mindful of the financial disparities in the lives of our children and step in to help during our lifetime when appropriate. Following our death, however, we are no longer trustees of our assets, and it would be outrageously presumptive to assume how the Lord will meet the financial needs of our children at a future date. Instead, we must elevate the importance of honoring our children at death by generally providing for an equal post-death and grace-based plan. I encourage you to trust God for the future needs of all your children, even the children who could benefit from a larger financial inheritance.

HONORING YOUR CHILDREN THROUGH A FINANCIAL INHERITANCE

Honoring your children through an unmerited financial inheritance is a costly endeavor. In summary, you should honor each child in the following ways:

1. Honor each child with an unmerited financial gift as a symbolic status symbol;

2. Honor God's plan for your family by providing for the financial needs of your minor (young) children;

3. Honor the marital relationships that each of your children have with his or her spouse;

4. Honor the relationships that your children have with their siblings; and

5. Honor the professional and ministry callings in the lives of your children.

The Lord honors the institution of the family and our role as parents. We provide for our children, regardless of their age and stewardship abilities, simply because we are their parents, and they are our children. If you have a wayward, pre-Christian "lost sheep" adult child, consider how an equal financial inheritance to that child would serve as a final blessing of encouragement to demonstrate your unconditional love towards that child. Rather than focusing on a child's stewardship deficiencies, we ought to focus on the opportunity to provide a lifelong symbolic blessing to our adult children through a symbolic financial inheritance.

ILLUSTRATIONS FOR APPLICATION

I offer the following three client illustrations to help consider how you should best honor your children.

The Spiritual Impact of Reducing a Successful Child's Share

Don had two adult sons, both of whom follow the Lord and are excellent financial stewards of assets. Don's older son, Blaine, was a Bible translator, working overseas for paltry pay. Don's younger son, Travis, was a successful financial manager. By reason of the significant disparity between the two sons' personal financial situations, Don decided that a significantly larger portion of his remaining assets at death would be directed to Blaine, with Travis receiving a smaller percentage. Don's two-fold message to his sons through this plan was as follows:

(1) Blaine's profession, as a God-honoring calling, was more laudable than Travis' profession, such that Don felt that he needed to bless the more "godly" professional decision by Blaine by giving him a larger inheritance.

(2) God apparently needed Don's money to provide for Blaine, since Don had the mistaken belief that there were no other avenues by which Blaine's needs could be met.

More than ten years after Don's death, Travis will tell you that he still feels the sting of receiving less than an equal inheritance from his father. While I am certain that Blaine allocated the larger inheritance amount for godly purposes, I am equally certain that God would have provided alternative means of providing for Blaine's financial needs outside of Don's inheritance.

Providing for a Sibling as Dad's Legacy

In contrast to the story of Don and his two sons, I wish to contrast the story of my widower client Raymond and his two sons. Similar to Don's family situation, Raymond had two sons, Terry, a successful real estate developer, and Aaron, a congenial man who had mental health challenges that precluded him from consistently earning a living wage. Not only had Raymond and his wife financially supported Aaron throughout Aaron's lifetime, but Terry and his wife also financially supported Aaron.

Towards the end of Raymond's life, I was blessed to be involved in planning conversations with Raymond and Terry. In this context, Terry engineered what I might consider a reverse "undue influence" conversation. That is, Terry advocated for his own disinheritance, but to the benefit of his brother Aaron. While Raymond was initially (and rightfully) opposed to the idea of disinheriting Terry, Terry ultimately convinced Raymond to do so mainly because Raymond came to understand that Terry would be financially supporting Aaron anyway. Rather than distributing assets equally at death between Terry and Aaron, all of Raymond's remaining assets would be earmarked to a testamentary trust for Aaron, with Terry acting as trustee of his brother's trust.

It is worthwhile comparing Don's family narrative with Raymond's family narrative. In Don's case, what if Don had directed that Blaine and Travis each receive the same percentage of remaining assets, but then separately communicated a desire that Travis use a portion of the inheritance to commit to his brother Blaine's ministry? The narrative of this plan would have been far more palatable to Travis. In Raymond's case, all three of the family members could buy into this multiplicative legacy: (i) Raymond felt good about providing for Aaron's needs, having been convinced by Terry that Terry felt adequately honored as an equal son, even in spite of being excluded; (ii) Aaron felt that not only the assets themselves but the testamentary structure would be helpful to him; and (iii) Terry loved the idea that his dad's assets could be directed to the good purpose of providing for his beloved brother. In your case, if you have children with widely disparate financial situations, consider what options you have to demonstrate an unconditional inheritance to each of your children that honors your relationship with each of them.

The Prodigal Child Trust

Suzanne and Ted have spent much time praying for the health, safety, and spiritual status of their prodigal daughter, Betsy. Betsy has always been a troubled soul. Betsy has come in and out of their lives since leaving home after failing to complete high school at age eighteen. When I worked with Suzanne and Ted to implement an estate plan, they had completely lost touch with Betsy, not having heard from her in the previous eighteen months.

Together with their other two adult children, both of whom are Christians, we worked with Suzanne and Ted to implement an estate plan. The plan requires that at the death of the surviving spouse, one-third of all remaining assets would be allocated to each of their three children. Taking a page from the Parable of the Two Sons, Suzanne and Ted structured the share for their prodigal daughter Betsy as a "prodigal daughter" trust. Under the terms of that trust, the two other children would "hold open" the one-third inheritance for the possibility of a family reunion. As trustees of this prodigal daughter trust, the one-third share earmarked for Betsy would be held open for at least five years following the second death between Suzanne and Ted. Just as with the father in Jesus' story of the two sons, Ted and Suzanne wish to provide every opportunity to allow their beloved prodigal daughter, Betsy, the opportunity to make contact with her siblings and claim her equal share.

If you have children who are not currently in communion with you or the Lord, prayerfully plan for an unconditional and honoring gift to the child at your death. If you would pay any financial price for your child to return, is it not worth an equal share of your remaining assets to attempt to purchase some goodwill with your prodigal child? If Jesus gives us permission to use financial wealth to "buy" opportunities for eternal, spiritual, and godly outcomes, you might attempt to create a similar structure for your wayward child.

REFLECTIONS
On Honoring Your Children

In the first chapter of this book, we reflected on how your identity in Christ ought to change how you are able to forgive others. In this chapter, we reflected on what it means to honor each of your children as your children. Using the questions that follow, reflect on how you might implement a plan that honors each of your children through an unmerited inheritance.

If you have minor children, do you have a sufficient amount of assets or life insurance to meet their basic needs if you died now?

Do you sometimes feel like your kids have not earned their inheritance, and that they need to "get their act together" before they deserve an inheritance?

Are you applying a standard of behavior to your children that you yourself are not able or desiring to meet for your own eternal inheritance?

Are you resentful that your children would likely receive a greater financial inheritance than you ever received?

Are you explicitly or implicitly directing your adult children to protect their current or future assets from their current or future spouse, such as through a prenuptial agreement?

What is more important to you: (i) the attention that your adult children are giving to you, or (ii) the relationships that your children will have with one another following your death?

Are you using the possibility of an inheritance to incentivized one or more of your children towards certain preferred behavior?

Are you upset that your children are not living up to a certain living standard?

7B: *Equity*

Provide equitably for your children by promoting a multiplicative mindset.

Jacob's gift to his son Joseph, a coat of many colors, was perhaps the worst fashion decision of all time. Aside from the plain fact that I don't understand why anyone would want to wear a coat of multiple colors, Jacob's obnoxious favoritism towards Joseph laid the groundwork for the subsequent debacles between Joseph and his jealous brothers. Jacob's lavish and conspicuous demonstration of unequal affection toward Joseph was clearly detrimental to his other children. The hurt and resentment that Jacob's other children felt toward Joseph was demonstrated in their hatred of him and their selling him into slavery. In this chapter, I review the legal rules applicable to lifetime transfers to your children and summarize how we might create a multiplicative mindset among your children as you support each of them equitably.

Expectations of Equitable Treatment

Psychologists who study successful sales techniques emphasize the importance of reminding the potential buyer of the scarcity of an object or service.[1] A "fixed sum" approach requires us to get ahead of other potential buyers of the same item or service because there is only so much to go around. Trust and estate disputes between siblings arise from a perception that mom and dad directed strictly equal financial distributions, but that a family member's [mis]behavior resulted in disproportionate distributions. I have been privy to conversations between sixty-something-year-old siblings that, if you didn't know any better, might be mistaken for conversations between eight-year-old siblings. A history of perceived favoritism extends to such pedantic matters as better toys as children, more valuable cars as teenagers, or more significant financial gifts to grown children.

The expectation among the family was that, because there was a "fixed

---

1 Robert Cialdini, *Influence: The Psychology of Persuasion* (Harper Business, 2021).

sum" of assets, each of the children should receive precisely the same amount.

Author Simon Sinek has distinguished between decisions based upon what he refers to as a "finite game" mindset and decisions based upon an "infinite game" mindset. Finite games are problems that assume a fixed mindset and worldview, a "zero sum" game in which there is a clear winner and a clear loser. In this finite game approach, an unequal gift given by a mother to a son for no apparent laudable purpose not only reduces the extent of the inheritance to the other children but results in resentments and damaged sibling relationships. This zero-sum game approach is the game of modern trust law, driving revenues of many litigation firms.

A biblical approach to equitable treatment of children should attempt to emphasize the eternal, godly, and spiritual benefits to your children in the hopes that we can achieve a *multiplicative* mindset. Under a multiplicative mindset, any non-recipient children might come to see how the unequal gift given to his or her sibling(s) achieves eternal benefits. They might come to have a joy in the knowledge of God's provision in a sibling's life. Just as importantly, the disproportionate gifts would have the multiplicative effort of freeing up the non-recipient children from any misperception of future zero-sum game financial entitlements. ***To the extent that unequal gifts are made to encourage our children to love Jesus wholeheartedly, and not to further a sense of entitlement, we will be playing an "infinite game" with financial assets.***

As a trustee of God's assets, we are obligated to provide for our children during our lifetime. You have the opportunity and the obligation to use assets to meet the needs of your children, even if the gifts are disproportionate. Lifetime gifts among one or more of your children during your lifetime when the needs are conspicuous to the other children creates the opportunity for family cohesion, a precedent for purpose-driven planning, not consumption-based, fixed-sum thinking. If you are articulating the reasons for disproportionate treatment during lifetime, you can mentor adult children in their relationships with one another and are far more likely to avoid future sibling resentment or disharmony between your children.

The precedent you set during lifetime with your children, even from an early age, will have long-term implications on how your children view transfers from you. Psychologists refer to the "anchoring effect" when referring to our cognitive bias in making a decision based upon the initial information we receive. If your adult children are "anchored" to the perception that they are legally entitled to one equal share of all your assets, regardless of the needs of other siblings, it will be difficult to move a beneficiary child off that anchored position. But if you have a lifetime precedent for demonstrating that gifts are made for the needs of children to achieve eternal, spiritual, and godly outcomes, your children can move an anchor of expectation from a strictly proportionate division to a multiplicative approach.

As the trustee of the financial assets in our possession, keep in mind that we ultimately answer to the Lord as the owner of our assets, not our children. We have the freedom to provide disproportionately to our children and charities in accordance with our duties as trustees of God's assets. In the case of an adult child who has experienced professional setbacks, unforeseen medical expenses, or costs related to a divorce, you have no legal duty to give your children equal gifts.

Ultimately, the responsibility for making the lifetime gifts is between you, the trustee of God's assets, and God, as the owner of the assets. You would be achieving important eternal, spiritual, and godly benefits in the lives of your children by making lifetime gifts to your child in a time of that child's greatest financial need.

Communicating Unequal Lifetime Gifts

For those of us with adult siblings, we have seen the eternal, spiritual, and godly benefit to our siblings and their families of the financial commitments made by our parents for our siblings and, now, their families. Even if you went to a less expensive school than your siblings, you appreciate the impact that your contribution made to your own human capital and can therefore be pleased with your parents' financial contributions to your siblings' human capital. Your parents' lifetime contribution to you and your siblings was multiplicative in nature because the financial contributions to each of you was based upon the purpose achieved.

You should therefore inform your children of disproportionate gifts whenever the knowledge of the gift among the non-recipient siblings is likely to create a multiplicative effect even among the non-recipient children and their families. If other siblings are aware of the need, and if they are Christ-followers as you are, they may be encouraged by the opportunity you have to make gifts to meet the need. If the knowledge of the disproportionate gift may cause undue embarrassment to a child, it is likely appropriate to keep the knowledge of the gift from all siblings.

You have no legal duty to your children to communicate the nature of unequal lifetime gifts as the lifetime gifts are made. Regardless of whether you decide to disclose the unequal gift at the time that it is made, you must be sure to disclose the gift to your professional advisors and, if the value of the gift is significant, to the IRS.[2] As discussed in the following chapter, you will also want to document the legal treatment of each lifetime transfer so that the transfer is accounted for following your death.

DOCUMENTING LIFETIME ASSET TRANSFERS

"Mom and I had a handshake agreement about the loan between us. We didn't have anything in writing." These are the types of admissions that will be subject to discussion after your death among the litigation attorneys representing your children. The relationship fallout after death usually arises by reason of a lack of proper documentation related to disproportionate asset transfers. Once the surviving parent dies, it is impossible for the parent to resolve the issue of whether an asset transfer was considered a loan or a gift. The rest of the family, as well as legal counsel, are left only with fuzzy and self-serving recollections. To avoid disagreements, it is critical that you and your spouse properly document the nature of a significant lifetime transfer.

A Loan

The most common point of contention among siblings following death is whether a transfer was a disproportionate gift or a loan. I believe that, in many cases, the parents understand the legal distinction, but simply cannot bring themselves to a decision. If the transfer was a gift, the recipient is entitled to receive the gift *without reduction* in his or her equal share of remaining assets. The loan agreement should be in writing, whether written by you, your child or your attorney. The agreement may be as simple as a signed letter from the child to the parent specifying the amount of the loan, the interest rate, and the terms of the repayment of the principal and interest. We commonly prepare promissory notes on behalf of a client family that requires the child to make interest-only payments for the term of the loan, with the ability to prepay principal at any time. Such a written loan agreement can be easily administered if the parent dies before the loan is repaid.

---

2 If the gift is more than the "annual exclusion amount," you should document the gift on a properly filed gift tax return.

In such an event, the loan becomes an "asset" of the trust or estate of the parent. Provided that the parent died with adequate other assets, the other children who did not receive the loan could receive other assets from the parent's estate to offset the outstanding amount of the loan. The debtor-child now receives the amount of the loan as part of his or her inheritance. Not very exciting, certainly, but a key part of this child's inheritance is the forgiveness of the outstanding amount of the loan. Through this structure, the child is provided the benefit of the distribution when they most need the distribution, while the children who did not need or want a loan are "made whole" following death.

Payment to a Child for Past Services

Conversely, perhaps a child has previously lent his or her time, money, or expertise to an asset of yours that has appreciated in value. If a portion of the value of your asset is by reason of the child's "sweat equity," you should document that sweat equity. Ideally, you will have repaid the child during your lifetime; but if that is not possible, you should document in writing the financial value of the sweat equity as a dollar amount or a percentage of the value. Commonly, clients will complain, "We can't do this! We don't know how to value our daughter's contribution to the value of the cabin!" Certainly, neither you nor your daughter in this event would have completed a time card or otherwise kept track of all the hours. This is a subjective determination made by you, not dictated by any legal or tax requirements. But if you die without specifying the value, how much more difficult will it be for your children to ascertain what should have been done? A biblical estate plan is not easily implemented in these scenarios, but these plans do result in a plan that is far easier for your children to implement after your death. If you attach a value to your child's past services, while your children may disagree with your valuation methodology, at least no Jacob and Joseph situation would arise following your death given that you demonstrated, in this act of valuation, an intention to be fair to all your children.

Compensation for Future Services

Aging clients often approach an attorney to direct that one child receives a larger percentage of remaining assets after death in exchange for the child's verbal promise to provide future personal care services. This plan, of course, assumes upon a certain future outcome, an outcome which would forseeably be thrown off by any number of variables. For example, what if the child is simply not able to care for a parent by reason of the child's health or family obligations, or the parent's health requires a stay at a care facility, or another similar event unfolds? When I query some of my clients about their stated intentions, it becomes clear that some of these clients are abiding by a secular approach of using the "future promise" provided by the child as the ostensible reason for rewarding the child who is now being far more attentive to the client than siblings. Under a secular approach, it really does not matter if and whether the "attentive" child provides any care. In reality, the aging parent is rewarding the attentive child for their current attention to the parent, not the promise of future services.

In these instances, the biblical approach should be to create a personal services legal contract between mom/dad and the caretaking child. Here, we are creating a legal structure to compensate the caretaking child for services rendered at actual financial "cost" to the caretaking child. This legal contract should set forth the terms of compensation to the caretaking child equal to what a third party-provider would charge for the same services rendered. The adult child can be compensated for actual services rendered as they are provided. Perhaps more importantly, the non-active siblings are made aware, on an ongoing basis, of the true costs involved in providing care and are therefore not reliant on the caretaking sibling to work for low or no cost, thereby preserving a greater financial inheritance to them.[3] By keeping everyone aware of the true costs of care, the family can collectively make decisions that are multiplicative in nature—such as deciding that a parent should indeed receive assisted living care, which is a better care alternative to staying in a child's unequipped personal residence, while also freeing up the caretaking sibling from the emotional and physical burdens of care.

Once you are no longer able to make your own decisions, your named power of attorney and health care directives take over as decision-makers for your finances and health care, respectively. Your named agent under the power of attorney has the legal obligation to make financial decisions on your behalf and to disclose all decisions to your other children. When these legal duties are coupled with the personal services agreement, you create a structure in which there is full disclosure of all financial decisions among your children and fair reimbursement to the caretaking child for time spent and out-of-

3 A tax advisor might note that these compensation payments are taxable income to the child, as opposed to the transfer being tax-free if characterized as a gift. However, the tax cost of this characterization is well below the legal fees associated with post-death litigation, not to mention the spiritual implications on sibling disharmony.

pocket expenses. The duties owed by the child to the parent and the child's siblings is governed by "fiduciary" legal principles, meaning that the child must act in the best interest of the parent. This structure creates the necessary "check and balance" on the power of attorney's activities as, among other obligations, the power of attorney is required to provide copies of all financial transactions to family members, if requested.

An Advancement as a Reduction in Future Inheritance

As an alternative to a loan arrangement with a child, you could document the existence of the disproportionate transfer as a lifetime gift, but direct that other children are "made whole" following death. In this event, you must document the unequal distribution within your trust agreement or will. Under the terms of that document, you must specify that such transfers must be considered "advancements" against the specified percentage of remaining assets that will be received by such adult children following the death of the surviving parent. In the absence of any direction in the estate-planning documents, any unequal lifetime gifts are **not included** in calculating an equal division of remaining assets at death. It might therefore be necessary to revise estate-planning documents to account for such unequal lifetime gifts and consider such significant lifetime gifts as an advancement against such child's share.[4]

IMPLEMENTING A PLAN FOR TRANSFER AT DEATH

Following your death, you have been relieved of your duties as trustee to care for your children—to provide them with ongoing eternal, spiritual and godly benefits. Unlike the opportunities presented during lifetime to make disproportionate gifts for the purpose of instilling wisdom to each child at just the right time, there is no opportunity for a feedback loop between you and your children following your death. As a result, we abide by our grace-based biblical stewardship prerogative of honoring each of your children through an equal gift.

In previous chapters, we summarized how you could identify and value your unique family assets. After identifying and valuing assets that are

---

4 In some states, it is possible to create a legally-binding attachment to your will or revocable trust, called an "Advancement List," that allows you to document which of your lifetime gifts should be taken into account in making an equal division of remaining assets at death. This Advancement List could then be updated, on your own, as you make gifts which you wish to be treated as an advancement against the child's share.

not given away during lifetime, you should create a legal plan for the transfer of your assets at death. Your plan might include a combination of four separate legal methods for the transfer of assets:

> directly to certain individuals regardless of third-party value;

(1) directly to certain beneficiaries, but incorporating a structure for the proper third-party valuation of the asset to "offset" for gifting of other assets to other beneficiaries;

(2) among a class of specified beneficiaries, with each beneficiary receiving individual assets without equalization for value; or

(3) among a class of specified beneficiaries, but with each of the beneficiaries receiving an amount having the same third-party value.

The remainder of this chapter summarizes a plan for each of these types of assets, and the worksheet to follow provides you the opportunity to sketch out how you wish for your unique assets to be distributed following your death.

Direct Distributions to Specified Individuals

You may have certain items that certain individuals should receive at your death without regard to the value of the item for "equalization" purposes among other individuals. A widow might direct that her only daughter should receive her wedding ring, regardless of value, and without an equalizing distribution to her two living sons. A mother might feel that her wedding ring is more valuable to a daughter for sentimental reasons more than for financial reasons, enough so that she feels it is unnecessary for her sons to receive other assets of equal monetary value.

Tangible Property. By law, you can direct the distribution of specific and unique items of tangible personal property according to a list that you would keep separate and distinct from your will (or Trust).[5] Through a list of this type, you can give legal direction as to who should be the recipient of specific items of tangible personal property. So long as you have a will in place that refers to the possibility of creating a separate tangible personal property list, you can periodically

---

5 Minn. Stat. 524.2-513. https://www.revisor.mn.gov/statutes/cite/524.2-513.

update a list of what items you wish to give to certain individuals. From a legal perspective, it is important to note that the recipients of these gifts receive these items regardless of value.

Real Estate, Cash or other Assets. By law, you cannot distribute assets other than tangible personal property according to such a "tangible personal property list." Instead, these assets must be distributed through a beneficiary designation for retirement accounts or life insurance policies, or through a will or Trust for all of your other assets.

Direct Distribution to Specified Individuals with Offsetting Distributions to Others

Some of our clients have a desire, for good reason, to give assets that have sentimental value or service value to one of their children, but desire to incorporate a value of the assets into equity considerations among multiple children. In this regard, attempting to quantify both a "third-party value" as well as a "family-value premium" is of significant benefit. You can transfer the asset to the chosen beneficiary but require that the asset is to be valued at a specific amount for purposes of equalizing distributions among children.

One common example is the family cabin scenario. Unlike situations in which the parents dictate a legal plan to require the kids to own and "enjoy" the cabin, some of our clients have a true multi-generational use property in the sense that one of the children has already developed a personal lifestyle involving the family cabin. In those situations, the clients should direct that the cabin is to be allocated to that particular child. In creating an equal division of assets at death, the parents value the cabin incorporating the true family value premium that exists with the property. In this manner, your child who is using the property can be honored by receiving the property, while still "paying" for the property through a reduction in amount of other assets received.

By Draft: Selection of Assets Regardless of Value

You might identify certain items, typically sentimental and/or household goods, which should be allocated to a "class" of named beneficiaries. This class (typically children, grandchildren, other family, and possibly close friends) would be given the equal right to choose among themselves, on a rotating basis, one item at a time, regardless of value, until all items are chosen. Unlike a closed-bid process, to be described shortly, this structure allows for those members of the class to freely choose items without regard to value without being constrained by any disparity in a personal financial situation. If you own items with sentimental value to more than one child, this structure assures your children that each of them have an equal right to receive an item without fear that she or he will be outbid by a wealthier sibling. At the end of the chapter, I have a simple worksheet to articulate those items that should be subject to a "draft" structure among your family.

By law, you can direct the distribution of undesignated tangible personal property by a separate tangible personal property list among a class of beneficiaries. This "class" can be a different group of individuals than the named beneficiaries of other assets, such as your remaining investments, retirement accounts, and home equity. The class is generally those individuals who are most likely interested in the sentimental value of the remaining tangible personal property items. In some cases, it may be appropriate to direct that tangible personal property defined as sentimental should be distributed among certain beneficiaries (*e.g.,* your children), while other items designated as service items should be distributed among other beneficiaries (*e.g.,* your spouse). In that manner, the individuals who could benefit from the sentimental items would have the legal authority to receive remaining sentimental property, while the spouse or others who could use the service items can receive those items.

By Auction: Closed Bid Option to Purchase Assets

Finally, certain of your remaining assets could be offered for sale by the estate or trust, with sale proceeds being allocated to the estate or trust. In these instances, it is common for the assets to be offered first to the family members before being offered for sale to third parties. If any family member has any sentimental connection to the asset or would benefit from the service value of the item, the family member can purchase the asset from the trust or estate. Especially for assets that have significant financial value (such as a family cabin), this structure creates the appropriate equity consideration for other family members to financially benefit from his or her portion of the sale proceeds. At the end of the chapter, I have a simple worksheet you and your spouse can complete to articulate those items that should be subject to a "closed bid" auction structure among your family members.

By law, the default legal framework is the last of the four methods referenced above. Therefore, if you or your children have sentimental value that requires special treatment of the assets, you should create a legal plan for the appropriate framework to address unique assets. In this manner, you can be certain to create a multiplicative effect on your children even after your death for difficult-to-value assets.

Praying for the Wisdom of Solomon

Allocating assets equitably among children might seem to require the wisdom of Solomon. On one occasion, King Solomon demonstrated his unparalleled wisdom by ruling on a dispute between two women.[6] Two women lived together and both had children at the same time. One morning, both women awakened to discover that one of the two children had died in the night. A dispute between them ensued as to whose baby was alive and whose was deceased. In order to ascertain which woman was telling the truth, Solomon feigned a directive to split the living baby in two. In response, only one of the women offered to give up the legal claim on the living baby rather than split the infant in two. Solomon announced that he had rightfully deciphered who was the true mother—the woman willing to give up the baby.

None of this planning is as important as the life of a child. However, providing equitably between your children will require you to ascertain the emotional and spiritual condition of each of your children, especially in the context of disproportionate gifts. You might follow Solomon's lead in taking steps to ascertain the true value to each of your children. Just as the one mother valued her child's life more than being "right," you might seek out opportunities to understand the underlying desires of your children in receiving assets from you. Through communicating with your children, you should manage your financial assets to encourage each of them towards a multiplicative mindset and with eternal, spiritual, and godly goals in mind.

ILLUSTRATIONS FOR APPLICATION

The following client cases illustrate the principles of this chapter and demonstrate how you might create an estate plan to create a multiplicative mindset on your children.

An Inconspicuous Post-Death Direction to Sell

My client Randy's construction business has seen both ends of the

6   1 Kings 3:16–28.

profitability spectrum. As a result of a few bad years, Randy has not been able to accumulate significant retirement savings. Only with a sale of the business to a competitor could Randy and his wife afford to retire. While two of Randy's five children are currently involved in the business, Randy has convinced me and others in the business that neither of his two children has the interest or the capacity to manage the business if he became incapacitated or died suddenly. From all appearances, Randy's two children have no significant emotional or sentimental stake in the company. Randy has rightfully elevated the importance of the financial value of the business (that is, the third-party value), above the need to distribute the business to his two children involved in the business (the sentimental value). Randy's current estate plan directs that if he dies before he sells the business, the Trustee is required to sell to a competitor for maximal return and not allocate the business to the two participating children. With this structure, Randy's wife would have the assets she needs for retirement. To the extent that assets remain following the second death between them, the assets from the sale of the company could be split among all five of his children. The two children who are current participating in the business can get on with their own lives and hopefully become more successful in other endeavors.

A Conspicuous Lifetime Sale to One Child

Before the COVID-19 pandemic in 2020, Sam was required to travel to and from all client meetings. By reason of the virtual meeting technology that rose to prominence beginning in the COVID-19 business world, his clients become comfortable with his virtual presence for his business services. Sam soon had more demand than he could handle. Sam hired additional employees, one of whom was his son, Ben. While Sam offered positions to his two other children, neither of them decided to leave their own careers to joint Sam and Ben.

Recently, Ben and Sam negotiated a sale/purchase of Sam's company to Ben. The purchase price was based, in part, on a professional appraiser's opinion of value. This value was reduced by a factor to account for Ben's inexperience. The entire transaction, including the value discount, was shared with Sam's two other children. The siblings responded positively to the plan, even though they were in some sense paying for the plan through a reduced inheritance. Each of the two siblings understood the value to Ben of finding his personal vocational calling, and the two siblings loved the idea of Ben retaining ownership and control within the family. Through this planning, Sam was able to achieve a multiplicative outcome among all three of his children.

Returning the Sweat Equity to the Son

My client Peter purchased land along the north shore of Lake Superior long before it became a popular vacation destination. While all four of Peter's children enjoyed the cabin there, it was one of his sons, Lonnie, who contributed "sweat equity." In addition to providing manual labor, Lonnie also contributed his skills as a licensed architect in designing one of the homes on the property.

As part of Peter's estate plan, Peter decided to "return" to Lonnie some of the sweat equity Lonnie had contributed to the property. At his death, Peter directed that all four of the children would receive a portion of all remaining assets. However, Lonnie's share would be twice the value as his siblings share. When Peter died a few years ago, Lonnie and his three siblings became co-owners. Once the property is ultimately sold, Lonnie and his family will receive twice the value as his three siblings.

REFLECTIONS
On Providing Equitably for Your Children

While none of my clients demonstrate the obnoxious favoritism that Jacob displayed towards Joseph, none of us have the level of wisdom of Solomon. We should reflect on what special considerations are in our unique family situation in the hope of creating a multiplicative mindset among our children.

If you have made lifetime transfers, have you properly documented the purpose of those transfers? Use the following spreadsheet to document those disproportionate gifts.

Do your children have an expectation of equitable treatment? What additional clarifications should be made to all your children so that no one child is singled out after your deaths for having received preferential treatment?

What steps have you taken to address the distribution of unique assets between your children? Use the spreadsheet below to document those unique assets.

UNEQUAL LIFETIME GIFTS MADE TO CHILDREN

RECIPIENT	DATE[S]	AMOUNT[S]	LEGAL TREATMENT: LOAN, GIFT, OR ADVANCEMENT

TANGIBLE AND SENTIMENTAL ITEMS

DRAFT: ASSETS SUBJECT TO DRAFT BY BENEFICIARIES	BID AUCTION: ASSETS SUBJECT TO CLOSED AUCTION

7C: *Wisdom*

Make lifetime gifts to develop wisdom among our children.

"Hey, kids, you had better enjoy Disneyworld…it was either this or college!" Comedian Jim Gaffigan

Proverbs 13:22 reads, "A good man leaves an inheritance to his children's children." Too many of us read this verse in the context of current secular assumptions about an optimal inheritance. We seem to think that the inheritance referred to by King Solomon is (a) of financial assets and (b) must be distributed out of financial assets that we own as of our death. A generation of Christian baby boomers must be released from the misperception that they are obligated to wait until their own death to leave a financial inheritance to their children.

In comparison to our secular neighbors, Christians should be more willing to release control—to transfer the stewardship of assets—to our children even during our lifetime. By releasing control earlier than our secular neighbors, we create better mentorship ministries to disciple our children during lifetime, we assist our children when our children are in most need of assistance, and we are better trustees of God's assets from a tax perspective. In this chapter, I summarize the benefits of making lifetime gifts to your children, generally, and provide an overview of the tax issues related to lifetime transfers.

Create Mentorship Opportunities

The comedian Jim Gaffigan's quip about the cost of a Disney World vacation is the reality of raising children. Many parents seek to instill godly character attributes through school, sports, and music programs. We might even venture into expensive vacations like the one apparently taken by the Gaffigan family, much to Jim's chagrin. But through all this, we should keep in mind our primary objective, which is to instill wisdom into our young adult children's lives in their formative years.

King Solomon, the richest and wisest man in the Bible, elevated the importance of wisdom above financial assets.

"How much better to get wisdom than gold, to get insight rather than silver."[1]

"Wisdom is good with an inheritance, an advantage to those who see the sun. For the protection of wisdom is like the protection of money, and the advantage of knowledge is that wisdom preserves the life of him who has it."[2]

Too many of my clients operating from a secular perspective fail to face the reality of our human frailty, brokenness, and sin. They live with the unrealistic expectation that their children, upon receiving a sizable inheritance without any previous training, will somehow possess the ability to make wise decisions. In contrast, Christians operating from a biblical perspective hold a distinct advantage over those who, from a secular perspective, hold realistic expectations about a child's stewardship abilities. None of us is born with the innate ability to manage financial assets, but rather must be mentored in stewardship abilities. The question is not *whether* our children will fail in finances, but *who* is there to guide them when they fail. Lord willing, we can be the ones to guide our children through failure and into godly wisdom.

If our children make financial mistakes with a lesser amount of assets in their twenties and thirties, the goal is that they will have learned from those mistakes before having access to more significant financial stewardship decisions in their forties, fifties, and sixties. As inadequate as we might feel for our own stewardship obligations to our children, God has placed us in a position to steward the opportunity and obligation of teaching our children, and so it would be far better for us to teach our children stewardship lessons as we are healthy and able. If we neglect this opportunity, then our children will need to rely on other (perhaps secular) mentors, and we have no certainty that those influences will present a biblical worldview. The most significant treasure we can leave to our children is biblical wisdom, we should take steps during our lifetime, at cost to our personal balance sheet, reputation, and even businesses, to create opportunities for wisdom for our children.

1 Proverbs 16:16.
2 Ecclesiastes 7:9.

Maximize the Usefulness of Your Financial Assets for the Benefit of Your Family

"What can I do to keep the government from taking my money if I get sick?" When my colleagues and I present on estate planning topics, questions about end-of-life costs top the list of most frequently asked questions. Many would prefer for their fellow taxpayers to pay for their medical costs rather than pay their own way.

As a Trustee of God's assets in our hands, we should look at our financial assets like a grocer views perishable fruits and vegetables— goods that must be used by specific dates. When God provided the Israelites with manna in the desert, the Israelites were directed to gather only the amount they needed for each day. When they tried to gather more than what they needed, they found that it spoiled and was useless. Why should we hold financial assets like some of the Israelites tried to hold extra manna, only to find it spoiled the next morning? Rather than waiting until the maximum usefulness of a gifted asset is past its prime, we should use the financial assets to support our children and grandchildren at a time of optimal usefulness of those assets.

The use of lifetime gifts, if given during young adult years, is more likely to go directly to purposes that most of us would consider laudable or appropriate uses of the assets. Younger adult children in their twenties and thirties have more significant financial needs for their personal living expenses and human capital costs than children in their fifties and sixties, assuming we do not consider the needs of grandchildren. In October of 2022, the median existing-home sale price in the United States was $379,100.[3] The average cost of a four-year undergraduate education at an in-state public institution was $102,383, while the average cost of a four-year undergraduate education at a private school was $281,004.[4]

While estimates vary widely on end-of-life care costs, we can say with certainty that such care costs can be very expensive. One report from 2016 indicates that for the 40% of Americans who died in the hospital, the average cost for that last month of life in the hospital was $32,279. Similarly, the care costs for a nursing facility were $21,221 for the

---

3 National Association of Realtors, as reported in the Wall Street Journal, Saturday, November 19, 2022.
4 https://educationdata.org/average-cost-of-college#:~:text=The%20average%20cost%20of%20 attendance,or%20%24218%2C004%20over%204%20years.

final month, and $17,845 for hospice.[5] If our end-of-life medical care costs are not covered by private insurance and public health benefits, these costs could consume a significant portion of remaining assets Therefore, financial gifts to your children when they are in most need of them, gifts that may have occurred years before your death, can create a far more fulfilling wealth transfer for the benefit of your family.

Root Out the Idolatry of Control

From a secular perspective, it is appropriate for us to retain control of a successful business, a second or third residence, and a significant investment portfolio. The retention of such assets allows you to not just enjoy the consumption standard, but perhaps more importantly, the reputational capital it affords. Whether at a country club, around the neighborhood, or even at church, we seek a reputation among a desired social circle, a reputation that we believe is predicated on certain assets. If life is indeed about dying with the most toys, then it is most appropriate for us to retain control of successful assets…we should literally die at our desks, and let our children and others simply passively glean from the harvest of our active work and successes.

From a biblical perspective, being unable to part ways with the control of successful assets might demonstrate an idol of the heart. An inability to surrender control likely demonstrates a core identity problem, a misplaced focus on the reputational capital that accompanies ownership and control of the asset. If our identity is in Christ, we ought to be willing to part ways with successful assets in the right season. Paul had reason to promote his own pedigree and did so before becoming a Christ-follower. But when Christ called Paul, Paul relinquished his past pedigree and even found that past to be an impediment to following Christ. "But whatever gain I had [in my past successes], I counted as loss for the sake of Christ. Indeed, I count everything as loss because of the surpassing worth of knowing Christ Jesus my Lord."[6] My clients who have made gifts to charity or children during their lifetime learn more about their own heart and inclinations toward the idolatry of control. In making gifts, we root out those idols, placing our identity more fully in God.

---

5 As cited by Arcadia Care Resources report, The Final Year: Where and How We Die. https://arcadia.io/resources/final-year-visualizing-end-life/
6 Philippians 3:7–8.

Minimize Taxes

Making lifetime gifts to children benefits your family to the detriment of Papa Joe and Uncle Sam. While not as important as the spiritual reasons for lifetime gifts, we should be aware of the financial benefits of making lifetime gifts. In this section, I summarize important tax rules related to income taxes, estate and inheritance taxes, and generation-skipping transfer taxes. I then provide three principles for Christians making lifetime gifts to children or grandchildren.

Income Taxes, Including Capital Gains

When you make a gift of cash, securities, or real estate to your children, you are not entitled to any deduction on your income tax returns. However, your children are not required to report, as taxable income, any gifts made by you during your lifetime. Similarly, following your death, your children or other beneficiaries should not report inherited assets as taxable income.[7] Once a child becomes an owner of an asset, that child is responsible for the subsequent appreciation, interest income, and other taxable events that occur with that particular asset. If a real estate property or investment had been gifted during lifetime, these taxes would include a "capital gains tax" due upon the sale of such appreciated assets.[8]

For many of my clients, even clients who are in retirement, the marginal income tax rate of the parents is higher than the marginal income tax rate of their adult children, especially if the adult children have little "tax credits" (children) running around the house. In instances in which the junior generation has a lower tax rate, it makes sense to send the assets "downstream" to the children, thereby saving the entire family some income taxes.

Estate Taxes and the Unlimited Marital and Charitable Deductions

Under current federal law, a taxpayer has the right to transfer at death a substantial amount of assets to family before paying any federal estate taxes. This amount, called the federal unified credit amount, has changed significantly over the past twenty years and is the subject

---

7 The large exception in this general rule is the receipt of tax-deferred retirement accounts, such as individual retirement accounts ("IRAs") and employer-provided tax deferred accounts, such as 401K and 403b accounts. See Internal Revenue Code section 409(a).

8 A capital gains tax is imposed whenever a capital asset sells at a price higher than the price for which the asset was originally purchased.

of many political campaign speeches.[9] In 2023, the federal estate tax exemption is $12,920,000 for each U.S. resident. In the absence of legislative action before 2026, the current estate tax rules sunset on December 31, 2025, such that on January 1, 2026, the federal exemption will be reduced to approximately $7,000,000 per person.

Assets directed to your surviving spouse at your death pass free of any federal estate taxes by reason of the "unlimited marital deduction." Those operating from a biblical perspective should be aware of a second deduction from federal estate taxes, called the "unlimited charitable deduction." By reason of this deduction, only those assets that are being distributed to children, grandchildren, or other family members will be subject to estate taxes.

Therefore, all wealthy Americans, particularly Christians creating a biblical estate plan, should be aware that the federal estate tax is only a "voluntary" tax that is paid, and if it is paid at all, it is paid at the second death. If our "default" plan is to provide for most of a vast estate to charity rather than children, then by reason of the unlimited charitable deduction, there would be no estate taxes due. However, if our default plan is to provide for family rather than charity, then those with substantial assets will have this voluntary tax imposed.

Federal Gift Taxes and the Annual Exclusion Amount

In addition to a federal estate tax, wealthy Americans must also consider the application of federal gift taxes. From the creation of the federal estate tax rules, Congress tied the federal estate tax rules to a federal gift tax so that wealthy Americans were left with the conundrum of paying a tax if the taxpayer wanted to pass assets to children—whether an estate tax after death or a gift tax during lifetime. Currently, the federal lifetime gift tax exemption is identical to the federal estate tax exemption, although that has not always been the case. The federal estate tax and gift tax exemption amounts are tied together through a "unified credit," which means that certain lifetime gifts made by a taxpayer that have the effect of reducing a taxpayer's federal gift tax exemption (called a "taxable gift") also reduce a taxpayer's federal estate tax exemption.

"How much can I give my kids before paying any taxes? Can I give $10,000 before having to pay taxes?" They nearly spew their coffee

---

9 The federal gift tax and estate tax is expected to raise $30 billion in revenues in 2026, which accounts for https://www.statista.com/statistics/217562/revenues-from-estate-and-gift-tax-and-forecast-in-the-us-as-a-percentage-of-the-gdp/.

in surprise when I answer, "You can gift your children nearly $26 million without paying any taxes." What clients have heard from their golfing buddies is a different amount, called the "annual exclusion amount." The annual exclusion amount is the amount which the tax code considers to be of a *de minimus* nature before the value of those gifts is deemed to reduce the lifetime unified credit. Under this rule, if a taxpayer makes total gifts of less than this amount in any particular year, such gift(s) would not be considered a "taxable gift."

The concern raised by some well-meaning advisors is that if the gift(s) to one child or grandchild exceeds the owner's so-called "annual exclusion amount," the client is required to file a gift tax return. But the filing of the return is not a tax liability, just an additional fee paid to your friendly law firm or CPA firm. The filing requirement allows for the IRS to track the gift for future reference. If cumulative lifetime gifts do not exceed the taxpayers' cumulative federal gift tax exemption, no federal gift tax payment would be due.

Generation-Skipping Transfer Taxes

Since the time when the modern federal estate tax and gift tax rules were implemented in 1916, tax lawyers have been looking for loopholes in these rules. Astute planners for wealthy clients recognize that for families who are wealthy at both the senior and junior generational levels, it is most advantageous for the senior generation to make gifts during lifetime or following death to "skip" the junior generation, the children, and provide directly to grandchildren, thereby avoiding estate taxes at the junior generation's death. In order to "close" the open loopholes of avoiding estate taxes at the junior generation, Congress instituted a "generation-skipping transfer tax" ("GST Tax") in 1976. Through this "GST Tax," wealthy taxpayers have a limited ability to skip children with lifetime transfers or transfers at death. Currently, the federal generation-skipping transfer tax exemption matches the federal unified credit of $12,920,000. As with the federal estate tax and gift tax exemptions, the GST Tax is a "voluntary tax" in the sense that GST Taxes are imposed only if, and to the extent, that significant assets are directed to grandchildren and trusts for the benefit of grandchildren.

Tax Principles for Lifetime Transfers

For those endeavoring to make sacrificial gifts during lifetime, we have nothing to fear in transferring assets during lifetime. The tax code is structured to benefit the families of those individuals who are willing to part ways with assets during lifetime. Three basic principles apply to lifetime transfers:

Principle 1: *Not All Transfers Are Gifts—Considering Intrafamily Loans*

First, keep in mind that lifetime transfers can be characterized to your children and to the IRS as loans, not gifts. Characterizing the transfer of assets to your children as a loan and not a gift presents a golden opportunity for you to assist your children in learning to balance a budget. From a legacy perspective, the transfer could achieve a specific legacy objective, such as the purchase of a home or assistance with educational costs.

From a tax perspective, if the amount of the loan (the "principal amount") is below $10,000, the parent does not have to charge interest on the loan, and no interest income needs to be reported by the parents on his or her personal income tax return.[10] If a loan is made for $10,000 or more, a minimum interest rate must be charged by the parent to the adult child. The interest rate can be any rate agreed upon by the parent and child, provided that the interest rate is no less than the minimum intra-family loan rate set by the IRS. This interest rate required by the IRS, called the applicable federal rate, is announced monthly and applies to loans made in that particular month.[11] By way of example, here are the rates for December of 2022:

SHORT TERM	MID-TERM	LONG-TERM
0-3 Years	3 to 9 Years	> 9 Years
4.55%	4.27%	4.34%

Your children would be legally required to pay down the debt to you, thereby allowing you to preserve some cash flow. In most cases I observe, the asset purchased by the child with the loaned amounts appreciates in value at a rate faster than the interest required under the loan terms. This is true of not only a home purchase, but also the benefit of the educational degrees obtained through loaned assets. This difference in rates of appreciation results in tremendous satisfaction to

10 Internal Revenue Code Section 7872.
11 https://www.irs.gov/applicable-federal-rates

the children and the parents alike.

Principle 2: *Do Not Fear a Gift Tax Return.*

Second, if you are in position to make gifts, and your children are in a position to receive gifted assets, the most tax-savvy gifting strategy is to make gifts of cash or other assets to children or grandchildren of an amount equal to your annual exclusion amounts. Those clients who, in my opinion, created the most tax-efficient estate plan are those who were not afraid to make gifts that even exceed the annual exclusion amount, and therefore require the filing of the gift tax return. Even if the amounts exceed the relevant annual exclusion amounts, it simply means that the clients must **file** a federal gift tax return to document the gift with the IRS. So long as cumulative lifetime gifts do not exceed the federal gift tax exemption amount of $11,580,000, no federal gift tax liability would need to be **paid**.

Principle 3: *Pass the Hot Potato*

Third, we should transfer assets by gift or sale before the assets appreciate. If you have played the game "hot potato," you know you don't want to be the one holding the hot potato—you want to pass it along before being burned. Similarly, if you own an appreciating asset, you will want to transfer ownership before the asset appreciates. Otherwise, your family will be forced to pay estate taxes when the asset is valued at its apex. If you can transfer an asset before that appreciation occurs, we can successfully pass the hot potato to our children without passing a higher tax burden. As Christians, let's be as "wise as serpents" and look for ways to transfer assets before the hot potato assets reach their zenith.

Wisdom Before Wealth

Ron Blue writes, "Wealth never creates wisdom. Wisdom may create wealth. If you pass wisdom to your children, you probably can pass wealth to them. If they have enough wisdom, then they may not need your wealth."[12] As trustees of God's assets, we should judge our stewardship success not by the size of our financial net worth at the end of our lives, but by our efforts to teach our children in wisdom. Let's place assets in the hands of our children while they are under our tutelage with the hope of instilling biblical wisdom.

---

12   Ron Blue, *Splitting Heirs,* Northfield Publishing, Chicago, IL. 2004. p. 70.

ILLUSTRATIONS FOR APPLICATION

These three client cases will illustrate the three most frequently utilized gifting strategies. In each of these cases, I want to emphasize not just the tax implications, but the more important eternal, spiritual, and godly impact of the asset transfers.

Educational Savings Plans ("529 Plans")

Oliver and Sylvia have always placed a specific emphasis on the value of education. Sylvia was an elementary school teacher, while Oliver wrote scientific manuals and journals for chemical engineering companies. Their two sons are now successful patent attorneys, both having obtained engineering and law degrees. In retirement, Oliver and Sylvia focus significant time and financial resources into educational endeavors, particularly for their five grandchildren. The Olivers have made sacrificial financial gifts for their two sons, and now for their five grandchildren.

To further the family's specific focus on education, we created a plan to implement special education shares for their five grandchildren. A college savings plan, also referred to as a "529 Plan," can be established through a sponsoring state government. The person creating the account can own and control an account and name a child or grandchild who will be the recipient of the educational funding as the "beneficiary." Once the beneficiary reaches the point of needing support for educational costs, the account assets can be withdrawn, and no income taxes are paid.[13] Only if funds are withdrawn for purposes other than educational costs would taxes and penalties be paid.[14] Commonly, clients will use their annual exclusion amount gifting rights to gift cash of up to $17,000 to 529 Plans for children or grandchildren.[15]

Oliver and Sylvia determined that a 529 Plan account is precisely the

13 So long as distributions are made only for educational costs, no income taxes are owed on such withdrawals. Estate tax rules permit the taxpayer making the gift to the 529 Plans to retain ownership of the account(s) without subjecting the assets to estate taxes at death.

14 If the child becomes the owner of the 529 Plan after your death and does not use the assets for educational purposes, the IRS imposes a penalty of 10% for withdrawals, in addition to taxes on the accumulated earnings.

15 Unlike other types of annual exclusion gifts, a taxpayer can "superfund" a 529 Plan account by making a one-time gift to a 529 Plan account equal to five years' worth of annual exemptions and consider the "super-funded" gift as being made ratably over those five years. Under current law, a taxpayer could transfer $75,000 to a 529 Plan. Of course, the taxpayer could not make any other annual exclusion gifts for the benefit of the designated 529 Plan beneficiary over the next five years.

type of inheritance that increases wisdom. They determined to stretch themselves by making significant gifts to each grandchild's 529 Plan during their lifetime. By reason of the fact that the 529 Plan assets must be used for educational purposes or be subject to taxes and penalties, Oliver and Sylvia determined that the gifting strategy was the best way to make lifetime gifts to achieve eternally significant outcomes.

Home Ownership

John and Mary's family and financial situation in 2021 was common among many of my clients. Their personal financial situation continued to improve, even better than they had originally expected at the beginning of the COVID-19 pandemic. Instead of keeping this appreciation in the market, John and Mary liquidated investments and loaned $300,000 to each of their two adult children. These loans were then used by each of the children to purchase personal residences. John and Mary charged each child a minimum interest rate low enough to make the payments manageable to the adult children. In John and Mary's case, they chose to forgive a portion of the first year's principal and interest payments that were due to them.[16]

You might follow John and Mary's lead in providing a loan or a gift in amounts sufficient to allow a child or grandchild to purchase a residence. In the case of a gift, the child would not be obligated to make payments to you, but the child would still be responsible for property taxes, utilities, and maintenance. Whether through gift or loan, using your assets during your lifetime would be a great way to transfer wisdom in your wealth. The transfer improves the child's financial situation without precluding the need for self-sustaining employment. A wealth transfer strategy of this type is likely to increase long-term wisdom as well as worldly wealth in the lives of your children.

Family Cabin Legacy

Shortly before Sterling and Mae retired, my law firm assisted with the creation of an entity called a "limited liability company" ("LLC") to hold their northern Minnesota cabin.[17] The LLC itself holds the

---

16 In many respects, the transaction could place the child in the same income tax position as if the child had obtained a conventional loan. If the parents record a mortgage on the property purchased by the child to secure the loan, the child's income portion of the loan payments to the parents would be deductible to the child on the child's personal tax return. A mortgage registration tax will be due on the recorded mortgage.

17 The LLC is a legal entity that has owners (called "members") and officers, such as the President and Treasurer. The LLC is then used to own the cabin property real estate, as well as a separate bank account to manage the expenses of the cabin.

cabin and the bank account used to pay the cabin expenses. Once the LLC was created, we assisted with gifting approximately 25% of the ownership of the cabin (through the LLC) to each of Sterling and Mae's two adult children. The LLC is an ideal planning structure because it allowed Sterling and Mae to gift the cabin at a lower valuation than if the cabin were gifted directly to their children.

Just a few years later, Sterling was diagnosed with terminal cancer. Sterling penned a moving narrative to his family that, among other instructions, provided direction on future family cabin decisions. Sterling emphasized that while they should continue to use and enjoy the cabin as long as possible, they should not be obligated to continue to co-own the cabin if the family situation changed and it became a burden.

A few years after Sterling died, one of the children went through a difficult divorce, and it became clear that the continued ownership of the cabin was too large of a burden on Mae. Based upon the change in circumstances and Sterling's guiding narrative, the family had no moral obligation to retain ownership of the property. When the cabin was sold, each of the children then received a significant cash payout. In keeping with the wealth narrative penned by Sterling, the two children then used proceeds to purchase their own cabins. You might choose to implement a plan like Sterling and Mae by creating a gifting structure to transition significant and unique family assets to the next generation.

REFLECTIONS
On Developing Wisdom in Children

Reflect on how you can use financial assets to demonstrate to your children that godly wisdom is to be valued above worldly wealth.

What specific assets could you use to teach your children to prize wisdom above worldly wealth?

How can you use some of your current financial assets to "buy wisdom" for your children, even if it is at financial cost to you?

What assets do you have now that you are in a position to gift to children and grandchildren?

If you have the opportunity to make additional asset transfers, prayerfully contemplate the potential eternal, spiritual, and godly outcomes that will result to you and to them in making the asset transfer. For each potential transfer, address the following questions:

Possible Outcomes for the Child-Recipient

What is the recipient's current capacity to learn wisdom from the transfer? Is the child in a position to be able to succeed, or will the efforts at stewardship fall flat? Even if the monetary value of the transferred asset is lost, is the child likely to learn from this experience?

What purposes will be accomplished in the life of the child, and are these purposes consistent with eternal, spiritual, or God-centered goals?

Possible Outcomes to You

Will the transfer make you more dependent on God? What eternal, spiritual, godly goals will be accomplished by reason of this transfer?

Will you be able to provide for yourself and your spouse if the transfer works out adversely to you and your spouse? What implications would an adverse outcome have on providing an inheritance to your children?

7D: *Limit*

Knowing that worldly riches impede spiritual vitality, establish limits to the worldly wealth transferred to your children.

"Enjoy your birthday, son. We have an all-you-can-eat pass to the baseball game tonight!"

A few years ago, my dad and I took my two living sons and my three nephews to a Minnesota Twins game to celebrate my ten-year old's birthday. That night, the ballpark was running a promotional event for a certain section of the right-field stands. For the ticket price, the holder not only gained entrance to the right field stands but also received the "right" to eat as many hot dogs, peanuts, ice cream treats and popcorn as one could possible fit in one's stomach. I quickly discovered the error of our ways after consuming just two bites of one hot dog. I realized that there was a reason these hot dogs were so readily being offered up to us—barely edible and certainly not worthy of a birthday celebration. My boys and nephews nonetheless plowed through these empty calories, while I silently regretted not accepting my wife's offer to make a home-cooked meal for us before we left for the park!

I am frequently recognizing my own mistakes in elevating quantity above quality. We fail to understand the principle of diminishing returns and make decisions based upon what is "more" rather than what is "good." As I frequently observe how our young adult beneficiaries spend the hard-earned assets bequeathed to them by their parents, I am reminded of this quantity over quality distinction. C.S. Lewis wrote, "It would seem that our Lord finds our desires not too strong, but too weak. We are half-hearted creatures, fooling about with sex and drink and ambition when infinite joy is offered to us, like an ignorant child who wants to go on making mud pies in a slum because he cannot imagine what is meant by an offer of a holiday at the sea. We are far too easily pleased."[1] At the Minnesota Twins game, my sons and nephews were drawn to the opportunity to enjoy limitless salt

---

1 C.S. Lewis, The Weight of Glory and Other Addresses.

and sugar but should have realistically expected that their ability to consume the meal was not unlimited, and the sensory experiences of the chips-and-popcorn buffet were inferior to the home-cooked meal.

A biblical estate plan intentionally considers the possibility of limiting an inheritance for our children because we perceive the danger of Jesus' teachings about money in the lives of our children. The frequency of Jesus' comments on money should cause us to stand up and take notice of Jesus' concern regarding how our love of money can "crowd out" our love for Him. More than warnings related to anger, sex, or truth, Jesus warns us that the desire for worldly wealth will replace our love for Him. Jesus explains that for the seed of faith planted among worldly wealth, "…the deceitfulness of riches choke the word, and it proves unfruitful."[2] Likewise, in responding to the rich young ruler, we see Jesus' view of how wealth "chokes" one's spiritual growth.[3] While the rich young ruler wanted to see how he could use his wealth to justify his own actions, Jesus saw through his façade. "One thing you still lack. Sell all that you have and distribute to the poor, and you will have treasure in heaven; and come, follow me."[4] The rich young ruler went away sad, and we are left with the impression that the man chose wealth over eternal life in Christ. We must be wary of the way in which worldly wealth creates a Faustian bargain—the ability to wield power to live a life that seems to be what the child wants, but in fact excludes the work of God from that person's life.

Jesus did not explicitly state that we should limit the size of a financial inheritance to our children. But Jesus' interaction with rich young ruler suggests the negative implications to our children for unfettered access to vast financial sums. The rich young ruler identified himself by his wealth and the "good works" that came from his wealth. Forced to choose between following God and identifying with his wealth, the rich young ruler chose the latter. One can only imagine the regret that he now feels. Some millennial-generation children are now reaping what was sown by their parents who chased the American dream—a disillusionment with secular desires for unending consumption. If our children ask for an inheritance, let us provide them with a financial inheritance that is good for them now, but without removing the possibility of an eternal inheritance in Christ. Given the warnings in Scripture, how can we possibly countenance placing our children in a

2 Matthew 12:22.
3 Matthew 19:16–30.
4 Luke 18:22.

position where they come to rely upon financial assets rather than on God's future grace?

The Secular Approach: Planning for the Black Swan

"We need to make sure we have enough to live on," my clients John and Jill told me during a meeting about their estate plan. While we would not sit up and take notice if these words came from the lips of most of our friends or neighbors, these words should never come from the lips of my clients, John and Jill. Together, this couple holds financial assets of $35 million in liquid assets. John and Jill were meeting with us, their team of advisors, about how to create tax-savings trusts. This couple was so risk averse, and so dependent on their need to have access to their own accumulated wealth, that they ultimately determined that our recommendations for gifting assets to trusts for children and grandchildren was simply too risky. After all, they reasoned, what if there is a worldwide pandemic and markets crash? What if the markets crash after they invested in certificates of deposit with the banks? They wondered if the $20 million they had in cash savings would be enough in that calamitous event. They were concerned that if the markets crashed, the federal government could become insolvent so that the FDIC insurance for the bank CDs didn't come through. They wondered what would happen if the markets crashed, the federal government became insolvent, our nation was invaded by another country, and our currency become worthless. Clearly, I was not going to be able to convince these "control-minded" clients that they should relinquish control simply to save their children estate taxes following their deaths.

Indeed, from a secular perspective, we should save up all our resources not only to meet every possible future scenario in our lives, but also every possible scenario that might arise in the lives of our children, grandchildren, and all subsequent generations. In short, under a secular estate plan, we should make the following plans:

- We should hoard assets. With more financial assets, our children are less likely to be adversely impacted by future events. Whether an increase in health care costs, negative investment performance, another worldwide pandemic, or a nuclear war, more financial assets means less anxiety about an unknown future.

- Consumption standards are the key metric of success. There is no spiritual benefit to your children for encouraging them to learn grit and determination in finding and progressing in a professional career. There is no spiritual benefit to your children to working through a career, or perhaps a couple of different professional careers, as they learn to trust God's provision for them.

- In a secular mindset, we have a responsibility to plan for scenarios that are not statistically probable—the "Black Swan" events.

The Biblical Approach: God Will Provide

Christians with substantial wealth have sometimes fallen prey to what I refer to as "retention indecision" related to future "Black Swan" events. Some Christians have a sense of duty or obligation about future calamitous events that are not foreseeable, but possible. Christians must create the appropriate legal structure to provide for those in their midst who either have a current need based upon health or other life circumstances, or even possible events with a fair degree of likelihood. But too many Christians fail to recognize the sovereign work of God in the lives of our family when considering future "what if" events.

When Moses led the Israelites through the desert, the benefit of the six-days-a-week provision of manna not only was a daily demonstration of God's gracious provision to the Israelites, but it also freed Moses from the significant logistical challenges that would have been associated with collecting, storing, and carrying significant amounts of food. Moses warns the Israelites, "Let no one leave any of it over until the morning."[5] God provided for their daily needs not only to meet those needs, but to demonstrate His character. I wonder how long the Israelites collected those daily rations before they realized that they had certainty as to God's provision for the next day, the next week, the next year. As Paul says, "Whoever gathered much had nothing left over, and whoever gathered little had no lack."[6] Jesus admonished his twelve disciples to travel lightly when proclaiming the gospel.[7]

In the absence of biblical promises to us, we would similarly take on significant burden for our children, acting like my clients John and Jill who felt like they had to plan for all possible scenarios. But even secular leaders and authors understand the conundrum—the

5 Exodus 16:10.
6 2 Corinthians 8:15, citing Exodus 16:19.
7 "Acquire no gold nor silver nor copper for your belts, no bag for your journey, nor two tuni s nor sandals nor a staff, for the labourer deserves his food." Matthew 10:9–10.

impossibility—of trying to plan for the Black Swan events, the events that are currently unforeseeable. Morgan Housel writes, "The correct lesson to learn from surprises is that the world is surprising. Not that we should use past surprises as a guide to future boundaries; that we should use past surprises as an admission that we have no idea what might happen next."[8]

Jesus promises that we will have trouble in this world.[9] This promise is equally applicable to our children, regardless of the extent of the financial inheritance provided to them. Trusting in the goodness and sovereignty of God means that we trust that God will provide our children with the daily manna, the financial needs that they will need, at just the right time and from the right sources. While it may inflate our ego to think that our children will have a sizable inheritance, consider the negative spiritual impact the continued retention will have on our children. By retaining assets for our children, we reduce the possibility that our children will seek the Lord's provision through their own personal career development. As we have seen in writing our own personal narrative, the loss of a child's opportunity to develop a personal career cuts the child off from the blessing of seeing God's work through the development of the child's own personal narrative.

Rather than leave assets for our grandchildren to address potential future "Black Swan" events, why not increase the chances of a positive spiritual outcome for your children by limiting the amount of the inheritance? If we want our children to become Christ followers and continue to be Christ followers, and if Jesus told us that wealth makes it more difficult for us to follow Him, why would we make it more difficult for our children to follow Jesus by making them wealthy? Providing unlimited assets to our children poses a far greater risk of "crowding out" their spiritual life than any risk of a lost opportunity to address a currently unforeseen future calamity. In comparison to our secular neighbors, a biblical estate plan requires us to be ready to limit the amount of the financial inheritance to our children because we recognize the adverse spiritual impact that a large financial inheritance will have on our children.

Creating a Cap on a Child's Inheritance

Create a plan to create an inheritance to achieve specific purposes in the lives of our children. This encourages your children to find a

---

8 Morgan Housel, The Psychology of Money, p 128.
9 John 16:33.

narrative of wealth and a life consistent with their life calling, thereby freeing them from the rich young ruler bondage of indiscriminate wealth. You could direct that only a certain asset, such as a business ownership interest or a percentage interest in a residential property, should be distributed at your death to your child. Alternatively, you could direct that each child would receive an amount of cash "capped" to a specific dollar amount. However, any excess or leftover assets owned by you would be legally directed to your church, your donor-advised fund, or specifically designated ministry organizations.

A Specific Gift

The most common types of specific gift assets are the family cabin, the family farm, the homestead, or the family business. Other variations on this "specific asset" theme include educational savings accounts (*e.g.,* 529 College Savings Plans), stock from your current or former employer, proceeds from the sale of your business when you retired, or even a specific life insurance policy purchased for this very purpose. Note the important difference between gifting the specific asset to the child for the child's ownership, and requiring the child to benefit and enjoy the asset through a trust structure requiring its continued retention.[10] The purpose of the specific asset gift is to bestow honor on the child in a limited and discernable manner and thereby allow the child to be blessed by the asset, either in its current form, or the liquidated proceeds from the sale of the asset.

A Pecuniary Bequest

Many clients "cap" the bequest to children at a specific amount, a type of gift called a "pecuniary bequest." The total value of the gift to each child should be enough to provide a true honor to each child and make a substantial difference in each child's life, but also not enough to allow the child to stop her pursuit of God's professional calling on her life. The child's lifestyle could be improved by reason of the gift, but the child's career and vocational goals should not be impacted. The amount is likely to change over time, depending on (i) the child's life situation, including professional advancement progression, (ii) the number of dependents in the child's household and (iii) cost of living factors.

If you believe that a grace-based estate plan requires you to give the same amount to each of your children, look first to the child who will

---

10 I previously discussed the "special purpose trust" structure in the Valuation chapter.

have the greatest financial needs in the future. Whether by reason of their family size, health situation, or ministry or professional background, ascertain an amount that would be appropriate for that child and her family. You can then replicate the same amount to your other children. As of March 1, 2023, in the city of Bloomington, Minnesota, the most common dollar amount I see among my Minnesota-based estate planning clients with substantial financial wealth is a gift of $1 million to each of their children.[11]

As with all other estate-planning decisions, you and your spouse should prayerfully consider the decision of whether to "cap" the total amount to each child and, if so, how much this "gift cap" should be for each of your children. This decision, in particular, is not likely a "one and done" decision, but a decision that must be continually reconsidered. As an upper bound to a "cap amount" strategy, I challenge the reader to consider whether any Christian should transfer assets to family and pay federal estate tax based on the current combined exemption levels of $24 million per married couple. Even for owners of family farms and family businesses, current business owners have ample opportunities to make lifetime transfers. Of course, this requires business owners to be ready and willing to relinquish control, which is fraught with emotional and spiritual difficulty. When politicians or your friends claim that the federal estate tax causes families to "lose the family farm," consider the likelihood that one or more secular assumptions about wealth and estate planning are also at play and contrast a biblical worldview with these secular assumptions.

Relationship Benefits to a Gift Cap Plan

"The Church Has Agreed to Pay for the Funeral Lunch and All the Accounting Fees."

A few final benefits to a "gift cap" plan are worth noting. In family situations with a history of disharmony, or where children are likely to disagree about a trust administration, a "gift cap" may have additional logistical and intra-family relationship benefits. If one or more charities are to receive all remaining assets, outstanding expenses and debts effectively reduce the share allocated to charity, not the specific gifts or "cap amount" shares allocated to children. Therefore, questions about the appropriateness of post-death expenses, trustee fees, and professional fees do not financially impact the children's inheritance

---

11 If your children are raising families on one of the coastal U.S. cities, you have good reason to adjust accordingly. Regardless, a gift of $1 million is a significant amount.

amount. These families would understand that not only is the church hosting your funeral luncheon, but it is effectively paying for it, too.

The gift cap plan might have a similar planning benefit during your lifetime related to your end-of-life care costs. If a "gift cap" plan is effectively communicated to children during lifetime, the children seem to be less concerned about end-of-life care costs and more concerned about obtaining the best care for mom and dad. Since the children know that leftover assets will be allocated to kingdom work at death, the increased care costs will not reduce his or her financial inheritance.

The gift cap plan would result in a greater amount of wealth being transferred to kingdom causes. Consider the impact on our global church and the Great Commission if we could start a movement among wealthy baby boomer Christians to cap the amount of the inheritance for their children. Certainly, God's plan will be accomplished, in His time, with assets He shall ordain. It would be a shame for you and your family to miss out on the joy of participating in kingdom causes. The counter-cultural and counterintuitive element of the gift cap plan is that it is not only more charitable than a "Black Swan" retention approach, but it is a superior form of estate planning in the lives of your children from an eternal, spiritual, and godly perspective. **I encourage you to *limit the gift amount to your children to a specific purpose or amount so that they receive the message, whether explicitly stated or implicitly understood, that gaining wisdom is more important than unfettered access to worldly wealth.***

You and your spouse should consider setting a specific amount and specific asset for each child so that each child (i) feels the blessing of receiving a financial inheritance, while also (ii) having the proper incentive to seek after the Lord and pursue his or her own professional and family calling. I pray that you and your spouse would endeavor to make the decision. Any attempt to find the right balance is the correct attempt, even if you are not successful in getting it exactly right. Once made, you should periodically review and revisit this amount.

ILLUSTRATIONS FOR APPLICATION

The following real-world illustrations may be helpful for you to consider whether to implement a "gift cap" plan for your children.

Specific Dollar Amount to Children; Remainder to Ministry

In a 2022 "Ask Pastor John" podcast, Dr. John Piper publicly shared his personal estate plan.[12] Pastor John, together with his wife Noel, chose a specific gift amount for each of their adult children that, "... is a significant, generous number, and yet a limited number that isn't the totality of the estate." Following the second death between them, each of their children would then become the owners of this specific dollar amount. Notably, Dr. Piper indicated that the rest of his assets are allocated to the donor-advised fund they established through the National Christian Foundation. As I will summarize in a subsequent chapter, the use of a donor-advised fund is an ideal structure for these situations. The donor (here, Dr. and Mrs. Piper) can direct not just specific distributions at death, but also appoint who it is that can carry out charitable giving following death. In summarizing his own plan, Dr. Piper cites the following benefits:

- Honoring your children with an amount that has a substantial and positive impact on the financial situation of the family;

- Limiting the amount of the gift so that each beneficiary is not overwhelmed by wealth; and

- Incorporating your desired ministry endeavors into your plan.

A Business Succession Plan with a Gift Cap

Allen will tell you how blessed he is by the opportunity to run the family business with three of his five daughters. Together with these three daughters, Allen owns and manages a successful technology business. Since these three daughters are already intimately involved in the business and hold key business relationships, the business is worth more to them than to a competitor. These three children already have a "family value premium."

Allen created a rather sophisticated plan with the help of legal counsel to achieve the following important objectives: (1) Allen's three daughters will continue to own and manage the IT Sales company after his death, (2) he will "gift limit" the amount to each of his five

---

12 https://www.desiringgod.org/interviews/should-i-leave-an-inheritance-for-my-children. I do not represent Dr. and Mrs. Piper. Dr. Piper did not disclose the "cap amount" for each of his children.

children, and (3) he will provide equally to all five children. [13] In Allen's case, we created a legal plan that would direct a total amount of assets to his five children. If the value of the business interests exceeded a certain amount, then the three daughters would be required to purchase the remaining business interests from the charity that is receiving the remaining assets.

If the Lord has blessed you with substantial assets or a business, Allen's estate plan is worthy of imitation. His "cap amount" assures that each of his children will not be overwhelmed by worldly wealth. His daughters are assured of an ownership interest in the business but would be required to continue to work out the plan. Perhaps most importantly, he provides the same amount for each of his five children, thereby bestowing on each of them the honor of an equal inheritance.

Creating a Narrative with the Gift Cap Amount

Phil and his two sisters co-owned a family business founded by Phil's late grandfather. Shortly before I commenced estate planning work with Phil and his wife, Sylvia, Phil decided to purchase a substantial life insurance policy for Sylvia and their four children. Just a few years later, Phil died in a traffic accident.

Over the next couple of years, Sylvia was able to successfully gift all of Phil's business interests to Phil and Sylvia's four children. While the gifts reduced Sylvia's personal financial holdings, Sylvia believes that the lifetime gifts placed her children in a better position to wisely steward the company.

By reason of the successful transfer of wealth, Sylvia determined to

---

13 Allen's plan directs as follows:

Each of the five children receives a total amount of assets at death equal to a "gift amount." This gift amount fluctuates based upon the value of the company.

While each child receives the same gift amount, the three daughters will receive company shares equal to the gift amount. His other two children will receive other assets equal to the gift amount. The gift amount changes with the value of the company so that the three daughters will be certain to collectively receive at least 20% of the value of the company. This minimum percentage assures the family that the daughters will have sufficient equity in the company to purchase the remaining shares from the donor-advised fund.

All remaining assets, including the rest of his IT sales company shares, are allocated to Allen's donor-advised fund.

Following Allen's death, if the shares of the company are allocated to the donor-advised fund, the three daughters will buy back the business ownership interest held by the donor-advised fund . Based on the cash flow projections, if the three daughters manage the company efficiently, the purchase of the remaining business interests can be fully purchased from the donor-advised fund over a five- to ten-year time period.

cap the additional inheritance amount each child would receive at her death, such that all of her and Phil's accumulated remaining assets would be allocated to their donor-advised fund. When it came time to determine the "cap amount," Sylvia chose as her cap amount the exact amount of the life insurance policy purchased years earlier. In Phil and Sylvia's case, there was no legal or tax significance to the amount chosen as the "cap amount"; rather, the cap amount itself reminded the four children, and the advisors for the children, of Phil and Sylvia's continuing narrative of purposeful planning.

Is there a particular number as a cap amount that would create a narrative of discussion and memorial among your family? If not, perhaps you and your family could creatively decide upon a cap amount that would create a narrative history for your family.

REFLECTIONS
On Capping an Inheritance Amount to Your Children

Reflect on whether it might be appropriate to update your estate plan to implement a "cap" to the amount allocated to your children.

Review your current financial asset inventory. Based on what you know about each of your children, how would each of them respond to receiving an equal share of all of your remaining assets?

What if you planned to give each child a specific amount (say, $100,000). Would that amount be appropriate, or would another amount? What eternal, spiritual, and godly impact would the receipt of another $100,000 have on each of them? Or perhaps another $200,000, $300,000 or $1 million?

What would be the maximum amount of assets currently on your asset inventory that, if you allocate to each of them, whether by lifetime gift or at death, would encourage each of them without raising a concern that they would end their dependence on God?

What specific assets could you give as a means of (i) capping the size of the inheritance while also (ii) providing a narrative of the story for the wealth? Do you have any of the following types of assets that might be used to achieve that goal?

- Lake property or farm
- Family residence with sentimental value
- Educational expense fund
- Shares of company stock

7E: *Trust*

Create the appropriate legal means to accomplish specific goals for your children.

"It turns out your friend is only **mostly dead**." So exclaims Miracle Max, the character played by actor Billy Crystal in the 1987 film, *Princess Bride.* Miracle Max, an underemployed magician, is called upon to resurrect the life of the movie's protagonist, Wesley. As it turns out, Miracle Max declares that Wesley is only "mostly dead," not "all dead."[1] After being revived by Miracle Max, the hero Wesley and his friends close out the movie by "storming the castle" and rescuing the damsel in distress from the evil prince.

You can decide to legally control how children or other beneficiaries benefit from remaining assets following death. In the words of Miracle Max, you can act as if you are only "mostly dead" following your real death by dictating a plan for distributions to your children from the grave. In this chapter, I explore the proper utilization of post-death trusts, or "testamentary trusts."[2] As in all other estate-planning decisions, we must seek an eternal, spiritual, and godly return when deciding upon the use of testamentary trusts.

Paul's View of Testamentary Trusts

In his letter to the Galatians, the apostle Paul likens the use of a testamentary trust to how the Old Testament law was intended as a placeholder, a bridge, until the new covenant was revealed in Christ. In Galatians 4:1–7, Paul writes,

"I mean that the heir, as long as he is a child, is no different from a slave, though he is the owner of everything, but he is under guardians and managers until the date set by his father. In the same way we also,

---

1 "If it turns out your friend is all dead," Miracle Max explains, "there is only one thing you can do, which is to go through his pockets and look for loose change."

2 A testamentary trust must be distinguished from a living trust. A living trust, also known as a revocable trust, allows for the owner of an asset to create a legal arrangement to minimize court involvement or certification requirement in the event of death.

when we were children, were enslaved to the elementary principles of the world. But when the fullness of time had come, God sent forth his son, born of woman, born under the law, to redeem those who were under the law so that we might receive adoption as sons. And because you are sons, God has sent the Spirit of his Son into our hearts, crying "Abba, Father!" So you are no longer a slave, but a son, and if a son, then an heir through God."

Under the law given by Moses, the Israelites were given direction on many aspects of the human life, from cleaning to eating to Sunday sabbath. Following Christ's life, resurrection, and the indwelling of the Holy Spirit, we are like adult children who no longer need to have an inheritance managed by the trustee. Through the Holy Spirit's power and direction, we can manage our lives outside the law.

According to Paul, a child beneficiary is "no different from a slave" in the sense that the slave cannot legally control inherited assets. A child under a trusteeship or guardianship is not "fully" the beneficiary of the promised inheritance because it is the trustee who manages the assets. A testamentary trust is a placeholder for the management of inherited assets, like the Old Testament law, until a child is of an age to be able to fully manage the inherited assets.

Our goal in making sacrificial lifetime asset transfers for the benefit of our children is to develop godly wisdom in our children. If the Lord directs, we will have lived long enough on earth to bring the tutelage to completion, and our children will have complete legal authority over their financial inheritance. In this case, our plan provides for a distribution to our children without any "legal strings attached." But if we die before our children are ready to succeed to the full management of the assets, we have a biblical directive, using the legal tools available to us under current law, to provide for our children by acting as if we were only "mostly dead."

The Modern Secular Approach to Testamentary Trusts

A testamentary trust is often treated by estate planners as a prophylactic for alleviating any possible inheritance problems for children. But a testamentary trust is not an end in itself, nor is it a panacea for all possible future problems. Before implementing a testamentary trust for our children, we should understand the secular assumptions underlying a testamentary trust.

Testamentary trusts are usually created to allow a trustee to make distributions for certain defined purposes, called an "ascertainable standard." For example, distributions can be made for the "health, education, maintenance and support" of the child. This standard allows for a trustee to make a wide range of distributions. These distributions have been defined by case law and years of trust administration experience to include health care costs and educational costs for the named beneficiaries (*e.g.,* children). Living expenses, such as rent, mortgage payments, and groceries, are covered under the term "maintenance and support." To properly implement this planning strategy, the trustee must understand the standard of living to which the family had grown accustomed and make sure that distributions are made for the benefit of the family consistent with that standard of living.

A trustee distributes assets to the beneficiary even if the beneficiary personally owns assets sufficient to meet their accustomed manner of living.[3] In these situations, the child's personally earned income would allow for the child/beneficiary to "double up" on a living standard—that is, to use trust assets to attain a higher standard of living. Alternatively, a child may view access to the trust assets as the reason to avoid gainful employment. In either case, the standard would place the child-beneficiary in a position of exceeding the consumption standards of the parents simply by reason of the inherited assets. Christians should be wary of the spiritual implications of creating a plan involving a testamentary trust with significant assets. When utilizing a testamentary trust, we should have a specific "end goal" for the dollar amount used to fund the trust or have other specific purposes in mind in creating the trust.

A Biblical Approach to Using Testamentary Trusts

Our goal in creating a biblical estate plan should be to encourage our children to attain to biblical wisdom, not necessarily a higher living standard. A testamentary trust plan should therefore be created to provide for a specific purpose and for a specific duration. While I am sure that other scenarios exist, here are a few scenarios when a testamentary trust structure might be implemented consistent with ESG objectives:

Beneficiaries with Insufficient Life Experience

A testamentary trust could be created for the benefit of children

---

3 The trustee can be required to consider assets already "reasonably available" to the beneficiary in determining the appropriateness of making distributions.

with insufficient life experience to personally manage a financial inheritance. Most commonly, we work with families to draft a plan to provide for a young adult's "health, education, maintenance and support," for a specific time frame. For example, if both parents died before the child reaches age twenty-five, a standard to provide for the child's "health, education, maintenance and support" would provide for that child's needs.

Specifically, this standard would allow for a trustee to meet the following types of expenses:

- "Health" includes medical and dental expenses, physical or mental therapy, and pharmaceutical costs. The trust could pay insurance premiums, deductibles, or direct costs not covered by insurance.

- "Education" refers to the payment of tuition at any primary or secondary school, including private school, as well as undergraduate programs, including trade or technical programs. It is deemed to include room and board costs but not graduate school.

- "Maintenance and Support" refers to distributions to assist the beneficiary in maintaining his or her standard of living.

This structure would be coupled with a plan to "cap" the total amount to children to an amount equal to their living expenses for the duration of the time that you would have supported them, had you then been living. This structure should be considered a stop-gap measure, to be used only until such time as your children attain financial wisdom and security. If your earthly life is long enough to see this process through to fruition, the legal provisions for such a testamentary trust can be removed, and you will be able to follow the admonition of the Apostle Paul in providing for a superior "outright" gift to your child.

Beneficiaries with Physical or Mental Health Challenges

A testamentary trust could be created for adult children with disabilities that preclude that child from earning a self-sufficient income. The use of a testamentary trust for such dependent and disabled children would abide by our biblical directives to provide for those in our household who are dependent upon us. **The specific type of trust would depend on whether the child is ineligible or eligible for public benefits.**

Ineligible for Benefits. If an adult child's disabilities prevent the child from working, a trust established for the "health, education, maintenance and support" of the adult child would be appropriate. Using your past financial history as a guide, you can calculate how much should be allocated to this trust to meet the child's expenses, accounting for the child's lifestyle needs and even the child's own life expectancy.[4]

Eligible for Benefits. A unique type of testamentary trust, called a "supplemental needs trust," would be appropriate for any children receiving government benefits by reason of a long-term disability. This trust would hold assets following your death for the benefit of a child with disabilities who is receiving "means-tested" benefits.[5] This type of trust is intended to supplement, but not replace, means-tested government benefits that are available to the adult child. If you are currently paying ancillary living expenses for a child who is already on such programs, this supplemental-needs trust would serve to cover such additional incidental expenses following your death. If a child's disability will be a lifelong disability, the amount allocated to the supplemental needs trust must take into account the benefits received for the benefit of the child.

Specific Future Purposes or Events

A testamentary trust could be created to pay for the costs associated with definite or planned future events.

If your child is enduring an alcohol or chemical dependency issue, a trust should be structured so that a trustee can make distributions to third parties to pay for recovery-related expenses. Once the child has experienced recovery from these issues, the assets could be distributed to the child as a "full inheritance." The trustee would manage the assets to preclude the assets being used to further aggravate the dependency situation.

If a child or grandchild has not yet completed primary, secondary, or undergraduate education, a specific gift of cash or other assets could be set aside to be invested, with the proceeds eventually being used to pay for such future expenses. Similar strategies have been employed for the

---

4 The amount allocated to the child's trust should be the product of: (1) your average annual contribution to your child's living expenses and (2) the child's remaining life expectancy, adjusted for expected annual growth rates in invested assets.
5 Unfortunately, I have seen too many well-intentioned parents create this type of supplemental needs trust when it is not applicable to their situation. A supplemental needs trust is appropriate only for those individuals who are certain to be on means-tested programs in the future.

following purposes:

- assisting the child or grandchild to attend graduate school, technical school, or seminary, but in no event any law school education;
- assisting a child or grandchild with a specific portion of the costs associated with a first wedding (*e.g.,* $20,000 for wedding costs);
- assisting with a specific amount of costs associated with the purchase of a home;
- assisting a grandchild, or a group of grandchildren, to receive specific types of school assistance, whether in the form of private school tuition, undergraduate tuition, or similar types of expenses.

As in other aspects of a well-designed estate plan, a testamentary trust would be appropriate for a specific time and season. While you might initially include testamentary trust provisions for your children, these structures can be removed once they have developed the requisite wisdom to accompany the wealth they will receive. If the Apostle Paul were reviewing your plan, he would characterize the inheritance as only fully realized once these testamentary trust provisions are removed. Or, in the words of Miracle Max, once the testamentary trusts are removed, you could then act as "all dead" instead of only "mostly dead."

ILLUSTRATIONS FOR APPLICATION

The following three case studies illustrate the implementation of biblically sounds testamentary trust strategies.

Children and Ministry Directions

Jake and Sara have three teenagers and a healthy investment portfolio. Jake and Sara have mentored their children about the important of ongoing financial ministry support. In creating an estate plan, we decided that their trust planning should incorporate a plan for the children to "tithe" out of their respective trusts.

Under their plan, if both Jake and Sara die, for any child who has not reached age thirty, a separate testamentary trust is established for said child to receive the benefit of ongoing discretionary distributions for the child's "health, education, maintenance and support." The trustee would also be obligated to work with each child to make charitable gifts to ministries mutually agreed upon by the child and the trustee of no less than ten percent (10%) of the total annual distributions made. For any child with such a trust once Jake and Sara are both in heaven, upon the child's thirtieth birthday, ten percent (10%) of the remaining assets are allocated to ministries chosen by the child, and the remaining ninety percent of the assets are allocated to the child as his or her full inheritance.

Cabin Trust

Rita and Ivan are retired clients with two adult children. They have owned a Minnesota lake cabin for many years, and they intend to own the cabin, cut the grass, bring the dock in, and deal with the mosquitos for the rest of their lives. Rita and Ivan's two children, together with their respective spouses, have also demonstrated by their time that they also intend to use the cabin as long as they are able. The children have agreed that, by reason of the sentimental value to both of them, they would rather co-own the cabin than split the proceeds from the sale of the cabin.

Rita and Ivan's legal documents direct that once both Rita and Ivan die, the cabin property and an additional $80,000 in cash is allocated to a trust. The cash will then be used to pay for utilities, property taxes, and maintenance costs of the cabin. The trust agreement provides that either or both of the children can direct the sale of the cabin and the distribution of remaining proceeds to the children. If you have unique assets that your children wish to co-own, you may consider the implementation of a special use trust of the type utilized by Ivan and Rita.

Indirectly Assisting Children Through Educational Costs

Craig and Diane are parents to one daughter, Audrey. Audrey has endured many setbacks in life, most of which have been self-inflicted. Audrey's two elementary-age children attend a local Christian private school. Craig and Diane are heavily involved in the lives of their grandchildren. They feel blessed to pay the tuition costs because Audrey could not otherwise afford to send her children to the school, which is particularly important because of how Audrey is espousing philosophical views contrary to her parents' biblical faith.

In order to demonstrate their unconditional love for their daughter, Craig and Diane are directing a portion of their assets "outright" to Audrey. Craig and Diane are making this bequest even while recognizing the strong possibility that the inherited assets will be used for less-than-laudable objectives. With the remaining portion of their assets, however, Craig and Diane have named a trusted friend as trustee of a testamentary trust for their grandchildren. The trust assets will be used for the ongoing educational costs of Audrey's two children. This strategy not only improves the ESG outcome of their grandchildren but would have the indirect benefit of benefitting Audrey's personal financial situation. Under this plan, Craig and Diane can honor their daughter through an unconditional gift, while also maximizing the eternal, spiritual, and godly outcomes for their grandchildren.

REFLECTIONS
On Trusts for Your Children

Reflect on whether you should implement any legal structures for how a family member receives an inheritance from you.

Are your children or other individual beneficiaries better suited to receive an "outright" gift of assets at your death, or is a "testamentary trust" more appropriate?

If you have not yet previously established a testamentary trust for children or grandchildren, for what purposes should the trust assets be used, and how long should the trust last?

If you previously established a testamentary support trust for your children, is it time to either (a) remove those provisions altogether, or (b) limit the total amount of assets allocated to the testamentary trust?

Are there specific needs that you would like to meet in the lives of your children or grandchildren?

If you have a child who is not currently following Jesus, how can you direct assets at your death to honor your child while also providing for laudable eternal, spiritual, or godly purposes?

LESSON EIGHT
Charity

Create a charitable giving plan that fulfills lifetime commitments, spreads joy in giving among others, and seeks optimal means to maximize eternal outcomes.

In charitable planning, as in other elements of estate planning, we apply an "already but not yet" approach. We are already a member of the kingdom of God, even while the Lord has yet to return to earth. Similarly, children can be honored in an estate plan, even though they have not yet received their inheritance. In this section, I apply the same biblical principles previously outlined, but in the context of our charitable giving. The focus is not on the types of ministries one might support, but on biblical purposes for giving, and how to create an efficient testamentary charitable legal plan consistent with those purposes.

These charitable giving principles are as follows:

- As a good trustee of God's assets, one must create a testamentary plan to honor the commitments made to supported churches and missionaries.

- If identity is centered in Jesus alone, and if assets are viewed as being owned by God instead of the holder, the opportunity afforded by charitable giving should be used to create a multiplicative effect of giving among our family and churches.

- In order to implement an eternal, spiritual, and godly ("ESG") charitable plan, life narratives consistent with God's eternal purposes should be elevated above any personal tax implications.

In this lesson, I outline these principles in the following three chapters:

- *Share:* What charitable giving commitments should be fulfilled by distributions of your assets following your death?

- *Joy:* Spread a contagious joy through your charitable giving.

- *Impact:* What strategies can you employ to create the biggest eternal impact on others through your charitable giving?

8A: *Share*

***Document your current charitable giving commitments as well as
your desires for post-death charitable gifts.***

What if the Good Samaritan were sued by the innkeeper? Imagine with
me a fictional alternative end to the Parable of Good Samaritan that
Jesus shares in Matthew 10.[1] Jesus shares that, while on a journey, the
Samaritan comes upon a man who has been beaten and robbed. Seeing
that the man needs care, the Samaritan takes pity on the injured man
and brings him to a nearby innkeeper whom he asks to care for the
victim while the Samaritan continues on his journey. Not only does
the Samaritan put down a deposit of two denarii but he also promises
to pay the innkeeper additional sums upon his return to the inn.[2]
The Samaritan tells the innkeeper, "Take care of him, and whatever
more you spend, I will repay you when I come back."[3] Such a verbal
promise could have legal implications under today's legal system. The
innkeeper presumably acted in reliance on the promise made by the
Good Samaritan and, at cost to himself, cared for the injured man.

In my extra-biblical hypothetical, what would be the legal ramifications
to the Good Samaritan if he had never returned to the inn? Perhaps the
Good Samaritan never returned because he was the victim of the same
robbers who had assaulted the man whom the Samaritan sought to
assist. In such a hypothetical scenario, who would then be responsible
for the expenses incurred by the innkeeper? If you know many lawyers
as I do, I'm positive you can think of a few attorneys that would have
been happy to sue the estate of the Good Samaritan, even though the
Samaritan himself had been assaulted and perhaps even murdered as he
went on his way.[4]

---

1 Matthew 10:30–37.
2 Matthew 10:35.
3 Id.
4 Attorneys spend three years in law school, and plenty of time afterward, thinking about such
odd hypotheticals. No theologian or pastor was involved in the creation of this extra-Biblical
hypothetical.

In my variation on the Parable of the Good Samaritan, we see an application of the legal doctrine of promissory estoppel. By law, under this doctrine, the individuals or charities that you promised to support could sue your estate after your death if (i) you had previously pledged to support the recipient, (ii) the recipient took proactive steps in reasonable reliance on your promise, and the promise was not kept. The U.S. Supreme Court has upheld this legal doctrine, creating legal obligations even though explicit contracts were never put in place.[5]

In reality, charities decline to sue families because (i) the ministry was not acting in reliance on the promise (*e.g.,* a $25 monthly gift is not enough to build the new sanctuary); and/or (ii) the amount of the gift is not worth hiring the high-priced litigation firm to sue the donor's family, especially considering the relationship fallout that would ensue from the litigation.

In your case, you may have pledged to a giving campaign but subsequently lost track of your commitment. You might have promised to support a ministry individual on a recurring basis but now cannot recall the amount or term of your commitment. As trustees of God's assets, we have an obligation to follow through with our commitments to minimize the disruption on those supported individuals and charities in the event of death. We should document ministry commitments so that we can be sure to communicate changes in the future, and to provide our fiduciaries with the information necessary to abide by those commitments if we die before they are fulfilled. We must, as believers, let our "yes be yes," and "no be no" in the sense that no legal agreements should be necessary between us and supported individuals or ministries.[6]

Record Current Charitable Giving Commitments

As trustees of God's assets, being accountable to God means that we document our commitments and create a means by which our chosen fiduciary can support those commitments. The template that closes this chapter allows you to document your current giving, any commitments you have made regarding that giving, the frequency of your giving, and contact information for the recipient organization so that your supported ministries will be made aware of your death. For those gifts tied to a specific pledge or commitment, provide details as to the amount, duration, and status of the pledge. You and your spouse

---

5   *Cohen v. Cowles Media Co.*, 501 U.S. 663 (1991).
6   Matthew 5:37.

should consider asking one other person, usually your named trustee or personal representative, to gather your records on charitable giving following your death. You should inform this individual of how to access these records following your death.

A Post-Death Charitable Distribution Plan for Your Assets

If you created a legally binding support pledge during your lifetime with one or more charitable organizations, your personal representative is legally obligated to fulfill the pledge following your death. The pledge is like a debt or other legal obligation that must be paid regardless of whether you listed the charity as a beneficiary under your estate plan or not. In most cases, however, your charity has not taken steps in reliance on your commitment; therefore, the commitment is not legally enforceable. Your appointed personal representative (if you have an estate) or trustee (if you have a trust) is therefore not legally obligated to pay the pledge following death. Instead, your fiduciary has a legal obligation to provide only for your named beneficiaries, even if everyone in the family agrees that it would have been your intent to continue to make charitable gifts at death. Your fiduciary has a legal obligation to fulfill charitable pledges *only if you have specifically directed* for the charities or supported individuals to receive certain amounts or percentages of remaining assets following death. To make your charitable objectives legally binding, use one of more of the following three testamentary (that is, post-death) charitable planning strategies.

(1) By Beneficiary Designation, by Will, or by Trust

First, you could provide specifically for the ministry through a legally binding designation within the legal documents comprising your estate plan. You might include a section in your will or revocable trust to provide that, if certain charitable giving commitments are not fulfilled at death, remaining assets must be used to fulfill those commitments. As noted previously, assets can pass at your death through different legal ways. It is important, therefore, that you have a general grasp of how each of your assets will pass at death, and seek legal help to confirm your legal plan. Your designation of charity to receive a fulfilling gift might take the form of (i) a beneficiary designation on a retirement account or life insurance policy, (ii) a provision for church or charity in your will, or (iii) a provision for church or charity in your revocable trust.

(2) To a Set-Aside Charitable Trust

Second, you could direct that an amount of cash assets sufficient to meet your charitable objectives are "set aside" in a trust-owned bank account at your death. This bank account, comprising what you could think of as your "charitable share," would be kept separate from your other assets that are directed to your family, or your "family share." Your family share would be allocated to your spouse and children or other family members. Your trust agreement or will would then name a fiduciary to be responsible for the set-aside charitable share. If this structure is incorporated within a trust agreement, the trustee would have the legal obligation to fulfill your charitable gifts.[7] By segregating the charitable assets from the rest of your assets, the other assets can be freed up for release to your family.

In many states, you can provide a simple written list of desired charities to your named trustee, who would then be legally obligated to follow through with fulfilling these charitable directions. This "set-aside" approach is the best option if you desire for specific individuals rather than charitable organizations, to receive some support after your death. Since a donor-advised fund, as described below, can support only tax-exempt organizations, a set-aside fund is your best option for supporting individuals in need.[8]

(3) To a Donor-Advised Fund

Third and finally, you could create a donor-advised fund (aka DAF) during your lifetime to manage your lifetime and testamentary giving. A DAF is an agreement established between you, as the donor, and any sponsoring organization that sponsors such funds. The sponsor is usually a large financial institution (*e.g.,* Schwab, Fidelity, etc.) or a public community foundation or university.[9] The sponsor must track all your contributions made to your DAF account, your directed distribution to desired ministries, and the sponsor's administrative expenses taken from your "account" or "fund." You might find it helpful to think of a donor-advised fund as a "charitable checking account" because once the assets are contributed to the DAF, the contributed assets can be used only for subsequent contribution to tax-

---

7 The variation on this theme is to simply designate a friend or family member as the beneficiary of assets and rely on his or her trustworthiness to follow your charitable inclinations. This type of arrangement has no legal support behind it and, more importantly from a relationship perspective, might result in mistrust arising among your children.

8 If not all the beneficiaries of this trust are tax-exempt charities, the trust itself would be subject to income taxes if the trust incurs income or capital gains after your death.

9 The National Christian Foundation is my preferred provider, which is where Heather and I have established the "Wessman Family Fund," our family's donor-advised fund.

exempt charitable organizations.

A DAF allows you to create a level of transparency about your current and planned charitable giving among a group of individuals you select. You and your spouse could name your adult children during your lifetime as your "fund advisors." As fund advisors, your children are incorporated into your lifetime charitable giving and will then be in an ideal position to follow through after your death with implementing your desired charitable objectives. Your successor fund advisors would be legally entitled to direct your charitable checking account assets directly to your chosen charities, or perhaps even make discretionary decisions regarding distributions to tax-exempt charitable organizations at death.

ILLUSTRATIONS FOR APPLICATION

Charitable Gifts in Disability and at Death

Christopher is a regular and generous contributor to parachurch ministries and local Christian schools and colleges. He has adequately documented the previous giving commitments he has made, and the amounts are outstanding under those commitments. Perhaps most importantly, Christopher has informed his son of these arrangements.

Following Christopher's recent 85th birthday, Christopher made two changes to his giving plan. First, he appointed his son as his power of attorney, with authority to continue to make charitable gifts if Christopher endures a period of mental incapacity. Second, he changed the recurrence of most of his gifts from annual to monthly. Christopher's thoughtful planning will certainly allow him to fulfill the commitments he made to charities. In your case, consider how you can disclose the nature of your gifts to your family, and if there are any arrangements you can make to make the fulfillment of those commitments easier on your family following your death.

Retirement Accounts to Charity

Ronald and Jane have deep ties to their alma mater Christian college. In addition to graduating from the school themselves and paying tuition for their own children to attend the school, Jane recently retired as a tenured professor at the school. Ronald and Jane wish to provide for their three children with 75% of their assets and direct the remaining 25% to their alma mater Christian college.

Not all assets are treated the same for income tax purposes. Children pay income taxes on tax-deferred retirement accounts, while tax-exempt charities do not. Therefore, if you desire to distribute a gift at your death to charity, and you own an IRA account, it is best to allocate tax-deferred IRA assets to charity to satisfy the charitable portion of one's planning objectives.

In Ronald and Jane's situation, approximately 25% of their total financial net worth is comprised of their combined IRA accounts. Their estate plan directs that following the death of the surviving spouse, 100% of their IRA assets (comprising 25% of the total assets) is allocated to the college, and 100% of all other remaining assets (comprising 75% of the total assets) to their children. Through this planning strategy, none of the beneficiaries pay any income taxes. In your case, you might apply a similar strategy with annuities or other tax-deferred assets to achieve a tax-efficient charitable planning strategy.

Donor-Advised Fund Giving

Scott has a host of mission organizations and churches that have received his generous contributions for many years. He has recently established a donor-advised fund ("DAF") for the purpose of receiving the investments that he would like to donate to charity. By reason of the frequent changes in his testamentary charitable giving, his estate plan provision could not keep up with these changes. Once Scott established a DAF, we were able to simplify Scott's estate planning structure. Rather than naming charities as beneficiaries under Scott's trust agreement and through his beneficiary designations, his estate plan was revised to name his DAF as the beneficiary of that portion of his remaining assets earmarked for charitable purposes. Through an agreement with the DAF administrator, Scott was able to direct that his brother would be responsible for overseeing the distributions from the DAF to his desired charities. You might likewise consider utilizing a DAF to fulfill your charitable giving commitments.

REFLECTIONS
On Documenting Your Charitable Commitments

Reflect on the charitable commitments you have made. If you died now, would your family have the clarity it needs to fulfill your charitable planning desires?

Specifically:

Are there individuals [e.g., family members] who are dependent on your needs now, such that, if you died suddenly, would lose support that they need to receive?

Are there missionaries who you would like to support following your death that would benefit from your having a plan in place for them?

You should disclose your current charitable giving commitments and your plans for the distribution of remaining assets at death. You can use the following spreadsheet to give your family direction on how your charitable planning commitments should be fulfilled following death.

CHARITABLE GIVING INVENTORY

CURRENT CHARITABLE GIVING					
NAME OF MINISTRY	FREQUENCY	AMOUNT	END DATE/ GOAL	CONTACT INFO	ADDITIONAL INSTRUCTIONS

TESTAMENTARY CHARITABLE GIVING					
NAME OF MINISTRY	AMOUNT	PURPOSE	MEANS OF FUNDING GIFT	CONTACT INFO	ADDITIONAL INSTRUCTIONS

8B: *Joy*

Spread a contagious joy through your charitable giving.

What if our charitable giving were contagious? According to
Malcom Gladwell in his bestselling book, *Tipping Point,* one of
the characteristics of whether a trend will gain traction and "tip" an
emerging trend into a widespread and exponential phenomenon is
whether it is "sticky" in the sense of being counterintuitive.[1] People
are more likely to remember, and then implement, the trend if the
principle is sufficiently contrarian. Gladwell points out that when it
comes to dining habits, music and fashion selections, our behavior can
create a contagious "stickiness" if it is sufficiency counter-cultural and
attractive.

In modern America, nothing is more contrarian than spending money
on anything other than oneself. Even in the church, charitable giving
is a paltry percentage of income.[2] Rather than looking at our personal
charitable planning as an obligation (what we "have" to do), or what
is necessary to support our favorite organizations (what the church
"needs"), what if we viewed our charitable planning as a means to
spread a contagious joy to others (what we "get" to do). We would
be sufficiently contrarian in our charity if we could be joyful in our
selfless giving.

In this chapter, I contrast secular and biblical purposes for giving. It is
my hope that we would examine the motives for our lifetime giving,
not only so that we can potentially realign our charitable giving, but
especially post-death ("testamentary") giving with biblical purposes.
From time to time, it may be necessary to revise our legal plan to align
our testamentary giving with biblical purposes.

The Apostle Paul's admonition in 2 Corinthians is what we have

---

1 Malcom Gladwell, *The Tipping Point, How Little Things Can Make a Huge Difference.* Brown
Books, 2000.
2 Christians gave 594 billion dollars in 2013, but that was only 1.5% of total income earned in
2013 of 33 trillion dollars. International Bulletin of Missionary Research.

in mind in our own charitable giving plan. "We want you to know, brothers, about the grace of God that has been given among the churches of Macedonia, for in a severe test of affliction, their abundance of joy and their extreme poverty have overflowed in a wealth of generosity on their part. For they gave according to their means, as I can testify, and beyond their means, of their own accord, begging us earnestly for the favor of taking part in the relief of the saints."[3]

Our charitable giving ought to be characterized by joy in participating in God's work. If we are giving as the world gives—for personal advancement of one's name, reputation, or career—we won't create a tipping point of a contagious joy of giving to family and the global church. A tipping point occurs when our personal charitable giving plan spreads the joy of giving to others. It might be started during our lifetime when we are sufficiently contrarian in providing for the favorite ministries of others, not our own, simply in order to increase their joy. Our testamentary charitable gifts could even encourage our children to participate in joyful contribution to ministry callings consistent with their life narratives.

SECULAR PURPOSES OF GIVING

While our secular culture applauds certain charitable giving purposes, such purposes are not necessarily aligned with biblical objectives. Let us review some common charitable planning purposes and compare them to biblical purposes.

To Increase Reputational Capital

"Hey, Heather, I am just calling to confirm you received my donation check....can you confirm you received it?" My wife is a planned giving coordinator at a Christian school and will receive calls or emails like this. Donor relationship managers at non-profit organizations know that they will receive these calls or emails if they are not on top of "thank you" notes and calls. If the organization does not quickly respond to donor gifts with gushes of appreciation, some donors will come knocking on their door looking for those accolades. Do these same donors call their utilities companies, asking them to confirm receipt of the check for their water bill? The human heart seeks to justify itself, and so the donor relations staff learns to anticipate the desire of the donor to receive the accolades of at least one human mouth. To one

---

3 2 Corinthians 8:1–4.

degree or another, all of us are guilty of desiring to receive the "atta boys" and "atta girls."

From a secular perspective, a donor requires an immediate return on her investment, albeit a return to one's "reputational capital." In modern-day professional development circles, no contingency is left unaddressed when it comes to considering opportunities to further a donor's reputational capital. Naming rights for the new library, the new wing of the hospital, or the new football stadium are all up for negotiation when it comes to a sizable gift. Development officers know the importance that large donors place on receiving a return on their "reputational capital." In contrast, Christians should be aware of the ever-present danger of self-promotion and the desire to be well-liked by reason of your good deeds.

Today, as it was in its original context, Jesus' admonition against giving for the purpose of seeking the affirmation of others in making gifts is completely countercultural. "So when you give to the needy, do not announce it with trumpets, as the hypocrites do in the synagogues and on the streets, to be honored by others. Truly, I tell you, they have received their reward in full."[4] When we give for the purpose of receiving the accolades of others, Jesus said that the receipt of the community's admiration is reward enough itself. If we give for the sake of "being seen as good," we will not receive any further benefit. My observation from my client interaction is that if this is our purpose in making gifts, we will be less likely to make repeating gifts, since even a nice bouquet of flowers, a thank you note or a hall named in your honor will ultimately create a sense of resentment in our hearts about the lack of admiration received.

A biblical charitable plan is premised upon giving out of gratitude for the great gift given to us in Christ. Rather than trying to take steps to implicitly remind people of our good past deeds, we should make gifts to encourage others to thank Jesus for His gifts of eternal significance to us.

To Create a Patronage Relationship

"We gave the school a $5,000 gift last year; why isn't our son Tommy in the top mathematics class?"

A second secular reason for charitable giving is to create a legal

---

4 Mathew 6:2.

or moral obligation to the donor from the recipient organization. From a secular perspective, there is no "higher authority" over the ownership of an asset. We have absolute rights over our assets. A gift could therefore be a means to "trade favors," whether receiving a benefit presently, or perhaps an implicit understanding that the donor or donor's family would receive benefits in the future. It was commonplace practice in the Roman culture of the Apostle Paul's day for wealthy donors to "sponsor" individuals of less financial wealth in a "patronage" relationship. You create a patronage relationship when you explicitly or implicitly state to the recipient, "I'll scratch your back today, and you scratch mine tomorrow."

God provided us with the assets, and as we "forward" these assets along to our desired charitable beneficiaries, we have no greater claim on those assets than the recipient beneficiaries do. The recipient of "our" gift is not obligated or indebted to us in any way because the assets given were never "ours" from the outset. If we think that God owes us something for "giving" to Him, we have another think coming. If the assets are already His to begin with, how dare we think that we can place God in a position of fealty to us by making charitable gifts?

The modern-day patronage system is seen in how high-profile or high-giving donors receive seats on the board or positions of influence, including the effective opportunity to dictate how the charitable organization should set its budget. With Solomonic wisdom, church leadership must carefully monitor its own motives in interacting with wealthy and wise leaders who are also donors. Are the elders listening to a donor because that person is a great leader with winsome strategies and ideas, or because that person has given lots of money? We must be careful to admit a leader to a position of leadership because of skills, not because of financial contributions. Otherwise, the church board is simply selling the board memberships.

To Prioritize Scarce Resources

"We must save the earth, because no one else will." Warren Buffett has publicly committed $1.5 billion in gifts annually to the Bill and Melinda Gates Foundation, and to "cap" the amounts of his fortune that will be allocated to his children upon his death.[5] Among other commitments, the Gates Foundation is committed to funding efforts

---

5 I previously discussed the Buffett 2006 charitable commitment in Chapter 1.

to manage population growth through birth control.[6] According to this view, we must assist mothers avoid pregnancies or end existing pregnancies to keep the population under control, thereby preserving a fixed amount of resources for the existing human population. It is therefore ironic that Warren Buffett's charitable giving will attempt to cut down the population of the human race, not encourage its flourishing. Rather than spread seeds of human flourishing to the ends of the earth, the gift will attempt to reduce the number of individuals consuming a fixed amount of goods so that those of us who are left can consume more.

In some states, laws require public charities to disclose the identity of significant donors.[7] If we have disclosure of our neighbor's giving, we can heap the appropriate level of blame or adulation on them, depending upon what we think of the outcome of the charitable objectives. If we have only a fixed level of resources, we must cast judgment on those who are wasting assets by mis-prioritizing the allocation of scarce resources. In an age of moral relativism, it is striking that certain charitable planning objectives are applauded as more laudable than others.

In contrast to giving under a "fixed sum" mindset, God promises a multiplicative effect of our giving. To the Corinthian church, Paul writes,

"As it is written,

> He has distributed freely, he has given to the poor;
>
> His righteousness endures forever.

He who supplies seed to the sower and bread for food will supply and multiply your seed for sowing and increase the harvest of your righteousness. You will be enriched in every way to be generous in every way, which through us will produce thanksgiving to God."[8]

God accomplishes His purposes regardless of our involvement; God is not dependent on Warren Buffett or Bill Gates, and certainly not us,

---

6 https://www.gatesfoundation.org/ideas/media-center/press-releases/1999/08/population-resource-center.

7 Certain states are enacting legislation to protect the identity of donors. https://www.thenonprofittimes.com/donors/at-least-10-states-going-after-donor-disclosure/. In 2021, the United States Supreme Court invalidated a California law that required public charities to submit lists of donors who gave more than $5,000 annually. *United States Supreme Court, Americans for Prosperity Foundation v. Bonta.*

8 2 Corinthians 9:9–12.

to accomplish His purposes. We give because He promises spiritual blessings of participation. If we don't give, God will use others— and it is we, the potential givers, who lose out on the blessing of participation. But if we give, we can connect the joy of giving with the narrative of how God has used our past sufferings, our success narratives, and even our stewardship setbacks to glorify God.

BIBLICAL PURPOSES OF GIVING

In contrast to secular purposes for charitable giving, the Bible outlines eternally significant purposes for charitable giving. These are as follows:

To Increase Our Joy in Participating in God's Work

We give out of the joy of being able to sacrificially participate in God's work in earthly ministries. When we become followers of Christ, our identity in Christ and the kingdom of heaven is the treasure of infinite worth, a treasure that results in day-to-day joy-filled exuberance, impacting every element of our financial lives. Jesus teaches us that, "The kingdom of heaven is like treasure hidden in a field, which a man found and covered up. Then in his joy he goes and sells all that he has and buys that field. Again, the kingdom of heaven is like a merchant in search of fine pearls, who, on finding one pearl of great value, went and sold all that he had and bought it."[9] According to Jesus, the distinguishing characteristic of our activities is that our joy in God supersedes all earthly pleasures.

In addition to every other aspect of our life, our financial decisions must be impacted by this joy in God. As Paul writes to the church in his second letter to the Corinthians, God increases our joy by the opportunity to participate in the work of God. Paul writes, "The point is this: whoever sows sparingly will also reap sparingly and whoever sows bountifully will also reap bountifully. Each one must give as he has decided in his heart, not reluctantly or under compulsion, for God loves a cheerful giver. And God is able to make grace abound to you, so that having all sufficiency in all things at all times, you may abound in every good work."[10] The more intimately we are involved in the ministry of others, the greater spiritual encouragement we receive from that participation. Rather than giving under compulsion, or being told which charities to give to, and how much we should give, we should

9 Matthew 13:44–46.
10 2 Corinthians 9:6–10.

give out of joy, knowing that God will only multiply our efforts. God promises not to multiply the number of digits at the bottom line of our financial statements, but the efficacy of the gifts given to charity, and to increase our own joy in the giving.

To Increase the Joy of the Receiver

In the book of Acts, we are told about how the earliest Christians considered the physical needs of their fellow believers as more important than their own legal rights to consume "their" assets.

"And all who believed were together and had all things in common. And they were selling their possessions and belongings and distributing the proceeds to all, as any had need. And day by day, attending the temple and breaking bread in their homes, they received their food with glad and generous hearts, praising God and having favor with all the people. And the Lord added to their number day by day those who were being saved."[11]

In the early church, we see that the believers were generous with one another and served one another's needs. They provided not just for the physical needs of the members of their own church but the physical needs of the far-away churches, even churches of differing ethnic backgrounds. Only the Lord knows how many believers in church history have been encouraged by anonymous gifts from Christian brothers or sisters.

After the death of our son in 2009, Heather and I founded Hope for the Mourning, a ministry that seeks to support recently bereaved parts. As a member of the board of this small ministry, I am blessed to have the opportunity to observe the generosity of friends who give to the ministry. Through their gifts, the givers have opened themselves up to the needs of the ministry, encouraging and supporting us in ways beyond just financial contributions. Their gifts have also served as a tremendous source of encouragement to those of us committed to be involved in the ministry.

To Support Individuals in Need

We are called to provide for those whom we see in our midst who lack necessities. Believers are called to not only pray for those in need, but also support those in our midst who lack the means to provide for their own necessities. Jesus taught that in providing food, clothing, and

11 Acts 2:44–47.

shelter to those in need, we act like we are providing for Jesus Himself, thereby demonstrating our love for Jesus and our true fidelity to Him.[12]

"If a brother or sister is poorly clothed and lacking in daily food, and one of you says to them, 'Go in peace, be warmed and filled,' without giving them the things needed for the body, what good is that? So also faith by itself, if it does not have works, is dead."[13]

Giving like the Good Samaritan could take the form of spontaneous, spur-of-the-moment giving or else structured giving for those in ongoing need of support.

"Spur-of-the-Moment" Giving

Giving spontaneous, spur-of-the-moment gifts to individuals with clear and demonstrable current financial needs is a good spiritual litmus test for a CPA or tax-minded planner like me. It seems these types of gifts are less difficult for those who, like my wife, are less immersed in the world of tax planning. Jesus admonishes us, "But when you give to the needy, do not let your right hand know what your left hand is doing."[14] I am often guilty of the very admonition that Jesus calls us away from. I have charitable giving goals in my mind, and when my wife or kids give cash to the man standing out at the highway median in the turn lane in the cold Minnesota winter, I realize there is no way to credit our contributions.

Spontaneous gifts allow for the right hand to give without the left hand; the gifts are not credited as part of the charitable budget. Such gifts are not tax deductible; they simply come out of our family's general fund. The $20 that is given is a demonstration of our joy in God. I have not yet discovered any now-deceased clients who are able to continue to give to the needy directly following death. However, many now-deceased saints had such an impact on others in their spur-of-the-moment giving that the estate plan must, in an eternal sense, be considered to include one's lifetime heart for the poor and needy.

Ongoing Dependent Friend or Dependent Family Member

When Paul instructs Timothy in the book of 1 Timothy about how Christians should provide for their family members, he notes that widows "who are truly widows" should be receiving the financial

---

12 Matthew 25:35–40.
13 James 2:16.
14 Matthew 6:3.

support of the church.[15] "But if a widow has children or grandchildren, [the children or grandchildren] must first learn to show godliness to their own household and to make some return to their parents, for this is pleasing in the sight of God."[16] By implication, if we have the financial means to do so, we are called on to support our parents or other family members who can't earn a living wage.

Once you are dead, you don't have that same obligation to provide for the panhandler, or the dependent friend or family member. You may, however, have created a legal or moral precedent for support for your dependent family member. If you have been a Good Samaritan, it is incumbent upon you to consider how you might finish the task you have started to support those who depend on the assets and income under your trusteeship. For my clients who represent family members at multiple generational levels, a "standard" legal plan will not be sufficient.

To Increase the Joy of Our Community

You might have friends who love to share with you the delight of newly discovered pleasures. Whether favorite recipes, podcasts, books, or new restaurants, some friends love to spread joy in newfound pleasures. Certain friends of ours love to share with us the joy of discovering a new ministry. We have been honored to join in the joy of contributing to these ministries, knowing the joy that the financial involvement has meant to our friends.

Our friends are sharing the genuine joy of participating in the work of the ministry, not "displaying their righteous deeds before men simply to be seen by men."[17] In his second letter to the Corinthians, Paul notes that he previously boasted to the church in Macedonia about the Corinthian church's generosity. In response, Paul tells the readers that the Corinthian church "stirred up" the Macedonian church.[18] Later on, referring to this same giving from the Corinthian church, Paul writes, "For the ministry of this service is not only supplying the needs of the saints but is also overflowing in many thanksgivings to God. By their approval of this service, they will glorify God because of your submission flowing from your confession of the gospel of Christ, and the generosity of your contribution for them and for all others, while

15 1 Timothy 5.
16 1 Timothy 5:4.
17 Matthew 6:1.
18 2 Corinthians 9:2.

they long for you and pray for you, because of the surpassing grace of God upon you. Thanks be to God for this inexpressible gift!"[19]

Giving conspicuously creates a danger of virtue signaling—that is, "practicing your righteousness before men." While only God knows the true heart intent of someone's charitable giving, it is possible to surmise the heart intent based on the nature and extent of the donor's desired disclosure. In the case of our friends, we have picked up their joy as our own and spread that contagious joy to others. Like a contagious disease, the conspicuous giving of our friends increases our joy in God.

Dead Men's Gifts

When it comes to charitable giving, you may have heard the admonition that, "Dead men don't write checks."[20] Randy Alcorn and others have rightfully emphasized the significant difference between lifetime and testamentary charitable gifts. Because of our sacrifice made during lifetime, only lifetime gifts will result in heavenly reward.[21] While I agree with Alcorn's approach to lifetime giving, we should nonetheless plan for the likelihood that we simply won't bounce our last check. A dead man can proverbially write checks through an estate plan. We must therefore create the appropriate legal structures to spread a contagious joy in giving. If structured properly, our estate planning structure should encourage others in their joy in participating in the Lord's work.

ILLUSTRATIONS FOR APPLICATION

You might already have individuals in your life who exemplify a joy in their giving. I offer three examples of clients who exemplify a contagious joy in giving.

The Four Sons and Their Donor-Advised Funds

Thor and Janet are friends and clients who are actively involved in several local nonprofits. As a planned giving officer, Thor speaks publicly to groups about charitable planning within an estate plan. In

---

19 2 Corinthians 9:12–15.
20 As cited in *Kingdom Giving; A New Perspective on Wealth.* Jerry Wear, The Great Commission Foundation, Campus Crusade for Christ, 2010. P. 75.
21 See Alcorn, Randy, *Money, Possessions and Eternity.* Tyndale House Publishers, Wheaton, IL, 2003, p. 120.

that context, Thor shares how he and Janet will provide for ministries following the second death between he and Janet. Thor jokes that while he and Janet have only three sons, for purposes of their estate plan, they have a fourth son, which is their "charitable share." Following the second death between them, they direct one-quarter of all assets to each of their natural sons, with their fourth son, charities, receiving the last one-quarter of remaining assets.

In Thor and Janet's family, all three of their adult sons are closely aligned on matters of faith and giving. As a result of this alignment, Jane and Thor feel comfortable directing that this charitable quarter share will be further split equally four ways, with each of the three son's separate donor-advised fund receiving one-fourth of the charitable share. If you follow the math, since there are three sons, and since each son's own donor-advised fund will receive one-fourth, each son's donor-advised fund would receive 1/16th of the entire remaining assets. The remaining 1/16 would then be allocated to Thor and Janet's own personal donor-advised fund. Through such a giving plan, Thor and Janet not only provide a plan for charitable objectives but spread the joy in giving by providing each of their sons the opportunity to contribute to their favorite ministry endeavors.

Multi-Generational Donor-Advised Fund

Eddie is a widower with two adult daughters. Eddie owns a townhouse and a significant investment portfolio. Similar to Thor and Janet's family, Eddie and his daughters are closely-aligned on ministry endeavors. In fact, Eddie and his daughters make frequent charitable contributions jointly through a family donor-advised fund. Eddie's legal plan provides that, at his death, his two daughters will receive all remaining assets at his death. Separately, Eddie has had numerous discussions with his two daughters about their shared desires to continue to support certain ministries. His two daughters have verbally committed to Eddie that they plan to contribute ten percent of all inherited assets to the donor-advised fund.

In Eddie's case, his daughters will *legally* receive the entire inheritance. In this case, based on the nature of Eddie's assets, his daughters will receive the entire inheritance free of any income taxes. In keeping with their verbal commitment to Eddie, the daughters will then be entitled to an income tax deduction for the value of their personal contribution (*e.g.,* 10% of the inherited assets) to the donor-advised fund. By reason of the alignment of values and the tax characteristics, the family is making wise use of the tax code for the benefit of the supported ministries.

Vision Cruises

Rick loves teaching pickleball to his friends, grandkids, and whoever else will listen, including his attorney. Even more than teaching pickleball, Rick loves sharing his contagious enthusiasm for building homes through Habitat for Humanity. Rick is so enthusiastic about Habitat that he regularly leads short-term mission trips for any family and friends who are willing to attend. Rick not only leads the trips but pays for them as well. While Rick calls these trips "Vision Cruises," he assures us that no cruise ships are involved. Rick and I worked together to provide that, at his death, a directed significant cash amount will be set aside to allow for friends and family members to participate in "Vision Cruises" for five years following his death. As much as Rick loves pickleball, I am certain that Rick's legacy will be spreading a contagious joy for internal mission work.

REFLECTIONS
On Charitable Giving

Reflect on how you might spread a contagious joy in giving at your death. If you and your spouse decide to make charitable gifts at your death, prayerfully consider how to best employ charitable giving to spread a joy among others in participating in gospel work.

1. Biblical Purposes for Current Testamentary Gifts:

In the previous chapter, you completed a spreadsheet of your current giving. On that spreadsheet, answer the following questions for each recipient:

Does the gift align with biblical purposes? If not, how can you revise your current giving to align your charitable giving with biblical purposes?

Are your charitable gifts being made without any sense that you are owed? Are you giving in anticipation that the charity or its administrators will "owe you one?" Does your family possess a sense of moral or legal entitlement over any charitable projects?

2. Alignment with Your Narrative of Success and Suffering

Return to the applications in Lesson 3 of this book, where we explored your unique narrative of suffering, success, and stewardship setbacks.

Having shared your stories of suffering, success, and stewardship setbacks, how can you connect these stories with your personal charitable giving?

What ministries give you unique joy in participating in light of your narrative of suffering and stewardship setbacks?

How can your testamentary giving fully leverage your narratives?

3. Alignment with the Life Narratives of Your Children

If you have adult children, determine how to create a testamentary plan to encourage your children in ministry endeavors consistent with their life endeavors.

What ministries are consistent with the life narrative of your children?

What ministries will your children likely be "growing into" in the next five to ten years? Would it be appropriate to provide testamentary gifts to those ministries so that they can experience the joy of your giving in the coming years?

8C: *Impact*

Implement charitable giving plans to maximize eternal, spiritual, and godly outcomes.

"Hopefully this will influence a new form of capitalism that doesn't end up with a few rich people and a bunch of poor people." Eccentric billionaire Yvon Chouinard is the founder of Patagonia, an outdoor clothing company. In his estate plan, Chouinard could have taken a more conventional approach. He could have sold his Patagonia shares, or perhaps gifted some or all the Patagonia shares to his two adult daughters. Instead, Chouinard gifted his entire $3 billion ownership stake in Patagonia to two entities. Since a 501(c)(3) organization is not allowed to engage in political activities or campaigns, Chouinard decided to form a 501(c)(4) organization, a type of nonprofit organization which is permitted to further environmental causes at a political level. While gifts to 501(c)(3) organizations receive a tax deduction, gifts to a 501(c)(4) organization do not qualify for an income tax deduction.

To be as "wise as serpents and as innocent as doves," we ought to be mindful of income tax implications of charitable giving. Income tax planning is not, however, a sufficient stand-alone charitable planning objective for Christians operating from a biblical framework. Jesus admonished us to "pay to Caesar what is Caesar's." The poor widow applauded by Jesus for giving her last mite had no worry about a charitable income tax deduction, both because she had no income to offset and because there was no charitable deduction in Rome for gifts to charities. *Our charitable planning objectives must be marked by an effort to impact others for eternal purposes, to support the joy of giving in the hearts of those around us.*

Whatever you think of the purpose of the gift, Chouinard must be credited for implementing a plan consistent with his life's narrative of environmentalism. Chouinard's plan elevates the importance of obtaining outcomes through political means above the personal tax benefits to himself. In Chouinard's case, he is willing to forego tax benefits to achieve outcomes consistent with his life's narrative. In our case, we can follow Chouinard's lead by elevating the full impact of the plan above income tax savings but do so in a manner consistent with biblical charitable objectives.

In this chapter, I summarize the eternal impact of various types of charitable gifts—the impact both on the giver as well as on the recipient ministry. To elevate the significance of the eternal outcomes, we focus first on the spiritual and relationship impact, and then turn to tax impacts. The types of gifts covered are: (1) outright gifts to your church and ministries; (2) restricted gifts to your church and ministries; (3) the use of donor-advised funds and private foundations, and (4) gifts directly to individuals. With each type of gift, I will first examine the eternal, spiritual, and godly impact ("ESG" impact) of such gifts. I then address the stewardship and tax impact of such gifts.

The ESG Impact of Outright Gifts

Our priority in charitable giving should be to give "outright" (that is, unrestricted) gifts to the local church. Paul admonishes us to give regularly and firstly to our local church, within which we have localized and regular fellowship. "Now concerning the collection for the saints: as I directed churches of Galatia, so you also are to do. On the first day of every week, each of you is to put something aside and store it up, as he may prosper, so that there will be no collecting when I come. And when I arrive, I will send those whom you accredit by letter to carry your gift to Jerusalem."[1] In the early church, the first believers took some of what they had, sold the goods, and laid the proceeds "at the feet of the elders."[2] In our member churches, we interact with others whose narratives are as different from ours as the callings to which each of us have been called as "hands and feet" of the body of Christ. Within the church, we have the joy of participating in the narratives of redemption that are occurring in the lives of our brothers and sisters in Christ. In writing letters to the various New Testament churches, Paul stated that he wanted to share what God was doing in the lives of various churches so that they could share in the joy of seeing God work and trusting God to meet their own needs in their own sufferings.[3]

---

1 1 Corinthians 16:1–3.
2 Acts 4:34–45.
3 Paul wants the Corinthian church to know what God had been doing among the churches in Macedonia. 2 Corinthians 8:1–2.

The act of transferring worldly wealth on a regular basis to our local church has ongoing and numerous eternal, spiritual, and godly ("ESG") benefits. For the individual givers, the "ESG" benefits might include the following:

- We reduce or perhaps even eliminate the pride that would have arisen if we gave directly to an individual. We give to the church, and the church becomes the means for accomplishing missional objectives.

- In giving financial assets to the church, our desires for the health of the church grows. "Money Leads, Hearts Follow."

- We learn of what God has done in the lives of others. We are open to the narratives of the other believers connected within our church communities. We realize that we do not suffer alone; that our stories of suffering, success, and stewardship setback are similar to the life narratives of others whom we can encourage through participation in ministry in the local church.

The ESG benefits to the church could include:

- The leadership of the church is encouraged by your financial commitment to the church and emboldened to take greater risks for the proclamation of the gospel.

- Gifts to the church place the leadership of the church in the legal position to use the contributed funds as the elders see fit.

- The elders are honored through the opportunity to make more and greater stewardship decisions.

- The members of the church, as well as outside observers, bring glory to God for how God used His resources through your giving to meet the expenses of the church.

God's ownership of His assets does not cease when you gift any of the assets previously under your trusteeship to your church. Your role as trustee of those assets is then complete, and the role of the church governance board has started. God calls our church leaders into the legal duties of overseeing God's assets that have been gifted to the church, duties that would include ascertaining the best uses of the gifted assets. The elders in our church are called to "shepherd those under their care."[4] We, in turn, are called to respect and honor them

4 1 Peter 5:1–4.

in their leadership roles.[5] Through a church governance structure, a church leadership board can gain more insight about the working of God in the lives of the church members than if it were a dictatorship, or if we were solely in charge. We could find ways to disagree with how our tithed offerings and gifts will be allocated within the church budget. But if our church is governed by biblical principles of accountability, we can be certain that God will use His assets for eternal purposes.

The ESG Impact of Restricted Gifts

"I don't want my hard-earned assets to be used to pay for resurfacing the church parking lot." A restricted gift is a gift made with conditions, such as for a specific something that the donor wants to see accomplished with the donated assets. From a biblical perspective, a restricted gift is appropriate when it is given in joy, without any sense of entitlement from the donor, and meets the true needs of the ministry. The donor and donor's family would experience the joy of participating in the work of the ministry, and in many cases have something concrete within the ministry to "point to." From the ministry's perspective, the acceptance of the gift would further its opportunities for advancing the cause of the ministry. But a restricted gift is also fraught with peril. From a secular perspective, a restricted gift is an excellent means of using one's wealth to leverage a desired outcome; to "buy" one's way into accomplishing personal goals. A restricted gift would not achieve eternal outcomes when one or more of the following exist:

A Sense of Entitlement. The directed gift should not result in the donor and donor's family feeling a greater level of entitlement over the ministry and its administration. Since the ministry and all contributions are owned by God, a wealthy donor ought to have no sense of entitlement to the charity because, "we paid for the new gymnasium." In these cases, even accepting a donor's condition provides the donor and the family a sense that they have a continuing ownership say within the administration of the charitable organization.

An Ability to Control Leadership. The directed gift should not be used to undermine the leadership of the church. Once the assets are contributed to the ministry, the leaders become the trustees of God's assets under their care and should be given full authority to make decisions to maximize ESG results for their members and employees.

5 An elder is "worthy of double honor." 1 Timothy 5:17–19.

Disparate Treatment. A restricted gift might also create an unbiblical precedent for favoritism within the church. Even the perception of influence could be problematic for the health of the church. We ought to be mindful of biblical directives to treat all members with equal honor, not elevating the wealthiest of Christians above those of modest means.[6]

Asymmetric Information: A directed gift may be the result of a mismatch between the donor's perceived needs of the ministry and actual needs of the ministry. Some donors are requesting gifts stuck in the past, gifts that have little use to the current needs of the ministry. In these situations, the donor's narrative of past blessing must be translated into a format that would allow the ministry to carry out the full story of what God had done previously through the donor. In other cases, an organization may sometimes be slow to recognize the needs of its constituent bodies, and the request for directed gifts may initiate communications that result in changes that positively impact the entire organization.

The ESG Impact of Donor-Advised Funds and Private Foundations

If a donor-advised fund or private foundation is implemented properly, these charitable strategies are an excellent means to spread the joy of giving to the next generation. The Christian clients I represent have used both the DAF and private foundation strategies as excellent giving vehicles to achieve eternally significant impact.

The Use of a Donor-Advised Fund

A donor-advised fund ("DAF") is the ideal legal vehicle for Christians seeking to organize their giving across multiple ministries. As summarized in the previous chapter, a DAF is a "charitable checking account" in which the donor sets aside assets of value including business interests, real estate, investments or most commonly cash contributions for subsequent disbursement among existing ministry organizations that have been approved by the IRS as "tax exempt." A DAF provides us with certainty that churches, parachurch ministries, and missionaries can continue to be supported following death.

The donor to the DAF will pay an annual maintenance fee to the DAF administrator. This DAF administrator will be responsible for

6 James 2:1–4.

assuring that only tax-exempt charitable organizations are receiving the disbursements. Administrators of most of the largest funds impose annual maintenance fees of approximately 0.60% to 1% of fund balances. In comparison to private foundations, most families will find that a DAF is a more efficient vehicle for charitable giving, taking into account the disparity in costs.

The Use of a Private Foundation

A private foundation is a stand-alone legal entity. If the stated mission of the organization is to further religious, scientific and community values, and the organization promises to apply its assets for the betterment of society generally rather than to benefit specific individuals, the IRS will grant the private foundation a tax-exempt status. A private foundation may make contributions to other tax-exempt organizations, or it may make contributions to individuals for purposes consistent with the foundation's objectives. Under current law, a private foundation must distribute at least five percent (5%) of its assets annually.

A foundation must have its own unique tax identification number, bank accounts, and tax returns. A foundation must establish a board of directors to run the organization. These board members must oversee all foundation matters, including investments and distributions. A foundation will need to file annual tax returns. In many cases, the private foundation is partially exempt from any income tax liability incurred on its investments.

ESG Considerations for DAFs and Private Foundations

Christians operating from a biblical perspective might make good use of either a donor-advised fund or a private foundation. In full disclosure, my family has a donor-advised fund with the National Christian Foundation. In utilizing each of these legal strategies, we should be aware of certain ESG risks with these vehicles.

The timeline for the use of the assets should be purposeful. Be aware of the risk that assets contributed to a DAF or private foundation might *sit idle,* and not be used immediately for eternal purposes. The noteworthy legal benefit of both these charitable planning strategies is that one can time the allocation of assets for ministry purposes at a different time than the distribution to the receiving charitable organizations. But joy in giving should be consummated as soon as possible, not unnecessarily delayed. If decision-makers are proactive about giving generously out of these accounts, the ministry organizations can immediately benefit. If decision-makers view the charitable checking account as just another barn to build to hold wealth, the joy will be lost.

The gifts should not be intended to challenge the authority of leaders in ministry. Under a secular estate plan, it is reasonable to create a DAF or private foundation for the specific purpose of dangling assets "away" from legal control of the charity in order to make sure the charity's leadership abides by the donor's requests. But if we are to abide by the Lord's direction that we ought to respect the leadership of our church and elders, we ought to be mindful of the natural tendency to use financial assets to attempt to control outcomes. Contributions to charitable organizations from a DAF or private foundation should encourage and embolden existing leaders.

The donors should attempt to broaden, rather than narrow, the opportunities for gaining insights into the Lord's work in areas beyond the normal scope of the donor's daily activities. Under a secular approach, there is no harm in keeping oneself insulated from the world, and to hold up the façade that the donor knows it all. In contrast, Christians should approach giving decisions with humility, attempting to learn from others and their ministry experiences. Donors should be aware of the possibility of losing opportunities to **broaden giving opportunities** by keeping the group of decision-makers relatively narrow.

GIFTS TO INDIVIDUALS

We have experienced the joy in giving not just to organizations but to individuals as well. You might be called to give gifts directly to individuals, whether because those individuals are in immediate financial need, or because you wish to help with achieving certain outcomes. If you make gifts directly to individuals, and not through the missions organization, there is no stewardship oversight on the contributions and no tax deductibility to you. This is true even if the form of the gift has the appearance of structure, such as through the popular "Go Fund Me" platform.

At your death, you would no longer have the joy in gifting to individuals. If, however, you have a history of providing for friends or family members in need, you should implement and communicate a plan to support those individuals following your death. You would then transfer the "joy of giving" from yourself to your designated trustee to continue to benefit these people. As noted in the previous chapters, you might include specific legal directions in your legal documents to provide directly for an individual, who then might oversee distributions to charities. You might consider, for example, providing a specific cash gift equal to $9,000, if you had been gifting $3,000 annually during your lifetime. Once the assets are received, the individual has no legal obligation to use those assets for the purpose that was explicitly stated. Even when the individual is using platforms such as "Go Fund Me," the individual has no legal requirement to use the assets in the manner that might have been advertised.

TAX BENEFITS

Beginning in the 1930s, churches and parachurch organizations received these tax benefits as part of what has been referred to as the "Grand Bargain." In exchange for providing churches and parachurch organization with exemption from taxes, churches provide services that would have otherwise been provided by government entities. Viewed from purely a cost-benefit analysis, a government benefits when religious organizations are providing services that reduce the cost of running state and local governments. In an era when Christians are perceived as outside mainstream society, and if fewer Americans are actually using the services of churches and parachurch organizations, we face a realistic possibility of our churches losing tax-exempt status. As with the early church under Roman rule, we cannot expect the Grand Bargain to continue. Let us, therefore, be ready to utilize the tax benefits of charitable giving while they are still available, but also be ready to continue to participate in charitable giving regardless of the tax deduction benefits.

Income Tax Deductions

Gifts made to churches and other religious organizations provide you, the donor, with an income tax deduction, subject to limitations based on your income.[7] As noted on the enclosed chart, gifts made to donor-advised funds and private foundations are also entitled to income tax deductions to the donor. Once the gift is received, churches are not required to pay taxes on earnings on that asset. In contrast, gifts made to individuals are not deductible to the donor.

Estate and Gift Tax Deductions

In general, gifts made to any charitable entity (churches, parachurch ministries, donor-advised funds or private foundations) are NOT

---

7 If the donor itemizes deductions, the donor is entitled to an income tax deduction equal to the fair market value of the contributed assets.

subject to estate or gift taxes upon the transfer. The tax code provides for a full "charitable deduction" for estate and gift tax purposes. Congress has agreed to bail out our stewardship failings if we make the same mistake as the rich fool, holding on to too much for too long, and dying with far too much. Let's prayerfully consider how to create more purpose-driven planning strategy that does not rely upon the estate tax charitable deduction.

In contrast to charitable deductions for transfers to charitable organizations, gifts made to individuals are not eligible for deductions from estate and gift taxes. An individual receiving a gift has no income tax reporting obligation. If the value of the total annual gifts given to individuals are at or below $17,000 per person ($34,000 if married), then it is not necessary to file a type of tax return called a gift tax return. As noted in greater detail in the previous chapters related to gifts to children, estate taxes are imposed if the total value of gifts to individuals exceeds the federal "unified credit" from federal estate and gift taxes.

RECIPIENT	LEGAL ACCOUNTABILITY / GOVERNOR	DONOR'S TAX DEDUCTION
Church	Yes; church leadership	Yes; cash up to 60% of AGI Non-cash up to 30% of AGI 100% deductible from estate taxes
Parachurch Ministry	Yes; ministry leadership	Yes; cash up to 60% of AGI Non-cash up to 30% of AGI 100% deductible from estate taxes
Donor-Advised Fund	Yes; fund administrator	Yes; cash up to 60% of AGI Non-cash up to 30% of AGI 100% deductible from estate taxes
Private Foundation	Yes; foundation board of directors	Yes; cash up to 30% of AGI Non-cash up to 20% of AGI 100% deductible from estate taxes
Individual	No legal accountability	No

ILLUSTRATIONS FOR APPLICATION

The following real-world illustrations may be helpful for you as you address how to implement a charitable giving strategy for eternal impact.

Supporting All the School's Stakeholders

A few years ago, the school where my children attend needed student technology upgrades. Several parents generously asked to make a directed gift to the school for the specific purpose of upgrading the technology. While the donors' desire was laudable, the donors did not recognize other financial issues that had been impacting the school leadership's financial decisions. At the time, the leadership was attempting to prioritize increasing the teacher's pay.

In this case, if the donors were allowed to proceed in upgrading the computer and science facilities, the teachers may have been left with the unfortunate impression that the computer science programs are more important than the staff. As it turned out, the leadership was able to raise the necessary funds to first address the teacher pay upgrades, and then subsequently address the upgrades to the school's technology. By communicating the situation among the stakeholders, the school was able to recognize the donors' laudable desire to upgrade the school's capabilities. All parties were able to achieve the desired outcomes for the benefit of the school.

Minimizing Parking Costs & Taxes

By the early 2000s, Jan Nunn, had accumulated a portfolio of real estate properties worth $50 million. Jan's oldest son, Joel, now manages the family's investment positions. A few years ago, a colleague of mine attended a charity breakfast event with Jan and Joel. My colleague noticed that Joel would pick up and leave the breakfast for a few minutes at a time, then come back again. Perplexed, my partner asked Joel about his departures. Joel admitted that he since he was not sure how long the event would last, he was leaving the event sporadically to put quarters in the parking meeting, one quarter at a time, to avoid overpaying the parking meter. In a classic example of the "millionaire-next-door" mentality, a man worth more than $50 million was taking it upon himself to leave the event to save less than a dollar in additional parking meter costs.

A few years ago, Joel and I met to implement his own estate plan. Joel is a strong advocate of small government and low tax rates. Joel decided to implement a type of plan that we often refer to as a "zero tax" estate plan, which directs that, at the owner's death, the maximum amount of assets that can pass free of estate taxes is passed to family members, with remaining assets passing to charity. By federal law, all assets passing to charity pass free of estate taxes. In Joel's case, he directed that the amount that would have otherwise caused tax if it had gone to family would instead pass to charities, thereby avoiding estate taxes at death. Appropriately enough, the charities named by Joel are all nonprofits seeking to reduce taxes in all levels of government.

Joel's plan, however, suffers from a lack of a binding narrative about his wealth. There are no unifying themes with Joel and his family about the use of wealth, generally, and charitable planning, in particular. Joel's narrative is simply that of tax avoidance or minimization. I hope to encourage Joel to provide more specificity to his son and daughter on their use of the assets before he passes. As of right now, however, his legacy is best symbolized by how we worked to save taxes as well as parking meter costs.

The Slush Fund Charitable Trust Strategy

Ryan is a business executive who supports many ministry endeavors that include both nonprofit organizations as well as individuals. Ryan's support of these individuals is difficult for his planners to handle. As soon as we think we have a grasp of his contributions, another ministry or individual in need comes into his life, and the plan needs to be revised.

Instead of attempting to update his will and Trust every time his support situation changes, we have developed a plan in which we will create a "set-aside" trust at his death. Ryan directs a lump sum of cash to a separate account. This separate account would then be administered to support not only the individuals he is then serving, but also the charitable objectives that he names. Ryan appointed a close friend from church as trustee, who will be given unlimited legal discretion to support those institutions and individuals whom Ryan supported at any point throughout his lifetime.

Ryan originally wanted to use the name "Slush Fund" as the name of this set-aside trust, but I persuaded him against such a title if only for banking compliance purposes. In Ryan's case, there is no estate tax or income tax deduction available to his Slush Fund trust, since his trustee has the legal discretion to make distributions directly to individuals (not deductible) or charitable organizations (deductible). Despite the fact that the assets allocated to the trust are not tax deductible to Ryan, the legal framework will achieve eternally significant outcomes because of the flexibility it affords to his designated trustee. In your case, you might likewise consider the best way of creating a plan for the fulfillment of charitable planning goals at your death.

REFLECTIONS
On Charitable Planning for Eternal Purposes

None of us can rival the financial net worth of a Yvon Chouinard. We can, however, follow his lead in implementing a charitable plan consistent with our personal legacy narrative. Rather than getting caught up with thinking about taxes (and parking meter fees!), we should keep our broader objectives in mind. Reflect on how you might implement a charitable plan to implement eternal, spiritual, and godly benefits

Supporting Your Home Church

Do you financially support your home church regularly?

How have your sacrificial financial gifts drawn your heart closer to the ministries of the church, its members, and its leaders?

Have you used past financial or ministry mistakes made by your church as the excuse for reducing or eliminating your support?

If your church loses its tax exemption so that you can no longer take an income tax deduction for your contributions, would you continue to contribute?

Directed Gifts

Are you placing specific restrictions on your gifts to your church or charities?

Do you have a sense of ownership in your church or ministry because of your volunteer hours or financial contributions?

Have you used a financial contribution as a test to see if the church leadership will go along with your desires for the direction of the church? Is your gift a "gift of no return," that is, a gift that if you don't get what you want, you won't return?

Donor-Advised Funds and Private Foundations

Are you involving a sufficient number of people in your ministry support decisions to optimate eternal impact?

If you have established a donor-advised fund or a private foundation, does anyone in your family have a sense of entitlement over contributed funds?

Is your family releasing a sufficient amount of assets now for ultimate kingdom impact?

If you own a sufficient amount of assets to justify creating a private foundation or donor-advised fund, have you engaged professionals to consider the best approach for your family's ongoing ministry giving?

Individuals

Are there any individuals in your life who would financially suffer if you died now and made no provision for them?

Are there any individuals in your life who would benefit from the opportunity to give away your assets to charity following your death

LESSON NINE
End of Life Care

We make end of life care decisions for the benefit of our community.

"Away from the Body, at Home with the Lord." For about twenty-four hours, our nine-month old son Micah had been kept alive by a ventilator. As I shared in previous chapters, Micah suddenly lost consciousness on the morning of July 26, 2009, the culmination of a series of events that started after he fell from his highchair three days earlier while eating his dinner. Those twenty-four hours seemed like three weeks for us, as my wife Heather and I agonized over how to manage not only the ventilator, but also our own prayers and hopes for the future. What were our obligations to keep Micah here on earth? How long do we keep him here? If there was no sliver of hope to see any brain activity, did we have an obligation *to him* to keep his heart beating? As pro-life Christians, were we obligated to keep his heart going indefinitely, even though there was no reasonable hope of any brain activity returning? Were we failing to trust in a miracle from God if we let him go?

It was in those difficult hours that our pastor, Kenny Stokes, in a gentle and humble spirit, encouraged us to trust that Micah was already in eternity, even as his heart was still beating. Based on Paul's description in 2 Corinthians 5:8 of "being away from the body, [then] at home with the Lord," we trusted that, because Micah lost brain activity on the previous day, he "left the body" on the previous day, and thereby passed into eternity well before he was even brought into the emergency room. Based on the assurance and trust that Micah was already in the presence of Jesus, we decided to remove the ventilator. The assistance we received in making that decision was supported by our community of believers. Since that time, our personal journey of wading into the deep waters of grief is inextricably linked to the support we have received from the community of fellow suffering Christians.

All of us will be called to endure and experience difficult end-of-life decisions. This chapter summarizes your end-of-life legal decisions, with a focus on how such decisions will impact your family and community. *Our end-of-life decisions should benefit our family and surviving community ahead of our comfort or reputation. Our decisions should elevate eternity by demonstrating the sufficiency of Christ to meet us in our sufferings and to allow us to grieve in the hope of the certain and coming resurrection of Jesus Christ.*

Every adult should have a legal document called a health care power of attorney, also called a health care directive. A health care directive accomplishes three important objectives:

- *Appointment of a Health Care Agent.* The person you name as your "Health Care Agent" would have authority to act on your behalf if you cannot make your own health care decisions. Your agent would interact with medical professionals in order to make important decisions on your behalf.

- *Sharing of Medical Information.* Medical providers are not permitted to provide family members with your medical records in the absence of your consent. The health care directive should authorize your agent to make informed decisions.

- *Desired End-of-Life Care.* You should specify end-of-life health care directions, desired living arrangements, desired personal interactions, and a desired level of medical interventions.

In a National Institutes of Health survey, it was reported that only

26% of adults have completed any sort of a health care directive.[1] This chapter seeks to encourage Christians to complete a biblically sound health care directive. Christians should take it upon themselves to be among those who have a health care directive in place. The chapter first examines the attributes of the appropriate health care decision-maker, called the "health care agent." The chapter next contrasts three different models for end-of-life care decisions. The chapter then summarizes certain relationship implications that commonly arise in end-of-life decisions and how we might elevate eternity in the hearts of our family in our dying days.

Attributes of Your Health Care Agent

If you have served as someone else's agent, you know that the role is not a mere ceremonial post. To achieve an outcome that is best for you and your community, your named health care agent must possess certain important attributes.

Consistency of Worldview. Your agent will have the legal authority to make your care decisions, including decisions that are in the "gray zone" from a legal perspective. When called upon to act, will your agent be willing to make decisions consistent with your views, not necessarily the agent's views? It is more difficult to ask someone with views disparate from your own to make these difficult decisions.

Family Relationships. Your agent will need to gather information and communicate with your family. If a relationship rift already exists between your children, the stress of your poor health will widen those rifts. Clients of mine with a rose-colored view of the world argue that this stress "will bring the kids together." In my experience, the opposite occurs. You might therefore name a health care agent who can effectively communicate.

Proximity: The appointment of someone within your community is your best option. Proximity cannot be sacrificed for the purpose of appeasing the expectations of others. In Proverbs 27, we read, "Do not forsake your friend and your father's friend, and do not go to your brother's house in the day of your calamity. Better is a neighbor who is near than a brother who is far away."[2] A Christian brother or sister who

---

1 https://www.ncbi.nlm.nih.gov/pmc/articles/PMC4540332/.
2 Proverbs 27:10.

is near, rather than a far-away blood brother or sister from a distance, is in the best position to gather information about your situation from medical care providers, communicate with other family members, and make informed decisions.

Active Engagement with Medical Providers. Finally, your agent should be tenacious in both desire and ability. That person should have an attitude of respectful stridency—to take the time to understand the course of care prescribed by your physicians. That agent also should be willing to ask tough questions, to conduct additional research, and perhaps ask for second opinions. The person should be generally willing to bend the edges of a physician's patience. An agent who is willing to ask tough questions about the necessity or benefit of a particular treatment or procedure is an agent who is most likely to implement your desired end-of-life care. Through your agent's communications, medical professionals can be kept accountable, assuring you and your family that the course of care being utilized is consistent with your desired intentions.

No one you name can perfectly serve as your health care agent. But by prioritizing in making your health care decisions, you'll more likely create an eternally focused outcome in your end-of-life care.

Specific Directions Regarding End-of-Life Care

About health care directives, Dr. Kathryn Butler writes, "While poetic metaphors may appeal to our hearts, they falter when we meet a mechanical ventilator, chest compressions, and feeding tubes."[3] A biblical approach not only seeks to provide as much clarification as necessary, but also seeks to elevate the eternal, spiritual, and godly implications of our end-of-life care decisions on our family. Since we are certain that God will never waste any of our sufferings, we can trust that God will use our suffering to positively impact friends and family members around us.

Your written directions can address the following types of questions and issues:

- Would you like to receive artificial nutrition and hydration?

- Would you like to receive or avoid treatments such as

---

3 When Flesh and Heart Fail: Why Believers Should Consider Advance Directives. Gospel Coalition, June 5, 2018. https://www.thegospelcoalition.org/article/believers-consider-advance-directives/

mechanical ventilation, antibiotics, and tube feeding? If so, how long should you receive these treatments?

- Would you like to spend your final days at home, even if it means receiving a lower level of care?

- Who should visit you in your last days?

A biblical end-of-life care framework should be focused on how your decisions support your Christian community. Our decisions should be markedly different from an individualistic approach that focuses on our comfort and reputation, while ignoring the positive benefits of our suffering on our community. Our decisions should also be characterized by a sojourner's desire for home, not holding on at all costs to a residency in a locale that has never been home. We should make decisions resting in the assurance that every aspect of the narrative of the end is owned by God.

Do It My Way

"I did it my way." Mr. Sinatra's famous song could be the theme of modern American life, especially when it comes to end-of-life decisions. One popular website is appropriately named "Planning My Way." If we owned our bodies, the length of our earthly days, and the narrative of our own lives, we would be justified in making decisions about the length of our life in a manner consistent with Sinatra's famous song. We would look for a way to sing a song of rebellion against the (perceived) straitjacket of cultural expectations and ritual. Our approach would be consistent with the famous poem, *Invictus*:

> "It matters not how straight the gate,
>
> How charged with punishments the scroll;
>
> I am the master of my fate,
>
> I am the captain of my soul."[4]

If we are the "master of our own fate," if we are the owner of our bodies and the author of our own narratives, we have the legal right to take our own life early. Some states allow for a physician to assist people in legally ending their lives. In the State of Oregon, as well as nine other states and the District of Columbia, it is possible to take

---

4 Invictus, by William Earnest Henley.

steps to proactively end your own life.[5] For example, under Oregon's "Death with Dignity" rules, a resident who has been diagnosed with a terminal illness can obtain a physician's assistance in terminating his or her own life.[6] Even in states where physician-assisted suicide is not (yet) legally permitted, various forms of suicide seem to be encouraged by some palliative care physicians. One physician encourages suicide through starvation. One recent method for suicide is called, "Voluntarily Stopping Eating and Drinking.[7]" If we are the captain of our souls, we have the right to starve ourselves, with little or no regard for how this impacts our family and community.

Our generation suffers from a chronological snobbery about suffering and death. As it turns out, we are not the first generation to die. Job suffered from extreme physical difficulty but never took his own life.[8] Job's wife encouraged him to end his own suffering by cursing God.[9] "Oh, that I might have my request, and that God will fulfill my hope, that it would please God to crush me, that he would let loose his hand and cut me off."[10] Let's follow the example of Job rather than Frank Sinatra as we wait upon the Lord. David was patient in waiting upon the Lord's provision for his kingship. David trusted that God would not ask him to take improper measures to become king; he was patient in waiting upon God. David would not kill Saul by his own hand to achieve God's purposes. May we, like David, wait on the Lord.

Take Extreme Measures

On the other end of the end-of-life spectrum, we might use modern medical means to prolong our earthly lives. Studies show that self-identified Christians are three times more likely than non-religious people to opt for heroic measures.[11] At least one pro-life advocacy group is seeking to redefine the legal definition of death in order to

---

5 https://deathwithdignity.org/states/.
6 The candidate for physician-assisted suicide must have a terminal illness diagnosis from two different physicians. The written agreement must be made by the candidate, and not a proxy/agent for the candidate. Oregon Stat. 127.800 to 127.897. See https://www.nolo.com/legal-encyclopedia/oregon-s-death-with-dignity-law.html.
7 Dr. Timothy Quill, Rochester, N.Y., a palliative care physician, has written the book, *Voluntarily Stopping Eating and Drinking: A Compassionate, Widely-Available Option for Hastening Death.* https://compassionandchoices.org/end-of-life-planning/learn/vsed/
8 My skin turns black and falls from me, and my bones burn with heat." Job 30:30.
9 Job's wife asks, "Do you still hold fast your integrity? Curse God and die" Job 2:9.
10 Job 6:8–9.
11 Holly Prigerson et al., *"Religious Coping and the Use of Intensive Life-Prolonging Care Near Death in Patients with Advanced Cancer,"* journal of the American Medical Association 301, no. 11 (March 18, 2009); 1140–1147, cited by Todd Billings, "The End of the Christian Life," p. 127.

exclude all brain deaths.[12] If successful, a person could not be declared "brain dead," such that a person with no brain activity would need to persist in a vegetative state on a ventilator until the heart and lungs stop working. While brain deaths account for only about 2% of deaths in the United States, the removal of "brain death" would create tremendous emotional difficulty for families such as ours.[13]

In religious circles, prolonging life seems to be the "spiritual" choice; it provides the opportunity for God to "respond" to our prayers for healing. If one believes that God responds to only the righteous person, then those who perceive themselves righteous have good reason to try to prolong life. After all, if God is obligated to heal someone because of good moral virtue, prolonging life provides God the opportunity to heal. Prolonging life is the virtuous route because it allows one to show others one's spiritual prowess. Other self-described religious believers taking extreme measures might simply want a noteworthy end; that is, to "go out with a bang."

For those of us who trust in Christ, we know that, in the words of the Apostle Paul, "We would rather be away from the body and at home with the Lord."[14] We can free ourselves from any sense that God "owes" us a certain end-of-life outcome. We can be certain that God accomplishes His purposes for us, even though we were given an emphatic *no* to our prayers for recovery and prolonged life. Therefore, let us approach our end-of-life days considering not just the length of our days, but the implications on our family. We can be confident that God has purposes for our lives that we don't fully comprehend but that will be achieved for the number of days He has ordained. According to King David, even the timing of our last breath is ordained by God: "…in your book were written, every one of them, the days that were written for me."[15] Since our story has already been interwoven into God's story, we do not need to prolong a life to create a noteworthy end-of-life narrative.

12 James Bopp, Jr., an Indiana attorney and the general counsel for the National Right to Life Committee, is seeking to amend Indiana law to remove the brain death as legal death.
13 A 2020 study published by Clinical Neurology and Neurosurgery, as cited in "Doctors and Lawyers Debate Meaning of Death as Families Challenge Practices," December 11, 2023, *Wall Street Journal,* https://www.wsj.com/articles/doctors-and-lawyers-debate-meaning-of-death-as-families-challenge-practices-11670761787
14 2 Corinthians 2:8
15 Psalm 139:16.

A Community-Based Approach to Suffering and Death

A biblical approach to end-of-life decisions requires us to live out our natural days, relying on the strength that God provides, for the benefit of our family and Christian community. In his second letter to the Corinthians, Paul emphasized the community element of suffering. Paul writes,

"But we have this treasure in jars of clay, to show that the surpassing power belongs to God and not to us. We are afflicted in every way, but not crushed; perplexed, but not driven to despair; persecuted, but not forsaken; struck down, but not destroyed; always carrying in the body the death of Jesus, so that the life of Jesus may also be made visible in our bodies. For we who live are always being given over to death for Jesus' sake, so that the life of Jesus also may be manifested in our mortal flesh. So death is at work in us, but life in you."[16]

Paul prioritizes the needs of the young church ahead of his own personal desires for earthly departure. His conspicuous and continued suffering then serves as an encouragement to us in our end-of-life suffering. Just as Paul subordinated his own desires to the needs of his community, we can make end-of-life decisions for the benefit of our Christian community.

The Spiritual Implications to Others

We suffer well if we use our physical suffering to encourage others who are in our community of believers to increase their trust in Jesus. The Apostle Paul wanted the early church to know about, and be encouraged by, his own sufferings. "Now I rejoice in my suffering for your sake, and in my flesh I am filling up what is lacking in Christ's afflictions for the sake of his body, that is, the church."[17] Our body must be used as an instrument of delivering grace to other believers who observe our steadfastness in faith in the face of suffering. Conspicuous suffering is an encouragement to others in their subsequent sufferings.

In her book, *The Lost Art of Dying,* Dr. L.S. Dugdale attempts to recover for modern readers the medieval art of *ars moriendi,* or the *art of dying well.* According to Dugdale, dying well means including the dying member in community, even through that person's dying day. The dying member receives the support and encouragement of the community; the individual community then prepares to die well.

16 2 Corinthians 4:7–12.
17 Colossians 1:24.

The dying member was the protagonist in a drama, with the rest of the community playing the supporting roles. In playing the supporting role, each of the members of the community anticipates becoming the lead. Dugdale writes, "Rehearsing made it easier to sustain a supportive community once death hovered. When someone died, there would be no guessing about what one should do or say."[18]

Together with all other Christians, we must endure periods of suffering even when we lack any sense of God's purposes in suffering. We lack polite and neat answers to these pressing questions sometimes asked with clenched teeth or tear-filled eyes. We are called to offer our humble bodies as the "jars of clay" that allow our communities to marvel at God's power. When our family or church friends come to support us and pray with us, there is no hiding that fact when we are feeling less than stellar. But through our sufferings, others can marvel at God's provision even in suffering.

In whatever suffering you endure, the beauty of Christian community is that we can suffer well together. When you come to rely on friends for support through past sufferings, you know what a blessing it is to rely on them during future sufferings. When it comes to our end-of-life decisions, our decisions may be a means by which "the life of Jesus also may be manifested in our mortal flesh...." We can trust that even when our physical body is dying, eternal life is at work in the lives of our family and church.[19]

The Spiritual Result on Us

As eternal beings, every opportunity we encounter that provides an opportunity for Christlikeness is not a wasted moment. C.S. Lewis writes, "Now there are a good many things which would not be worth bothering about if I were going to live only seventy years, but which I had better bother about very seriously if I am going to live forever." [20] Moment by moment, suffering by suffering, God grows godliness in us. We might be called on to live longer than we would wish simply to increase our personal trust in God.

The Apostle Paul apparently experienced some chronic pain, and despite his requests, the Lord did not take it away from him. In response to requests for physical healing, God promised to meet Paul in Paul's physical suffering. "For my grace is sufficient for you, for

18 Lydia Dugdale, *The Lost Art of Dying,* (New York: HarperOne, 2021) 53.
19 2 Corinthians 4:12.
20 C.S. Lewis, *Mere Christianity* (San Franciso: Harper, 2001) 74.

my power is made perfect in weakness."[21] When Paul writes, "To live is Christ, and to die is gain,"[22] I wonder if he means that God's presence will continue with you in life circumstances. When you endure significant sufferings or grief, you are able to leverage the past experiences to trust in God's provision for the satisfaction of the next ones.

Our final days make us yearn for the body that we will clothe on the other side of eternity. "For we know that if the tent that is our earthly home is destroyed, we have a building from God, a house not made with hands, eternal in the heavens. For in this tent we groan, longing to put on our heavenly dwelling, if indeed by putting it on we may not be found naked. For while we are still in this tent, we groan, being burdened—not that we would be unclothed, but that we would be further clothed, so that what is mortal may be swallowed up by life."[23] Our final days create a desire to depart the earth, with its pain, suffering, and dysfunction, and finally be birthed into our new life, with our new tent, with our new body.

Relationship Implications

Well-intentioned clients sometime create relationship hardships through certain end-of-life decisions. In my law practice, two sets of end-of-life decisions often result when clients elevate personal preference or financial considerations above relationship implications.

Minimizing Health Care Costs

First, negative relationship implications often arise when parents attempt to protect personal assets from being used for medical care costs. We often hear the refrain, "I don't want the government to take all my money for medical care." If your end-of-life care costs are not covered by insurance, whether public or private, you and your spouse are personally responsible.[24] You might decide to gift your assets to your children so that these assets are not "countable" assets when it comes to determining your eligibility for state-sponsored care. Alternatively, or additionally, you might forego care treatments or options because of the cost.

---

21 2 Corinthians 12:9.
22 Philippians 1:19–26.
23 2 Corinthians 5:1–4.
24 Some individuals think of the "nursing home taking my money," when in fact it is the local governments who require us to use our own assets first to pay for additional medical care costs before means-tested government programs, such as medical assistance, will provide benefits.

Some adult children are of the opinion that their parents should receive the best possible care, regardless of cost. Historically, patients receiving care through Medicaid/medical assistance receive a lower level of care then "private pay" patients—patients who use personal assets to pay for living expenses and care. If you had gifted assets to your adult children for the purpose of "protecting" those assets for purposes of an end-of-life expense spend-down, they may face a moral quandary. If one or more of your children believe that they have a personal obligation for your care, they may end up thwarting your intentions by using gifted assets for your care costs.

These situations could create difficult moral and emotional decisions for your children that may lead to disharmony among them. One or more of your children may use their personal assets to pay for better or private pay care. Another child or children will emphasize your austerity in giving away your assets, or withholding medical treatment, as your direction that no assets be used for your care, even to your detriment, and to the anguish, of your other children. In these situations, retaining ownership of your own assets for your own care costs has the *practical* effect of reducing the financial obligation that your children would pay out of their own assets, even though your children have no *legal* obligation for such debts.[25]

One final note on this subject is sure to spark disagreement among readers. The narrative presented to your children about the purpose of your lifetime gifting will impact how your children view end-of-life care. Some of our adult children are told that they are "spending their inheritance" during the parents' lifetime on educational costs, home purchases, or other laudable objectives. In these cases, the narrative set by the previous gifting history was not centered around the avoidance of medical care costs. The narrative was previously set to achieve laudable objectives. In contrast, if the first time a parent makes a gift is in an attempt to avoid medical care costs, the children are placed in a no-win situation. In situations without a guiding family narrative, the siblings will likely disagree about the extent of medical care. As one adult child once said to me, "I thought we would be cheating the system, but as it turned out, we are just cheating our mother out of better care." I am generally in favor of retaining assets to "pay one's own way" so as to avoid any disharmony among children.

25 In the United States, the debts of a parent are not transferable to the children.

Benefiting Family Caregivers

A common refrain among clients in our office is, "I want to be carried out of my house 10 toes up." Dying at home is preferable over a noisy and sterile hospital for many reasons, including a greater opportunity to interact with your community. However, depending on your health conditions, dying at home may not be possible. Even if it is possible, though, we should wisely anticipate the relationship implications to your family of your dying at home. Will your surviving family members benefit from your dying at home, or will your dying at home create relationship strains among your community?

From time to time, I meet with the adult children who, at great financial and emotional cost to themselves, provided care to their dying parents. For those who were expecting compensation for their services, these surviving adult children invariably express disappointment about the insufficiency of this compensation. In a recent study conducted by Fidelity Investments, 62% of caregivers reported being occasionally overwhelmed with financial stress. The average leave of absence from a caregiver's professional career taken by caregivers was 20 months, and 53% said the time away from work was longer than expected. When they did return to work, 37% earned less, and that reduction in pay averaged 40%.[26] In another study, in cases where extreme measures were taken to prolong life among those suffering from cancer, the surviving caregiver was three times more likely to suffer from severe depression.[27] Clearly, these survey results show that adult caregivers suffer a significant financial toll personally when they leave their professional careers to care for aging parents.

If you desire to live at home, clarify whether family members are planning on providing you care. You might head off any potential issues by not even allowing a willing family member to provide your care. If family members are willing to provide care, clarify with your entire family that your family caregivers will be compensated not based on actual time and costs incurred at market rates rather than receiving a certain asset or a greater percentage of remaining assets at your death. To avoid future family disharmony over any perceived sense of favoritism, the family caregiver should be paid no less than a third-party caregiver so that the entire family can be fully invested in

---

26 Statistics cited by Chris Taylor, "Caregiving brings financial as well as emotional stress." Star Tribune, June 13, 2021.
27 Atul Gawande, *What Should Medicine Do When It Can't Save You?* The New Yorker, July 26, 2010.

your care. Otherwise, when your caregiver is paid less than fair market rates, the rest of the family members/beneficiaries financially benefit to the expense (both financially and emotionally) of the caregiving family member.

A family member should not be provided any special treatment as a beneficiary of your estate plan in anticipation that the person will serve as a caretaker, whether in the form of the receipt of a specific asset or an increased percentage of remaining assets. While we might assume a certain course of care or longevity, we simply cannot know with any degree of certainty the length of our days or how extensive our care-receiving needs will turn out to be. We should therefore not implement a plan to provide disproportionate distributions to our children based upon assumptions subject to far too many variables. The symbolic importance of an equal inheritance to your children is far too important to leave it to chance.

The Financial Implications

Whatever level of personal suffering we experience, those sufferings would be eclipsed by Job's sufferings. All of us will lose our health and life, but none of us will experience all possible forms of suffering simultaneously, as Job was. When faced with significant end-of-life care costs, we could shake our fist at the government for failing to pay for our end-of-life care costs. Alternatively, we could mirror Job's humble response. "Who among all these does not know that the word of the Lord has done this? In his hand is the life of every living thing and the breath of all mankind."[28]

As the owner of our financial assets, God has the right to "waste" His financial assets on our end-of-life care costs. If God chooses to prolong our lives through a four-year bout with dementia, God effectively "spends down" your child's inheritance. We are simply not our own; God owns every part of us, from our bodies to how the length of our days might impact the size of our inheritance. We must use our bodies for the good of our families and our church communities.

End-of-Life Decisions with Eternity in View

Our end-of-life decisions ought to be markedly different from those of our secular neighbors in the following important respects:

---

28 Job 12:9.

- *We allow God to determine the length of our days.* Since God owns it all, we must not take our lives before the end of the days determined for us. We must be mindful of how our broken vessels of bodies provide extraordinary opportunities for Christlikeness among our community of believers.

- *We trust in the certainty of God's promises in Christ.* We can make end-of-life decisions in the best interests of our family and our church without any obligation that we receive a miraculous cure in order to receive justification. While we can "fight the good fight" to the end, our victory is certain regardless of the outcome of our last illness.

- *We allow our broken bodies and cluttered minds to be used to reflect God's glory.* We owe it to our fellow brothers and sisters in Christ to lend them our broken, weak, failing bodies so that they can see the glory of God being manifested in our final days.

- *We are not opposed to using our assets on our medical care expenses.* Since God is the owner of financial assets as well as our bodies, it's God's problem, not ours, if God calls us to spend what we consider to be far too long in an assisted living facility, spending His assets on long-term care.

- *We address the relationship implications that our decisions would have on our family.* End-of-life decisions should not assume upon a certain future. We will have events that occur in life that are unexpected. An estate plan should be well-designed to withstand all future plan changes.

ILLUSTRATIONS FOR APPLICATION

The following three illustrations might be helpful in considering how to benefit your community in your end-of-life care decisions:

Telephone Tag

Marian simply could not bring herself to name anyone other than her sister, Martha, as her health care power of attorney. While Martha and Marion had a good relationship, Martha lived on the other side of the country. When Marian developed health issues rather suddenly, Martha was simply not in a position to meet with her sister's care providers and gather information necessary to make informed decisions.

Marian's friend Lori lived locally and checked in on Marian daily. Unfortunately, medical care providers were not able to share information with Lori because Lori was not authorized as Maran's health care agent. On a few occasions, Lori would call Martha simply to ask Martha to call in to the hospital and collect information from care providers. This information would then be relayed back, by phone, from Martha to Lori. In hindsight, it would have been far more efficient for Marian to name Lori as her health care agent so that Lori could have provided "boots on ground" directions. .

Unfounded Assumptions about End-of-Life Care

Nancy and Larry are a delightful and successful couple now in their nineties. Nancy and Larry have three adult children and many grandchildren and great-grandchildren. Two of their three children live on the east coast. Their third child, Blake, now lives in the Twin Cities residence previously owned by Larry and Nancy. Larry and Nancy only recently moved out of their beautiful Minnesota lake property residence and into an assisted-living residence.

When I first met with Nancy and Larry about ten years ago, Nancy and Larry involved their son, Blake, in many of their estate-planning decisions. Blake was then in his fifties, having recently endured a business bankruptcy and a divorce. When we initially created a plan, it was the stated intention of Blake to live with Nancy and Larry and to provide personal care to them at end of life. Based on this understanding, Nancy and Larry gifted the ownership of the lake property residence to Blake.

Recently, Larry and Nancy met with me to update their plan. I learned that while Blake continues to live in the lake property, he is generally living his own life, busy with new business endeavors. Blake never really provided care to his parents and provided no indication that he was willing to do so presently. Nancy and Larry have now updated their plan to treat the gift of the lake property to Blake as an advancement against Blake's one-third share that he will receive once they are both dead. Of course, none of these changes would have been necessary had the original plan provided for an equal distribution of remaining assets at death.

No Guiding Narrative for Care Costs

Henry had a lifelong aversion to government intrusion in his life. When

Henry's friends told him about their plans to "keep the government from taking their money" for health care costs, Henry likewise followed suit. Henry took it upon himself to make gifts to his three children so that he could "make himself appear poor" in the eyes of the government. While I did not represent Henry in this planning, I am told that he relished the idea that the government would not be able to take "his" money for his care costs.

As it turned out, Henry lived longer than he expected. When he needed care, it turned out to be far more expensive than even his children had contemplated. Since Henry's children had not planned for this scenario, they had not set aside the gifted assets in separate co-owned or co-managed accounts. Two of his three children felt that Henry's wishes were clear, and that no assets should be used to provide for Henry's care. The third child felt otherwise, and used personal assets to pay for Henry's rent and other personal expenses. While Henry intended to keep the government from "taking his money," the end result was that one of his children personally paid for his end-of-life care costs. .

REFLECTIONS
On Your End of Life Care

Reflect on how you can articulate your end-of-life care desires with an intention to elevate eternity in the hearts of your community. You and your spouse may use the following questionnaire to give direction on your end-of-life care decisions. Regardless of whether you use your own living will or express these preferences using the questionnaire, you should take steps to communicate your directions to family.

PAIN CONTROL

I would like my pain controlled by medication, in this manner:

☐ I wish to be as comfortable and free from pain as possible.

☐ I believe that pain is a part of life. I would rather experience pain than be administered medication to an extent that I am no longer able to interact with loved ones.

☐ _____

_____

LIFE PROLONGING TREATMENT

I would like life prolonging treatment if:

☐ I will be able to socially relate to loved ones even if I have some physical limitations.

☐ My continued longevity would encourage family or community members by reason of a significant family event or the possible reunion with a family member or friend.

I **do not** wish to have life prolonging treatment if:

☐ My agent has determined that my family and support system will not benefit from my continued longevity, and continued treatment will only prolong death.

☐ _____

_____

ARTIFICIAL NUTRITION AND HYDRATION

☐ When I can no longer take food or fluids orally, I do not want any nutrition or any fluids by any artificial means, whether by tube or intravenously or otherwise.

☐ If necessary, I wish to receive intravenous fluids, but under no event should I receive any type of nutrition by tube feedings.

☐ I do not view food and water as medical treatment. I want food and water provided by whatever means are necessary to keep me alive.

☐ _____

_____

CARDIOPULMONARY RESUSCITATION (CPR)

☐ I want CPR under any circumstances.

☐ If I have an incurable terminal illness or injury, I do not want CPR.

☐ _____

_____

DIAGNOSTIC PROCEDURES

If I am terminally ill:

☐ I do not want any diagnostic procedures.

☐ I wish to receive blood work and any non-invasive imaging, but not invasive procedures (e.g., spinal tap, thoracentesis or biopsies).

☐ I agree to any diagnostic procedures, including invasive procedures, but only if it will prolong my life or allow my physicians to take further steps to improve my condition or reduce my pain.

☐ I am willing to receive any diagnostic procedures if it serves to improve medical knowledge generally, and not necessarily my particular condition.

INTERACTION WITH FAITH COMMUNITY

☐ I wish to have visits from my faith community even if I do not appear to understand or cannot fully participate.

☐ I wish for the following people to visit with me:

_____

_____

☐ I have the following additional directions to my faith community:

_____

_____

MY PREFERENCES FOR CARE WHEN DYING

If a choice is possible and reasonable when I am dying, I would prefer to receive care:

☐ Home

☐ Hospital

☐ Nursing Home

☐ Hospice services

☐ Palliative care facility

This is the name and address of the facility I would like if possible:

_____

_____

LESSON TEN
Testament

Use legacy letters to provide written encouragement to your Christian community about important matters of faith.

"I have fought the good fight, I have finished the race, I have kept the faith."[1] Paul's letter to his protégé Timothy, now referenced as 2 Timothy, is seen by many biblical scholars as Paul's closing admonition—his own version of his "last will." Paul emphasizes that his life work in the promulgation of the gospel was worth the cost of losing out on all other pursuits. In this last letter to Timothy, Paul takes the opportunity not to outline his own achievements but to encourage Timothy in gospel hope.

A comprehensive estate plan includes not just legally binding documents and directions, but also *legal decisions delegated to successors*. While contemporary legal last wills provide only legal directions, a last will historically includes words of testimony, points of policy conviction, and desires for specific family, business, and ministry matters. You may follow Paul's example of 2 Timothy by leaving written instructions, instructions serving eternally significant purposes.

In this closing chapter, I summarize decisions left to others because they yield greater eternal outcomes if made by others. I previously summarized the importance of sharing life narratives of suffering and

---

1 2 Timothy 4:7.

success with your family. I now turn to the use of non-legally binding written directions made by you, commonly referred to as *legacy letters* or ethical wills. In this chapter, we cover legacy letters in the context of (1) your funeral planning, (2) the management of a financial inheritance left to family, and (3) ministry and faith statements. Through these directions, you can encourage your family, friends, and church to wisely steward your affairs following death.

YOUR FUNERAL

Being no stranger to suffering himself, Paul says Christians are *"sorrowful yet always rejoicing."*[2] Pastor John Piper, among others, encourages Christians to live in a *sorrow and joy paradox*.[3] The paradox of Christian hope is that we can simultaneously be both the saddest yet most joy-filled people on earth. A funeral service presents the opportunity for us to demonstrate this sorrow and joy paradox. In our sadness, we fully recognize and grieve the spiritual, emotional, relational, and physical implications of sin and death in this world. After his friend Lazarus died, Jesus honored his friend in expression of genuine grief.[4] If Jesus wept after the first of Lazarus's two deaths, shall we not also expect our family to grieve our passing? We should allow our family to recognize and honor our family's sadness at our passing, but also encourage them in the joy we have because of our unshakable hope of the coming resurrection. Our funeral or memorial rituals should serve as the means to proclaim joy in this resurrection hope.

I offer the following three principles in applying a *"sorrowful yet always rejoicing"* approach:

- Recognizing the reality of grief in your family;

- The opportunity to use the symbolism of burial; and

- Opportunistic appointments.

Recognition of Grief

Following the death of my oldest son Micah in 2009, we created the Hope for the Mourning charitable organization to assist fellow grieving parents. We have learned of the importance of healthy grief. Every

2 2 Corinthians 6:10.
3 Pastor John Piper has preached that Christians ought to be simultaneously both the saddest, as well as the most joy-filled, people on earth.
4 John 11.

family grieves in a different manner, but no family has ever benefited from taking a stoic approach to their grief. We have seen many families grieve well. We have observed many parents who tried to "stuff" their grief in unhealthy ways. **Recognize your family's tradition and memorial as a stabilizing force.**

During the COVID-19 pandemic, I was saddened to see many families delay any funeral services for the ostensible reason of the pandemic. "Funeral services to be held at a later date" was the common refrain on obituaries from 2020 and 2021.[5] The pandemic was merely the excuse for families to proceed with a trend that has been gathering for quite some time—to avoid traditional funeral services and instead hold more informal gatherings, such as a "celebration of life" or private dinner parties.

A biblical estate plan realistically recognizes the grief that we justifiably feel when we lose a loved one or friend. You suffer from misplaced modesty if you want your family to have a "celebration of life" dinner and move on as if nothing worthy of grieving has occurred. When responding to my expression of sympathy following his mother's death, an adult son was clearly in this "let's move on" mindset.

"Happy Pizza, Cory, Happy Pizza…Cory, don't keep saying, 'My condolences.' It makes me really sad. Say, 'Happy Pizza!' or something else."

This family member made it clear that there was no redeeming hope for his now-deceased mother. "Well, she had a good run, but now it's all over" was the best he could say. This son's approach to grief was to avoid it. If you encourage your family to take a Happy Pizza approach, then while the dinner party might be fun for one night, your family will have simply delayed the inevitable grief that will come. My "Happy Pizza" clients are the ones who epitomize the secular mindset of avoiding grief. Our secular clients and your secular friends will take proactive measures to avoid the pain, to minimize the loss. Having walked alongside many fellow grieving parents over the past fourteen years, I can relate to the desire to numb the pain of loss through all sorts of worldly distractions.

---

5 FEMA estimates that only one-third of the families who lost a loved one to COVID and were therefore eligible to receive federal reimbursement for funeral expenses actually incurred funeral costs. https://abcnews.go.com/Health/million-deaths-350k-families-asked-fema-funeral-cost/story?id=84694884

Our Happy Pizza neighbors, if pressed, must admit that they have no logical grounds for arguing that death is anything other than one part of an evolutionary process. But we know that death is not the way life is meant to be. Paul Tripp writes, "Death is the enemy of everything good and beautiful about life as God planned it. Death should make you morally sad and righteously angry. It is a cruel indicator that life is broken; it is not functioning according to God's original design." The rituals we have conducted for generations should not be dispensed with because we think it would be "too sad" for our surviving family members. Your family is profoundly saddened by your loss, and they are better served, in the long run, by directly confronting their grief through funeral or memorial services.

When planning our son's funeral in 2009, we chose worship songs that we associated with our short time with our son on earth, as well as hymns sung at the family funerals. In a time of unspeakable loss, there was comfort in the familiarity of the promises contained in those favorite worship songs and hymns. You might provide your family with a list of hymns, songs, or passages that you and your family have found meaningful. Familiar family rituals will provide your family with a sense of stability in grieving, even while looking ahead in anticipation to the coming resurrection.

The Symbolic Benefit of Bodily Burial

Our eternal destiny is secure regardless of the status of our earthly bodily remains after our death.[6] While the disposition of our bodily remains will have no eternal impact on us, the symbolic disposition of our bodies in burial might provide some solace in grief to our families. **The burial of our body could symbolize to our Christian community our hope of our future resurrection.**

Today, cremation is the cheapest and most environmentally friendly option for the disposition of bodily remains. In 2022, the average cost of a reviewal and burial in the United States was $7,848.[7] The average cost of direct cremation is $600, and the cost of cremation with a funeral is $3,700.[8] Perhaps as a direct result of this cost differential, the

---

6 It seems that Paul was certain about his eternal destiny in heaven and with Christ regardless of how he would be executed. "Whether I surrender my body to the flames, but have not love,..." (1 Corinthians 13:3).

7 https://nfda.org/news/statistics.

8 https://www.neptunesociety.com/state/minnesota#:~:text=What%20is%20the%20average%20cost,a%20cremation%20with%20a%20service.

cremation rate was projected to be 57.5% in 2022. [9]

Cremation originated among religions that emphasize the evils of the physical human body. In the ancient world, only the Chinese, Hebrews, and Egyptians buried their dead; all others cremated the body. Greeks believed that the soul was freed from the evils of the physical body by the death and subsequent cremation of the physical body.[10] Cremation was seen as the symbolic destruction of the evil body and the return of our souls to a cosmic, pantheistic "being" of which we have been a part. Cremation is a symbolic annihilation of the body, a destruction of that which kept us from our true identity.

In direct contrast, Christians have historically preferred burial because of the symbolic demonstration of the physical body being resurrected. We are fully aware that our bodies will decay in the ground. Christians were nonetheless buried because of the symbolic demonstration that God will raise us again, albeit in a bodily form far superior to the form in which our bodies went into the ground. Viewed from the time frame of eternity, our bodies are merely resting, sleeping until the second coming.[11] At that time, our deformed and decayed bodies are the seeds that will eventually be sown into our eternal, heavenly body. Upon Christ's triumphant return, "Christ will transform our earthly body to be like his glorious body, to be like him as he is."[12]

Historian Stephen Prothero describes the symbolic distinction between cremation and burial as follows:

"The American way of burial deals with the decay of the material body via preservation. Embalmed, coffined, and buried, the preserved dead are said to be merely sleeping, patiently awaiting a future bodily resurrection, perhaps in a coffin designed to provide eternal protection from the elements…The American way of cremation confronts decay very differently…by accelerating, not arresting it. Rather than preserving the corpse through embalming, cremation annihilates it through incineration. Confident that the true self is spiritual rather than material, they welcome the swift

---

9 https://nfda.org/news/media-center/nfda-news-releases/id/6012/turning-to-tradition-more-than-a-quarter-of-americans-embrace-religion-in-post-covid-funeral-planning
10 Prothero, p. 7.
11 Pastor John Piper argues that our burial symbolizes the sowing and sleeping. https://www.desiringgod.org/articles/should-christians-cremate-their-loved-ones.
12 Philippians 3:21.

fragmentation of the body into ashes."[13]

By law, any written directions made for the disposition of your remains are legally binding. This can be accomplished within a health care directive, but any written direction will suffice. Likewise, your desires for anatomical gift of your organs can be made through any signed written statement, including a will, driver's license, health care directive, or donor card. Notably, you can refuse anatomical gifts following death, so long as such refusal is in writing. In the absence of a written refusal made by you, your family has the legal authority, following your death, to donate your organs.[7]

My wife Heather and I have requested a preference that our bodies be buried in a traditional manner in the same cemetery as our oldest son, Micah. We recognize that this traditional burial is more expensive and cumbersome than a simple cremation. But as grieving parents who have struggled in grief and pine for Jesus' second coming because of our own son's passing, *we prioritize symbolism above cost savings.* Jesus defended Mary's extravagant anointing of Him at Bethany, elevating the symbolism of her act above Judas' concern about the financial cost. Taking our cue from the anointing of Jesus' body at Bethany, we cast our lot fully in the hope in the physical resurrection of the dead upon the second return of Jesus Christ. "For the creation was subjected to futility, not willingly, but because of him who subjected it, in hope that the creation itself will be set free from its bondage to corruption and obtain the freedom of the glory of the children of God."[14] You might decide that it is worth the extra cost of burial to demonstrate to your family your hope in your future physical resurrection.

Opportunistic Appointments

"To each person in attendance at my funeral, I hereby give a cash gift of five hundred dollars ($500)."

This provision was properly executed by a trustee represented by our firm. As stated in the trust agreement, every person in attendance at the funeral received $500. Apparently, the decedent had a history of being ignored or offended by friends and family. The decedent therefore took the opportunity presented by his own funeral to reward those who he felt appropriately honored his memory. No, the terms of his

13 Stephen Prothero, *Purified by Fire: A History of Cremation in America.* (University of California Press, 2001) 4–5.
14 Romans 8:21–22.

trust agreement were not disclosed ahead of his funeral, but the trustee arranged for video recordings to substantiate attendance. In this case, the decedent was getting in his "last word" to his family. The decedent desired to benefit those who brought him honor and punish those who dishonored him by their absence.

We will not attend our own funeral, keeping score. If we make any decisions or directions about our own funeral, it should be to opportunistically appoint those who we believe would be honored to lead. Any instructions left behind should be only to honor those designees whose leadership would heighten the chances for spiritual engagement by the funeral participants.

DIRECTIONS FOR FINANCIAL ASSETS TO FAMILY

"What did Dad want us to do with all this money?" A legacy letter, made by you during your lifetime, would encourage your family through clarity of purpose following your death. Clients have used legacy letters in various contexts and updated these letters as their life situation changes.

Directions to a Named Guardian of Young Children

Parents with young children should prepare a legacy letter to your named guardians to cover important parenting decisions. The directions to your guardians could cover issues such as: (1) your desires for the educational opportunities provided to your minor children, including public, private, or homeschooling options; (2) the desired residency of the guardian and children, including where the guardian would be willing to relocate if they agree to move in order to take on the guardianship, (3) how a guardian's children should be treated financially with remaining funds owned by you, and (4) your desires for your children in maintaining contact with certain family members or friends, such as grandparents, aunts, uncles, and cousins. You could provide specific direction to your guardians as to family vacation expenses or other unique or unusual expenses.

Use of Inherited Assets by Children

Once each of your children has reached adulthood, your legacy letter may change to address new and updated life circumstances. A legacy letter could be used to provide direction to your adult children on the desired use of a financial inheritance.

An implicit obligation may be in existence for a family to retain ownership of a unique asset. In my Minnesota-based law practice, this often involves a lake cabin. A legacy letter can be used to articulate the intentions of passing the ownership of the cabin to the family. If the ownership becomes a burden rather than a blessing to the family, a letter is useful to clarify whether the children are allowed to sell the cabin. A letter might provide children the moral freedom to sell such assets, whether that is immediately after the death of the surviving parent, or upon the occurrence of a certain specified event in the future (*e.g.,* a financial hardship or change in family circumstances).

In cases where liquid assets are left to adult children, I recommend that parents provide children with encouragement to consume inherited assets for certain purposes. Providing your children with this encouragement will free them from inaction on account of indecision. Many, but not all, of our clients leaving their children with unfettered legal access to assets would deem the following list to be an appropriate use of inherited assets.

- *Health care, generally:* The financial assets could be used to pay for medical care for the beneficiary and her family. This could include such items as health insurance premiums, deductibles, and out-of-pocket costs.

- *Living expenses in the event of long-term disability:* If a beneficiary experiences a long-term health condition that precludes earning a living wage, assets could be used to pay for not just medical expenses, but all living expenses.

- *Careers with insufficient income:* If a beneficiary is earning a wage, but not earning enough to meet living expenses consistent with a pre-determined living standard, inherited assets can be used to meet that shortfall.

- *Care provider:* If a beneficiary's calling is to serve as a full-time or part-time care provider, whether for the beneficiary's own children or perhaps other family members, inherited assets could be used for living expenses to offset the fact that the child is not engaged in the work force.

- *Grandchild's costs.* A grandchild's educational costs, including private school education, undergraduate education, or even graduate school. Some have specifically provided for Bible camp, sports activities, or music endeavors.

- *Family vacation fund.* Adult children and their families could be encouraged to take a vacation together. Some clients have dedicated a certain amount of assets (*e.g.,* $20,000) to a family vacation fund, to last for as many years as the fund will allow.

- *Missions trip expenses.* A child or grandchild could be encouraged to use assets to fund a mission trip.

The letter might address how a child and her family should order the consumption of the inherited assets vis-à-vis personally accumulated assets. For example, assets dedicated from an inherited account for a family's vacation fund could be used and consumed before a child's own assets for such purpose. In contrast, inherited assets should be used for living expenses only if personally earned income is insufficient.

In cases where a testamentary trust structure is established for the benefit of children or grandchildren, a testamentary letter provides the trustee with necessary directions. The legal standards used for directing trust distributions are often too broad. A legacy letter, though not legally binding, is an ideal means of providing a trustee with direction as to how each individual beneficiary might benefit from trust assets.

A legacy letter is a Do-It-Yourself ("DIY") project; the estate planning attorney should not draft the letter. These types of letters can be frequently and easily reviewed, revised, and updated without involving legal counsel. As your family's needs and circumstances change, you should revise your legacy letters accordingly.

FAITH AND MINISTRY STATEMENTS

Finally, a legacy letter might also be used to provide a faith statement and closing encouragement to your family and faith community. In his Last Will and Testament, Billy Graham directed as follows:

I ask my children and grandchildren to maintain and defend at all hazards at any cost of personal sacrifice the blessed doctrine of complete Atonement for sin through the blood of the Lord Jesus Christ once offered, and through that alone. I urge all of you to walk with the Lord in a life of separation from the world and to keep eternal values in view.[15]

Billy Graham's Last Will and Testament became public after his death

---

15 https://www.christianpost.com/news/billy-grahams-will-and-testament-released-to-public-asks-family-to-defend-gospel-at-any-cost.html

in 2018. His will includes legal directions for the transfer of assets as well as these closing admonitions to his surviving family. Historically, Christians might have included a statement of faith in their wills as a "Last Testament" to their faith. In today's legal environment, I rarely see such statements in a will or a trust agreement, but not because there is anything wrong with making such explicit acknowledgments of faith. (I assure you that attorneys, more than any other profession, need to hear the Gospel!) Depending on the type of assets you own, your will may not be seen, having no legal purpose. A legacy letter is therefore the appropriate means to provide your family a statement of faith or a faith pronouncement.

Your statement of faith might be structured as:

- An assurance of your faith in Christ;

- An encouragement to each of your children in their relationship with Jesus;

- Your faith story or testimony, or

- Your reasons for hope in the coming resurrection.

Policy Directions

A legacy letter can also be used to put in a final word on important policy matters. These directions might be related to something in your home, in a ministry, or in your church. In Acts 20, Paul speaks to the elders of the Ephesian church for the last time. Paul anticipates the spiritual warfare that is ahead for the church. "I know that after my departure fierce wolves will come in among you, not sparing the flock; and from among your own selves will arise men speaking twisted things, to draw away the disciples after them. Therefore, be alert, remembering that for three years I did not cease night or day to admonish everyone with tears."[16] Paul admonishes the church to continue fighting the good fight, even in his absence.

You might use a letter to address theological or doctrinal issues that you anticipate arising in the near future. You might anticipate how doctrinal changes in ministries you currently support might cause a change in direction within those ministries. If ministries currently supported by you see "mission drift" after your death, and if your family has the legal authority to change course with charitable

16 Acts 20:29–31.

contributions after your death, your legacy letter would provide your designated agents some framework to retain authenticity to your beliefs.

Last Blessings to Children

Closing words to your spouse or child could be particularly impactful when read following your death. A letter might be prepared and saved to send final words of encouragement, affirmation, or forgiveness to loved ones. These letters might be sent to those who have a "relationship debt" still outstanding. Ideally, of course, you will have gone to your brother or sister on these matters as they occur, but I have seen clients who have not yet closed out a difficult chapter of life address this issue within a letter.

Memorial Contributions

Finally, you might use a legacy letter to provide guidance on post-death memorial contributions. We experience joy in freely giving to those missional organizations that we believe in and are consistent with the memory of the deceased. A legacy letter might therefore be used to provide friends and family suggestions, but not direction, as to charitable beneficiaries. You might also consider delegating this task, via legacy letter, to a family member or friend who would be honored by your designation of her to make these decisions.

Your Narrative of Faith

The Heroes of Faith cited in Hebrews 11 followed God's leading in faith even though each of them lacked knowledge of the entire story. Each of these heroes carried on in faith without a complete understanding of how their part of the story, including their sufferings, served to achieve God's purposes.[17] Each of them continued in faith, and it was credited to them as righteousness.

In the words of the Apostle Paul, we currently "look through a glass darkly."[18] We cannot know with precision when we will die, who will survive us, or how much money we will have at death. We also don't know the way in which our stories will impact others. We can be certain that God will use our life stories as part of God's broader story. As Christians, we ought to be more willing than our secular neighbors and friends to engage in an ongoing communication of our narrative

---

17 "And these died, not having received the fulfillment of their promise" (Hebrews 11:39–40).
18 1 Corinthians 13:12

precisely because our story has been created by God and is ultimately intended to bring glory to Him.

ILLUSTRATIONS FOR APPLICATION

The following three illustrations taken from my law practice may be applicable to your own planning as you create one or more legacy letters for your children.

Appointing a Family Funeral Director

Karen wanted to honor all four of her children by assigning each of them a task at her death. One son, Derek, is not blessed with organizational skills or financial background. Derek is a public speaker, gifted story teller, and a presenter of the gospel. So, Karen designated her other three children to each of various fiduciary duties as part of her estate plan and named Derek by a legacy letter signed by Karen as her "Family Funeral Coordinator." Following Karen's death, the family looked to Derek for all funeral arrangements. Derek arranged the service, burial, and meal. Derek also shared stories from Karen's life and the gospel presentation to friends and family in attendance at the funeral service.

Consumption Standards for Grandchildren

Dick's business had expanded into several states before his death in 1995. Dick made numerous wise gifting decisions, including the transfer of business interests for his children and grandchildren. One business was transferred to irrevocable trusts for the benefit of his grandchildren. These trusts are legally governed by irrevocable trust agreements that include the legal direction for how the assets in the trust must be handled for the grandchildren.

Recently, a disagreement arose between the two trustees administering these irrevocable trusts for the grandchildren. One trustee determined that distributions of cash to the grandchildren was appropriate considering legitimate expenses by the grandchildren. A second trustee disagreed, stating that the distributions would allow for the grandchildren to exceed a standard of living not contemplated by Dick. The tax planning strategy involved here was perfectly implemented, but neither of the trustees can know for certain what Dick wanted. In your case, consider your overall planning desires for children or grandchildren. You should use a legacy letter to outline your desires for trust distributions and to what degree your assets should be used to exceed a current standard of living. Even if your situation involves a smaller estate, your family will benefit from a legacy letter to provide your trustees (in the case of a testamentary trust) or beneficiaries (in the case of an outright gift) direction on the use of inherited assets.

Theological Directions

Peter was a well-respected faith leader who held leadership positions in both his church and parachurch organizations. Following Peter's death, his name was used by a group as a means to advocate a new campaign. As documented by several letters that I would characterize as legacy letters, Peter's beliefs were diametrically opposed to the new campaign. Based on these letters, we were able to convince the campaign organizers to cease use of Peter's name. If you anticipate that issues may arise related to your ministry or work, you might create written legacy letters to address important social or theological issues in your church or family. Even following your death, your legacy letters could serve to encourage your family and your church in matters of faith and life.

REFLECTIONS
On Leaving Legacy Letters of Testimony

Reflect on what written directions you can leave behind to your family to achieve eternal, spiritual, and godly outcomes. Complete the sections below to provide your family with your preferences for post-death arrangements.

Immediate Arrangements & Funeral

Organ Donation:

> Would you be willing to be an organ donor? (Yes/No)
>
> Do you have special directions for organ donation? If yes, please specify.

Disposition of Body:

> Should your remains be cremated? (Yes/No)
> If yes, should the ashes be buried or spread?

Location of buried remains/ashes or where ashes are to be spread:

Funeral and Memorial Directions

Favorite family worship songs & hymns:

Location of funeral:

Other desired arrangements:

Individuals responsible for memorial and their roles?

Family Directions

If you have young children who would need a guardian if both you and your spouse died, what important parenting direction would you like the guardian to know?

If you own a unique asset (e.g., business, cabin, or theology book collection), would your family benefit from directions as to the use and/or sale of the unique asset? If so, how can you go about leaving directions to encourage them?

If your children will inherit assets through a testamentary trust, on what types of expenses should your trustee use the inherited assets?

If you have adult children who are receiving an outright inheritance ("no strings attached"), on what types of expenses should your children use the inherited assets?

Faith

Would you have any family or friends who would be encouraged by a statement of faith, to be read after your death?

Are there any friends or family who would benefit from a word of encouragement from you if you died suddenly?

What theological or policy matters do you anticipate arising in the next five to ten years, and would your faith community benefit from your speaking to them on these subjects?

CONCLUSION

"Well, I'll be dead, so what do I care what happens to my assets when I die?" Numerous clients express frustration when attempting to understand, and then outsmart, the IRS tax code, a copy of which can be used for your next weight-lifting session. If our entire existence is a mere forty to seventy years, and if we have no accountability to God for use of assets, an estate plan is an unnecessary act of charity. After all, emotional ties to our spouses and children are merely the product of evolutionary development. We must "eat, drink, and be merry, for tomorrow we die." Even our dependent children should be left to battle it out with their siblings; to the fittest, luckiest winner should go the spoils.

For those who have been called to faith in Christ, we have been redeemed from a meaningless toil to an eternally significant earthly existence. Christ's redemption means that we "…were ransomed from the futile ways inherited from your forefathers, not with perishable things such as silver or gold, but with the precious blood of Christ, like that of a lamb without blemish or spot."[1] Christ's death was the death that needed to occur for us to receive an eternal inheritance.

"Therefore he is the mediator of a new covenant, so that those who are called may receive the promised eternal inheritance, since a death has occurred that redeems them from the transgressions committed under

---

1 1 Peter 1:18–19.

the first covenant. For where a will is involved, the death of the one who made it must be established. For a will takes effect only at death, since it is not in force as long as the one who made it is alive."[2]

Christ died the death that was required for the will to be implemented. The relevant will that has been read is the will of God. We have been bought by the blood of Jesus, once and for all time, into the eternal inheritance of heaven. The will of God is that each of us who has been called by Him have received an eternal and complete inheritance.

With the assurance of our eternal inheritance, we have the freedom to complete an earthly estate plan to achieve eternal outcomes and for the benefit of our Christian community. We use financial resources to maximize eternal return in the lives of our families and communities. We share our stories of success, suffering, and setbacks with our family and friends so that they can marvel with us at God's sustaining grace. We bless our children by pronouncing blessing upon them and provide a financial inheritance properly ordered below Christian institutions of marriage, family, and work. We use charitable gifts to multiply the joy of giving in others. We make end-of-life decisions for the benefit of our community and leave behind instructions to bring honor to God. We are ready to implement an estate plan now, not assuming on a future that only God knows.

While in Philistia, Abraham made a covenant with a local landowner at Beersheba, then planted a tamarisk tree. Abraham "...called on the name of the Lord, **the everlasting God**."[3] The Hebrew term for God used here, *Olam*, emphasizes the attribute of God's *everlastingness*. The tamarisk tree is a slow-growing tree, but a tree that can live up to 400 years. By reason of the tree's slow growth, Abraham could never have seen this monument come to full fruition. Abraham's tree eventually died, but the planting of the tree symbolized Abraham's dependence on God's everlasting blessing. In like manner, the legal and financial decisions you make with your temporal goods can likewise serve as our tamarisk tree, a monument to our identification in the everlasting God. I pray that you would plant your tamarisk tree by planning your estate for eternal purposes.

2 Hebrews 9:15–17.
3 Genesis 21:33.

Made in the USA
Columbia, SC
27 November 2024

47783408R00159